The DITCH CANDIDA COOKBOOK

Your All-in-One Guide to Simple Recipes For
Living Healthy without Candida.
(Second Edition)

Rebecca Austin

The Ditch Candida Cookbook
By: Rebecca Austin (Coach Green)
Healthy Homestead Living
A division of Strive 4 Savvy, LLC
©2017 & 2019 Strive 4 Savvy, LLC
Second Edition

All rights reserved. No part of this book may be reproduced in any form without the written permission of the publisher, except in the case of brief quotations embodied in critical articles and reviews.

Cover design done by Strive 4 Savvy, LLC
Typesetting, book layout, compilation, photography, and publishing done by Strive 4 Savvy, LLC. All photographs used in the book are either the property of Strive 4 Savvy, LLC or public domain.

Published by: Strive 4 Savvy, LLC
Edited by: Jordan Willson & Christina Ellison

ISBN: 978-1-7345928-0-1

Disclaimer: As with any diet changes, additions, or substitutions it is recommended to use good judgment and if need be ask for the advice of your healthcare provider. The author of this book is not a certified nutritionist, nor healthcare professional. The ideas, concepts, and opinions expressed in this book are intended to be used for educational purposes only. None of the information provided is intended to offer medical advice of any kind, nor is this this book intended to replace medical advice, nor to diagnose, prescribe, or treat any disease, condition, illness, or injury.

Author and publisher claim no responsibility to any person or entity for any liability, loss, or damage caused or alleged to be caused directly or indirectly as a result of the use, application, or interpretation of the material in this book.

Acknowledgements

A book isn't complete without an acknowledgements page. And yes, I'm one of those people who actually likes to read the acknowledgements when I pick up a new book. Writing can be a difficult task, and putting your thoughts into words, then sharing them with the world is a vulnerable position in which to find oneself. No book comes together to be published without a great deal of work, support, mentorship, and love.

First, I'd like to thank my Father God who is always with me. He has been my strongest supporter in these projects, directing my paths and guiding me where I needed to go when I faltered.

Nothing could have happened in this book or any of my companies without all the love, patience, and sacrifices of my husband, Andy. You are amazing, baby and I am so thankful God brought us together.

Special thanks go out to my guiding light and driving force, my beautiful and talented daughter Megan. You give me so much purpose. Your smile, your hugs, and your laughter never cease to bring me such peace and joy.

I wouldn't be where I am today without the wisdom and love of my dear mom, Joyce. I miss you every day and look forward to the day I get to see you again in Glory.

Big hugs and thanks go out to my two sisters-in-law, Angela Breedlove and Amy Austin who first introduced me to the world of cultured foods and set me on the right path many years ago when my health needed a serious reset. Your knowledge and willingness to share was an inspiration to me that spearheaded the founding of Healthy Homestead Living so we could spread the word on a more global scale.

Sincerest gratitude goes to my friend and mentor, Dawn Roller, who always has such a big heart for people and who always knows when to push me a little harder to strive a little higher. Success never comes without incredible support through a powerful Inner Circle and I am so blessed you saw something in me that at one time I didn't even see in myself. We've come a long way since those first days at the university, yet even then God had bigger plans for both of us.

A word of thanks to my mentors, Tamara Lowe with Kingdom Builders Academy and James Wedmore with Business by Design. Your encouragement and your willingness to push me a little harder to stretch outside my comfort zone have helped me grow in ways I never knew were possible. Through your guidance I have come to embrace the discomfort so I can do what God intends so others may benefit. You are both truly anointed and I am so blessed by all you share with me.

To all my followers on my website **www.healthyhomesteadliving.com,** my blog, my social media pages and my videos, I offer my biggest thanks. For without you, Healthy Homestead Living would be nothing more than an idea. Thank you for all your comments, feedback, shares, discussions, and love that keeps me going; always looking for bigger and better to share with you so you can live a life of peace, joy, harmony, and abundance.

A special note to the guys out there (aka hubbys).

The following is a letter written by my hubby to your support system... A little perspective from my biggest skeptic...

To all the dude's.

    I never.... ever thought for a second that I would be writing a testimonial about anything and especially a cookbook. But this is no ordinary cookbook! I'm not one for long-winded speeches or sales gimmicks to get someone to buy something . Also I won't promise if you do this or that, your results we be this or that. That's not my reasoning for writing this. So I'll get to the point. I love to eat....alot! I love sugar! Ice cream, sodas, candy, junk food....if it has sugar and tastes great, I'm good with that. I'm sold on delicious, quick, fast and easy. So what's in our American diet that doesn't have ;-&#)% loads of sugar or other flavor enhancing chemicals in it? So my choices to eat what tastes great are virtually unlimited. None of which equates to most things healthy.

  In 2015 I was diagnosed with a very rare tumor in the base of my skull. And by God's grace and the help of an amazing team of surgeons I have overcome cancer. Note, I'm not saying that my poor eating habits was the cause of me getting this tumor, although it may have had something to do with being 40 lbs overweight. I have no clue to why or what may have caused my tumor. But I will say it made me pay a whole lot more attention to what I put in my body. So having said that.. changing my eating habits was incredibly hard to do even though I know the health risks to not changing my lifestyle.

  When my wife Rebecca introduced me to what candida is, how it grows in your body, the symptoms that are linked to an overgrowth of candida and a simple test to find out if I did have too much of it, I was intrigued, and after testing, ...yes I definitely had an overgrowth of candida.

Now my personality insists, ok I've got a problem. Let's fix it and fix it now. So when I asked how, the answers to that question were words I didn't want to hear!

A diet with no sugar... none...not of any kind. No bread, no fruit, no grains, no beans, no nothing was all I could hear. Now, I'm not so interested. I NEED MY ENERGY. And I only want good tasting food. Rebecca assured me that if I would try this with her she could create and modify recipes that would fit into the criteria of a candida diet. So I agreed (kicking and screaming to be precise).

  After being her guinnea pig through the processes of experimenting and taste testing these recipes I have created a " husband approved " scale to these recipes. Obviously all our tastes aren't the same but hey, who doesn't like ice cream?

  So to all those fellas (or gals) whose spouses want to go on a candida diet, I encourage you to try it together and support each other. If you're anything like me, the proof's in the pudding. And after sinking your teeth into just a few of these dishes, like me, you won't be as skeptical as I once was. Fighting candida for me has been a piece of cake. Mmmmmm, did I just say *cake*?

Happy healthy eating!

Andy (aka Hubby)

Foreword:

The original release of *The Ditch Candida Cookbook* was created by working closely with a local Chinese Medicine doctor who specializes in candida and has years of success through clinical studies with his patients. The majority of the contents of this book remain unchanged, however since the initial publishing, God placed it on the heart of the author to publish another book, based in scriptural guidelines on diet, health, and nutrition. As a result of writing that book, and the research that went into creating guidelines from God's Word, there were a few adjustments to suggestions offered in this book. The primary adjustments being what God says in Leviticus about meats and which meats are considered unclean. These include all pork, shrimp, crab, and other shellfish. We still include the recipes in this book containing those ingredients, however it is encouraged to listen to your body and your spirit on if you want to consume these foods. Any recipes that include bacon can be substituted for turkey bacon. Turkey sausage can replace pork sausage, or use the recipe listed in this book to make your own breakfast sausage.

If you are interested in further reading, check out *The Theologenic Diet: What the Bible Says About Diet, Health, & Nutrition"*, by Rebecca Austin, available at www.HealthyHomesteadLiving.com or Amazon.

It is our hope and prayer that you find these books as valuable resources on your journey to health and a better lifestyle.

Contents:

Chapter 1: Welcome 8
How do we Ditch Candida? 10
The Candida Cleanse Protocol 12
Foods to Enjoy! 14
Tips on Eating Out 16
Words of Encouragement 18
Chapter 2: Setting Up Your Kitchen 19
Chapter 3: A Word About Die-Off 23
Chapter 4: Kids and the Candida Cleanse 25
Chapter 5: Adapting Recipes & Common Substitutions 29
Chapter 6: Sugar & Candida 31
Chapter 7: Efficiency Tips 32
Chapter 8: Money Saving Tips 34
Chapter 9: Eating Out 36
Chapter 10: Navigating the Holidays 38
Eggs and Breakfast Recipes 39
Soup and Stew Recipes 55
Vegetable Main Dish Recipes 85
Vegetable Side Dish Recipes 101
Chicken and Poultry Recipes 118
Beef Recipes 137
Pork Recipes 155
Seafood Recipes 165
Snacks 179
Desserts 195
Dressings 222
Spices 245
Condiments 252
Beverages 264
Menu Plans 274

Chapter 1: Welcome to the Ditch Candida Forever Journey!

Congratulations! You are reading this book because you have made the important decision to take your life back and find better health and vitality!

Food has become such a central part of our lives that in some cases, it controls us. Food related illnesses continue to rise in numbers, food addictions affect an alarming number of the population, and obesity has become more the norm. You pretty much can't turn on any media, be it television, social media, or even radio without being bombarded with both food-related marketing campaigns that tempt us to buy their products or food related weight loss programs with super models and body builders, catering to our desire to look like them. Our culture has become heavily food-centered. Food is used as rewards even starting with our kids like ice cream and candy when they behave well or get good grades. Family events, holidays, and birthday parties are almost always centered around the table. Comfort food is considered acceptable when we have emotional upsets. Going out on dates generally involves dinner and a movie (with popcorn and candy). Even business meetings often are conducted over lunches, dinners, or catered events. So when food is so central in our subconscious minds, it is no wonder that we struggle with making good food decisions.

Add that to the constantly conflicting reports from the various nutrition centers, highly paid marketing campaigns, and expensive supplement companies trying to sell you their latest, greatest miracle product, we are left feeling more confused and frustrated

Growing herbs and vegetables is a fun and easy way to add flavor and nutrition to your table.

than ever…which then ends up with more comfort food in the form of ice cream, chocolate, starchy foods, or bag of something processed.

Sound familiar? I for one finally got fed up with all the commercialism associated with the food industry and couldn't help but feel that there had to be a better solution. I was sick and tired of being sick and tired. I badly wanted to shed the extra baby weight that was sticking to me after the birth of my daughter. I wasn't sleeping well and couldn't understand why I was waking up several times each night, then unable to fall back to sleep for what seemed like hours. I never seemed to have enough energy and there were times when my brain didn't seem to want to function very well. I dealt with the discomfort of seasonal allergies and occasional skin rashes and eczema that would cause terrible discomfort. I had terrible hormonal problems each month with incredibly painful menstruation yet chalked it up as "typical." Then, as a final straw, I found a lump in my breast. I asked friends, colleagues, and various professionals for their opinions and was given a huge range of answers which left me more confused than ever. However, as a natural thinker, I knew there had to be a logical reason for my health challenges and there had to be a solution.

So, I set out on a quest. A journey to find answers and make sense of all the jumbled messages, conflicting doctors' prognosis, marketing slogans, ad campaigns, sales gimmicks, so-called-better-for-you-high-priced "healthy" foods, and supplements galore that are out there. I interviewed doctors, nutritionists, homeopathic doctors, chiropractors, and countless individuals just like you and me who had both successes and failures with finding health. Finally, through the Grace of God, I met with Greg Hollingsworth from Acupoint Health Clinic who was able to give me some answers with solutions. In a nutshell, I had Candida….

….Candida….Such an ominous little word for the cause of my health issues…and the cause of an estimated 80% or more of the American population's health issues! So what exactly is Candida and more importantly, how do you eliminate it?

What is Candida?

Before I could effectively go to war against this enemy combatant that I now knew was the culprit of my woes, I had to do some recon and size up what I was up against. Everyone has some candida in their bodies. Candida is a yeast that resides primarily in the digestive tract and is kept under control by the beneficial bacteria and yeasts in your gut. However, certain triggers can cause candida to grow out of control, such as excessive use of antibiotics, birth control pills, and stress. During conditions such as these (and others), candida can mutate into a more aggressive fungal, bacterial, and parasitic forms that start causing major problems. Left unchecked due to a weakened immune system and/or gut flora, the candida starts reproducing and essentially taking over your body. Doesn't sound very pretty, does it?

Well, to be frank, it isn't! As a result of this candida overgrowth, your body then tries to regain balance but once out of control, candida is an aggressive parasite-like organism that doesn't give up easily. A slew of health problems can often result, ranging from skin rashes, yeast infections, depression, allergies, immune disorders, hormone imbalances, and even cancer…among other health challenges. Do I have your attention now? I hope so! Because getting your candida under control may be the single most important thing you could do for yourself. By ditching the candida, you can take your life back and feel better than you have in years! Is it easy? I wish I could say yes, but I promise it will get easier as you progress in your journey. Is it worth it? You betcha! So hang in there and persevere through the program. You can do this! It is our goal in writing this book to make your battle against candida easier with tactical support every step of the way!

You CAN do this! One simple step at a time!

The journey of a thousand miles begins with one step.   -Lao Tzu

How do I know if I have Candida?

There are a couple scientific tests you can do in order to find out if you have candida, but there is a simple at-home test you can do on your own that is very accurate. We call it the Spit Test. Candida, if you have it, will be found in your saliva. Saliva is

Work with your Healthcare Professional

It is important when fighting candida to work with your healthcare professional. He or she will be able to monitor your health, offer support, and prescribe important medicinals, herbs, and oils that will help you in your fight.

It is also recommended to consult with a colon hydrotherapist as a healthy colon will make a huge difference when progressing through the "die-off" process.

lighter than water and therefore, like oil, won't mix well with water and will float on the top. Candida on the other hand, is five times heavier than water and will sink. Therefore, we can determine our level of candida by testing our saliva in water to see if it floats or sinks. Follow the following instructions to test your level of candida:

1. As soon as you wake up in the morning, before you eat or drink anything, get a clear glass and fill it with water. Don't use tap water as tap water generally contains chemicals that will interfere with the test. Let the water settle a minute until it is still.
2. Collect saliva in your mouth and spit into the glass.
3. Watch the saliva for the next 15 minutes to an hour and observe what it does. Depending on your level of candida, you may see a few different things, all indicating a candida problem.
   - Your saliva stays at the top and you see thin or thick strands that look like strings sinking downward.
   - Your saliva stays on top, sometimes sliding to the side of the glass, and looks cloudy or has bubbles.
   - Your saliva sinks all the way to the bottom of the glass.
   - Your saliva is suspended in the middle of the glass either in specs or in strings.
4. If your candida levels are in balance, then your saliva should be relatively clear, with no bubbles, and no sinking, stringy 'legs', or sliding to the side of the glass. Your saliva should stay floating in the center.

How do we ditch Candida?

Now that we know *what* we're fighting, we need to take a closer look at *how* we can win against this alien invader so that we can once again enjoy energy, balance, vitality, sleep, mental clarity, and health! The approach may vary depending on which doctor or healthcare professional you ask. The internet is inundated with suggestions and tips for eliminating candida with some discrepancies between theories. The cleanse program we offer here is the one we personally used with success. The protocol is not mine,

Make health your hobby!

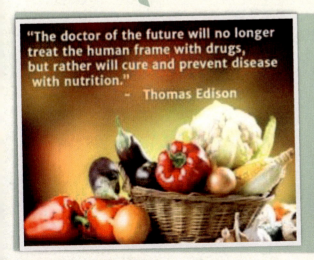

"The doctor of the future will no longer treat the human frame with drugs, but rather will cure and prevent disease with nutrition."
   - Thomas Edison

I was at a business conference one time years ago when I met an interesting gentleman who was in his 80's and looked as young and spry as if he was just turning 50. We struck up a conversation and I asked him his secret. He said something that has changed my life forever afterward. He said he makes health his hobby. He said that we all have hobbies, and the purpose of hobbies is to fulfill us…to have fun and enjoy life. He said he made the decision to make health his hobby so that it was always fun, always a new adventure, always something to look forward to rather than dread. From that day forward I have made health my hobby, from gardening to cooking. Try making health your hobby and have fun with what you learn, the time you get to spend in the kitchen, the recipes with which you get to experiment, and the results you subsequently get to feel.

Eat to Live! Don't live to eat.

How to Ditch Candida, continued....

rather the guidelines given to me from my healthcare professional. It is **highly recommended** that you work with a trusted healthcare professional when fighting the candida fight, as you will greatly benefit from the additional support and guidance, as well as additional herbs and oils that boost the immune system and encourage die-off.

So let's dive in and take a look at what your plan of attack will be over the coming months. First, I'll talk about what you want to eliminate, but don't dwell on that. Focus on what you CAN have and enjoy great foods with confidence, knowing you are supporting your healing while eliminating candida forever!

The Candida Cleanse Protocol

What to Eliminate:

- To begin, the most important thing you can do for your body and to start eliminating the candida overgrowth is to immediately eliminate ALL sugar from your diet. Candida LOVES sugar and feeds off sugar in your body. This includes any and all sugar forms and substitutes including corn syrup, high fructose corn syrup, honey, agave, coconut sugar, brown sugar, powdered sugar, fructose, dextrose, or any other ingredient ending in "-ose". The only exceptions are Stevia and limited amounts of Xylitol. Stevia is an herb that doesn't affect your blood sugar or internal glucose levels. In your Candida Cleanse, we recommend using stevia liberally. You may find yourself craving sweets and stevia will help satisfy that mental craving without jeopardizing your cleanse. Xylitol is also acceptable; however some people have digestive reactions when taking xylitol such as bloating, diarrhea, gas, and abdominal cramping. If you experience any adverse reactions, eliminate xylitol and stick with stevia.
- You'll also want to eliminate all processed foods from your diet. Processed foods have been packaged for convenience and storage. As a result, nutritional value is compromised. Excess sugar and salt are often added to make up for the loss of flavor when nutrition is lost (because the nutrient dense parts of the food are also the parts that spoil the fastest).
- During your Candida Cleanse, you want to avoid all grains and legumes. This includes wheat, rice, millet, amaranth, quinoa, spelt, all beans (except green beans), and peanuts. If you're used to a diet

A Little Word About Stevia

Stevia is an herb that can be up to 100 times sweeter than regular sugars. For this reason, a little bit goes a long way. If too much stevia is used, the flavor can turn more bitter than sweet. If you're new to working with stevia, or if you've tried it in the past with less than satisfactory results, I encourage you to give it a try again but use it sparingly. Liquid tends to be less bitter than powdered varieties, and you can control the quantities better with drops.

We did find a brand called "Stevia in the Raw" which is a cup for cup equivalent to regular sugar. When baking, we found this version of stevia to be easier, especially if trying to convert one of your favorite recipes to Candida Cleanse ingredients.

With ice cream, herbal teas, almond milk, and other recipes that are "softer" or "liquid" in nature, stick with the liquid version. Sweet Leaf Brand Stevia comes in a variety of flavors which also lends some variety to your dishes.

Let food be thy medicine, and medicine be thy food. -Hippocrates

rich in heavy carbs, eliminating bread and pasta may be a challenge at first, but I have included some great alternative recipes in this book to help you adjust.
- Due to Candida's voracious appetite for sugar, you are also going to avoid all fruits during your cleanse. Despite the fact that fruits are generally good for you and loaded with phytonutrients, vitamins and minerals, they also contain fructose which is fruit sugar. The only exceptions to this rule are the occasional lemon or lime zest (zest only and not the juice). Zest of fresh lemons and limes are acceptable but limit it to once or twice a week.

That being said, it's easy to feel like there's nothing left you CAN eat. Don't be disheartened like my husband was, however. There are many options left for you and with a little practice, you will be amazed at how much easier it gets.

Now for the Foods to Enjoy!

Vegetables

The cornerstone of your Candida Cleanse will be lots of vegetables (with the exception of corn or regular potatoes…because they are too starchy and turn to sugar in your system, feeding the candida. Sweet potatoes are ok, though, and are used in some of my favorite recipes). Vegetables are loaded with nutrients and fiber which will help give you energy while combating the candida. Vegetables are best lightly steamed, sautéed, roasted, or baked. Raw vegetables should be avoided, especially for the first part of your cleanse, as they can be difficult for your already tired digestive system to break down and digest. Adding a healthy fat like coconut oil, grass-fed organic butter, or ghee to your lightly cooked vegetables makes the nutrients more absorbable and readily available for your body.

You can also enjoy lacto-fermented vegetables. Lacto-fermentation is an age-old preservation technique where the natural bacteria in the vegetables increase; creating a dish that is easily digestible and loaded with probiotics. Most commonly known lacto-fermented vegetables include sauerkraut, kimchi, and pickles (no vinegar varieties) but you can lacto-ferment just about any vegetable.

Be sure to refer to the Vegetables chapter in this book for tips, tricks, preparation and cooking ideas, recipes, and a list of vegetable favorites.

The goal should be to have approximately 40-50% of your plate or dish consisting of vegetables.

Note: Mushrooms, although technically a fungus and not allowed on some candida diets, are classified with the vegetables on our Candida Cleanse and are perfectly admissible. Mushrooms can be medicinal and are a delicious addition to many recipes. Choose fresh mushrooms and avoid canned. Reishi, Shiitake, Crimini, Portabella, Winecap, and Oyster are a few of our favorites.

Greens & Microgreens

Often lumped in with vegetables are your greens and microgreens, yet we feel they deserve a classification all their own. Greens and microgreens are powerhouses in nutrients. Greens include lettuce, arugula, chard, kale, collards, wheatgrass, barleygrass, and other grasses and also includes sea vegetables and greens like spirulina, chlorella, kombu, dulse, kelp, and hiziku.

Microgreens and sprouts are the result of planting a seed and growing it to the baby plant stage. Common microgreens include alfalfa, broccoli, kale, mustard greens, arugula, and just about any vegetable sprout. Avoid spinach, as most spinach is too harsh on your tender digestive system while combating candida.

Meats

Red meats supply the body with much needed vitamin F and help the body produce red blood cells. The key with meats is to proportion them correctly. Our digestive systems do best with about 4-6 oz. of meat at one time. The most common mistake is to eat too much, combined with heavy starches (meat and potatoes) causing digestive upset. Choose red meats that are pasture-raised, grass-fed, organic and white meats that are free-range organic. Avoid processed meats like sausages, sandwich meats, and kielbasa due to the sugars, nitrates, and additives that you will inevitably find in the ingredients.

Eggs

Enjoy farm-fresh organic eggs for breakfast or any meal of the day or add eggs to your baked dishes. And don't be concerned with cholesterol. Eggs, especially farm-fresh free-range eggs have actually been shown to LOWER cholesterol in some scientific studies.

Dairy

Dairy is allowed on the Candida Cleanse but in small quantities. Dairy can be mucus-producing so avoid dairy if you are experiencing die-off symptoms or have any dairy sensitivities. Raw, organic milk products are best. Enjoy butter, cheese, yogurt (no sugar), sour cream, and kefir. Check out our recipes for homemade whipped topping and make your own Ice Cream using Stevia.

Nuts

Nuts are allowed on the Candida Cleanse with the exception of peanuts (which are actually a legume). Be sure to purchase only raw, organic nuts and soak them 12-24 hours prior to consuming to increase digestibility. Refer to the Snacks section in this book to learn how to soak nuts for optimal nutrition. Nuts offer great substitution ingredients like nut milks, nut butters, and nut flours.

Note: Coconut is generally lumped into the "nuts" category and is acceptable in small doses on the Candida Cleanse, however it is technically classified as a fruit so use coconut products sparingly. Coconut oil is allowed and recommended during your cleanse. Coconut Aminos make a great soy sauce substitute.

Herbs and Spices

When transitioning to a diet devoid of sugars and grains, herbs will become one of your greatest allies. Herbs add flavor and nutrition to your recipes. Choose fresh organic herbs when possible, or start growing your own. Many herbs grow very well in pots in a sunny location like a kitchen windowsill. Some of our favorite herbs include dill, basil, cilantro, parsley, oregano, lavender, and mint.

Use garlic as liberally as you can in your recipes. Garlic is a powerful candida deterrent and will boost your Candida Cleanse. Ginger, horseradish, onions, shallots, chives, fennel, and peppers are also excellent additions.

Healthy Oils & Fats

Oils and healthy fats are used in many recipes on your Candida Cleanse. Choose healthy oils such as Olive, Coconut, Avocado, and Grass-fed Organic Butter or Ghee (clarified butter). When cooking with oils, be sure to choose an oil or fat that can handle the heat you are using. Generally as a rule of thumb, healthy oils and fats for cooking are those that are solid at room temperature. This includes Coconut Oil, Organic Butter, and Ghee. Lard, if from a good organic source, can also be used occasionally.

Liquid oils will all become toxic if heated and therefore should be avoided in cooking. Feel free to experiment with a variety of liquid oils for salad dressings, condiments, and on your vegetables such as Olive Oil, Avocado oil, Pumpkin, Sesame, Safflower, Walnut, Macadamia, Sunflower, Almond, Hazelnut, Hemp Seed, and Flaxseed.

NEVER consume canola oil. Canola oil is highly toxic to our bodies and will slow down your healing. Also avoid peanut oil, corn oil, rice bran oil, soybean oil, and vegetable oil as they are made with ingredients otherwise not allowed on the Candida Cleanse.

Bone Broth

Homemade bone broth is one of the best secret weapons in your arsenal. Broth contains collagen and gelatin which supports healing of the digestive tract while providing valuable nutrients needed for healing. Check out the

Tips on Eating Out

Just because you are focusing on certain foods instead of others for awhile doesn't mean you have to live like a hermit and feel tied to your kitchen. Quite the opposite. Feel free to eat out as often as you like! Just follow our simple guidelines offered in our chapter on "Eating Out" to help you stay on track and stick with the recommended foods that will best help you in your journey of getting healthier and balancing your gut!

Soups section (page 55) to learn how to make your own bone broths. We recommend adding a little bit to every meal.

Vinegar

During the first several weeks of your Candida Cleanse, it is best to avoid Apple Cider Vinegar. ACV (Apple Cider Vinegar) is made from apples, which is a fruit and is not allowed. The exception to this rule is when making your own homemade bone broths, you need a couple Tablespoons of ACV to pull the minerals from the bones during cooking. Small quantities such as this are acceptable since the benefits of the bone broth far outweigh the possible side-effects of the ACV.

A vinegar you CAN use regularly is a well-aged, quality balsamic vinegar. Be sure to check out the chapter on Condiments for more ideas on dressings, toppings, sauces, and accompaniments.

Water

Be sure to drink lots of fresh, oxygen-rich water while on the Candida Cleanse. Water is your best friend and will assist in flushing toxins and die-off. A good rule of thumb is to take your current body weight, divide it in half, and that number is how many ounces of water your body needs on a minimum to stay hydrated. More is better. If you're not used to drinking water, try infusing it with fresh cucumber or herbs like basil, mint, or lavender.

Celtic Sea Salt

The only salt you should use in this program is Celtic Sea Salt, which is the only form of salt that is truly from the ocean and contains the perfect balance of minerals your body needs. Salt is required by the body for hydration and mineral absorption. Although Real Sea Salt and Himalayan Pink Salts contain minerals, they don't have the same balance of minerals. Stick with Celtic Sea Salt only during your Candida Cleanse.

Words of Encouragement

Life if filled with choices, and each choice we make has consequences both good and bad. What better choice could you make than health? Our bodies are beautifully and wonderfully designed by our Divine Creator and He wants you to be healthy, ...to live a life of happiness, vitality, and prosperity.

As you go through this cleanse, celebrate the small successes. Be encouraged by each step you make. Know that every day you make good choices is a day closer to your goal. Persevere and you will find that it gets much easier each day. And then one day you will suddenly wake up and realize that you have won the battle and ditched candida forever!

I believe in you and God is with you!

Chapter 2: Setting Up Your Kitchen

Now that the recon is in, the next phase of your battle is to prep your weapons. Let's take a quick look at your kitchen.

If you're like me when I first got started, you might be feeling a bit overwhelmed right about now. Rest assured that just like anything new, it gets easier over time and within the first couple weeks you'll have a routine established. While you're getting started, here are few things I found out through trial and error that may help you:

1. Encourage your family to do this Candida Cleanse with you. It's so much easier when you have an internal support group with your family and definitely better when everyone is eating the same meals and ingredients. There is a good chance that they could benefit from the cleanse anyway, since an estimated 80% of Americans are suffering from candida overgrowth!

2. Eliminate any and all temptation in your kitchen. Sugar is a powerful addiction, sometimes being compared in strength and reactions to heroin and cocaine! So just like any addiction, remove as much temptation from your home as possible to make it easier on yourself. Bag up those off-limits groceries and give them to a needy family, donate to a church or food program, or give to a friend or family member. That way you can start fresh without worrying about resisting the urge to get into that candy, cookie box, bag of chips, soda, pasta, or other temptations that will derail you from your fight.

3. Take an inventory of what you have and what you will need, both in food items and kitchen tools. There's no getting around the fact that you will be doing regular cooking during this cleanse and a clean, efficient, well-stocked kitchen is so much more enjoyable to work in. A well-stocked kitchen means more convenience and time-saving, which are cornerstone in a successful program. Here are a few of the kitchen tools we consider particularly beneficial during your cleanse (and for the rest of your life)…which are worth the investment if you don't already have them….

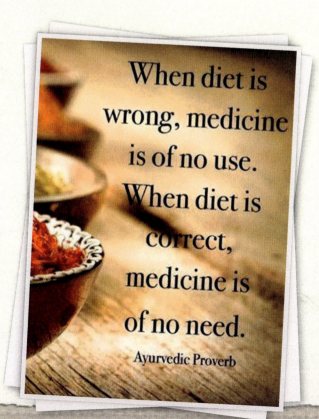

Vitamix or other Powerful Blender: Whether it's smoothies, soups, or making your own nut milks, having a good blender will be a cornerstone of your kitchen. We use ours literally every day and even take it with us when we travel. I made the mistake of thinking I could go the cheaper route and bought inferior blenders for years, only to have to

Our Weapons of Choice:

Don't worry if you don't have these, but they're worth the investment if you can add them.

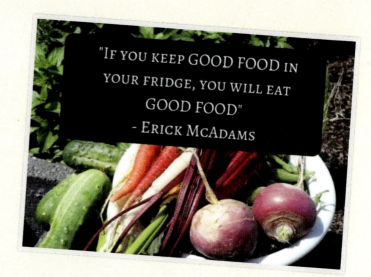

replace them again or be disappointed with the blending quality. After investing in a good blender, I was amazed at the difference and so much happier with the results. I found myself saving time and effort, and a good blender opens the doors to recipes that inferior blenders just can't handle.

Power Pressure Cooker: A more recent addition to our kitchen is a power pressure cooker, and I can't say enough good things about it. The power pressure cookers on the market today are easy, safe, and have pre-programmed cooking settings, timers, and keep-warm settings to make your life easier. Pressure cooking retains more nutrients in the food than any other cooking method, even steaming or sautéing. Plus, it is FAST! I've taken roasts from freezer to table in about 45 minutes using this awesome tool. Our Power Pressure Cooker is used almost everyday because it makes my life so much easier! Much like a Crockpot, I can throw ingredients in before I leave for work in the morning and have a delicious dinner ready when I get home. And, it's a handy appliance for making nourishing bone broth! I'm all about fast and easy, and the Power Pressure Cooker really does make my life easier and my time in the kitchen shorter.

Toaster/Convection Oven: The toaster oven is a great replacement to the microwave. We made the switch last year and I love the difference. The toaster oven makes many recipes so much faster and easier to prepare. Unlike the conventional oven, the toaster oven uses less energy, takes less time to preheat, doesn't heat up the whole house in the summer when cooking meals, and has many cook settings for a variety of recipes. Whether it's roasting vegetables, baking meats, casseroles, or quiches, or reheating left-overs, the toaster oven is a handy addition to any kitchen!

Food Processor: Until I started my Candida Cleanse, I didn't use my food processor very often. I'm not sure why, now that I see how much easier a food processor can make your life. Chopping, slicing, and pureeing becomes a breeze and super easy. Making your own almond butter, sunbutter, or cashew butter becomes a snap (see recipes). Make healthier mayonnaise from fresh ingredients (see recipe).

Dehydrator: Not a required appliance, but certainly a handy one, the dehydrator holds a regular place on the counter in my kitchen. A dehydrator opens the doors for many great snacks, which is often the hardest thing to adjust when starting a Candida Cleanse. Common snacks of the past often would

Every job is easier with the proper tools.

contain grains or fruit so having the ability to make your own crackers, dried veggie chips, jerky, and healthy nuts makes a huge difference! The dehydrator is beneficial especially with nuts. Nuts need to be soaked before consuming to release enzyme inhibitors to become more digestible. After soaking and draining, nuts need to be dehydrated to make them nice and crunchy again. When purchasing a dehydrator, be sure to invest in one that has a temperature setting so you can adjust the temperature to the best drying temps for each food for best nutrient preservation.

Ice Cream Maker: No, this isn't a required appliance for the Candida Cleanse, but my husband says it is. Ice Cream sure makes life more enjoyable! When you feel like you have to give up so many of the treats you used to enjoy, it's so uplifting to get to enjoy ice cream occasionally, especially on special events and birthdays. I use an ice cream maker that doesn't even require any salt. You just freeze the basin ahead of time, pour in the ingredients, and turn on the power. About 20 minutes later, I have fresh homemade ice cream that I make with Stevia instead of sugar. See the recipe in the dessert section for full instructions and flavor variations.

Kitchen Tip: Try to Stay Organized

When it comes to time savings and quick/easy recipes, having a clean organized kitchen really makes a difference. I know it's not easy, and I'll be the first to admit that I fall short here at times especially on those busy work days or crazy-take-the-kids-all-over-town days. There's no denying, though, that a well organized and clean kitchen is so much easier to work in and you can be so much more efficient.

Delegate this task if you find it a chore. Keep your counters clean. Having a menu plan and a grocery plan will make your life so much easer. Have snacks on hand for quick energy or those "gotta have something" moments.

Most importantly, have fun with it!

> YOU DON'T HAVE TO COOK FANCY OR COMPLICATED MASTERPIECES - JUST GOOD FOOD FROM FRESH INGREDIENTS.
> -JULIA CHILD

Proper Preparation Prevents Poor Performance.

Good Knives: When my husband and I got married many moons ago, one of the wedding gifts I received was a quality set of kitchen knives. Wow! I've been cooking since I was about 10 years old but for the first time in my life I had some really nice knives and oh, what a difference! When you are cooking every day, especially with lots of vegetables, it makes a HUGE difference when you have good knives that are sharp. If budget is a challenge for you, invest in one good chef's knife or Sudoku knife then add other knives later. I can't stress enough how worth it a good knife is … and I know you'll thank me!

Be sure to refer to our Weekly Menu Plan section for additional tips on what to do each week for time-saving tips and for helping establish your new routine. The key to success in the Candida Cleanse is plan ahead, know your plan (battle plan), and then stick to the plan as much as possible. We've tried to make it as easy as possible for you with our sample Weekly Menu Plans. Enjoy!

Chapter 3: A Word About Die-Off

As you progress through your Candida Cleanse, you may experience what is often called "Die-Off" or "Detox" Symptoms. Ranging from mild to severe, many individuals deal with some form of discomfort ranging from flu-like symptoms, headaches, skin rashes, stomach cramps, diarrhea, depression, fatigue, muscle spasms, brain fog, and trouble sleeping. Although these symptoms are uncomfortable, rest assured that they are perfectly normal and as your body adjusts, they WILL get better. Learn to embrace the discomfort and feel good that it's a good sign that you are making progress! Think of it like when you spring clean your house…it always looks worse before it looks better. Here are a few things you can do to help with die-off to help you feel better…unless you're one of the lucky ones who avoids die-off symptoms:

- Remember, the body uses three main channels to detoxify…through the bowels, the lungs, and the skin. You need to have at least two bowel movements a day (preferably 3-4), break a good sweat, and breathe deeply for optimum support of your natural detox processes.

- Aloe Vera Juice can naturally support your entire digestive tract and assist with candida die-off symptoms. Use only high quality, pure Aloe Vera and start with about 2 oz with water right before bedtime.

- Take a detox bath at least once a week. To your bath water, add ½ cup Apple Cider Vinegar, ¼ cup Bentonite Clay, and ½ cup Celtic Sea Salt or Epsom Salts. For a more relaxing bath, add a few drops of Lavender Essential Oil.

- Use Sesame or Coconut Oil and do Oil Pulling at least once every day. Oil pulling is a technique where you draw oil through your teeth using a sucking and swishing method. Carefully draw the oil between each set of teeth, both top and bottom. The whole process takes about 20-30 minutes. Do NOT swallow the oil and do not spit oil out in the sink or toilet as it can cause problems with your plumbing, especially if you have a septic

Cravings can be a powerful battle in this war against candida. A tip that I found helpful when battling cravings, is always have some "treats" on hand that will help you through the mental battle. For example, stevia sweetened dark chocolate, cinnamon spiced nuts, cashew cake batter pudding, or stevia sweetened ice cream. That way you can still "indulge" without jeapordizing the protocol and your progress.

Food is essential to life; therefore make it good. -Anonymous

system. After your Oil Pulling session, discard oil in the trash. Oil pulling is an effective method of killing bacteria and yeasts in your mouth, including candida. This process is especially beneficial if you are dealing with bad breath or problems with your gums.

- Use an infrared sauna. FAR saunas are different from the steam saunas, using infrared heat rather than moisture. Infrared heats your tissues deeper and you will get a good sweat, helping flush your body of toxins through the skin.

- Consider getting a colonic one or two times during your cleanse, especially if you have suffered from constipation for a long time. Find a reputable colon hydrotherapist in your area who understands candida and your needs during this cleanse.

- Use a rebounder (mini-trampoline) to keep your lymphatic system moving. Generally about 15-20 minutes per day of *light bouncing* are all you need to encourage a healthy lymph system. Consider getting a Lymphatic Massage if you are needing additional lymph stimulation.

Be sure to work closely with your healthcare provider when experiencing die-off symptoms. Although normal, they may also indicate other underlying issues other than die-off. Your healthcare provider can help you more easily navigate this battlefield while supporting your detox systems, in particular the liver, kidneys, gall bladder, colon, and skin.

It is also very important to stick to the Candida Cleanse Protocol. Temptation is strong, but each time you indulge you are only feeding the candida and making it stronger. Each battle you win over temptation and cravings, the shorter the war will last in duration. So hang in there and persevere. You can do this!

Chapter 4: Kids and the Candida Cleanse

Kids can have candida overgrowth, too! Here are our tips on how to support your kids during their Candida Cleanse, too.

If you have kids on the Candida Cleanse, you're faced with a few extra challenges because our culture revolves so much around food and sugar. Whether it's birthday parties, holidays, family get-togethers, play-dates, school treats, or other events….sugar, processed foods, and grains take a center stage all too often. Your kids will need extra support during their transition on this cleanse. The good news is that kids tend to bounce back faster than adults. They are already wired for growth, cell repair, and healing with youth on their side. A recent study done by the University of Texas showed astonishing results by cutting sugar from kids' diets for just 10 days! In this study, improvements were seen in blood pressure, blood sugar levels, attention spans, bowel regularity, sleep, and a host of other health improvements. So feel confident. Encourage your child that this Candida Cleanse is only for a short time and remind them that they will feel so much better when they're done!

Here are a few tips to help your kiddos as they win the fight against candida:

1. Make it fun and focus on what they CAN eat! Your kids will mirror your attitudes and emotions, especially when it comes to big changes like this. Be the cheerleader, the coach, the general, the teacher, the counselor. Listen to their opinions and gently encourage them through this process.
2. Encourage them to try new foods. In our home, we like to make an adventure out of new recipes and I let my daughter know that it's ok if she doesn't like something… but she does have to give it a fair try first.
3. Include your kiddos in the menu planning, grocery shopping, and food preparation. Not only do kids love helping out, but you're sharing valuable life skills with them in the process!
4. Use lots of color and visual appeal on their plates. Kids are more sensitive than adults to visual appeal of their foods. Take the time to make shapes or smiley faces in their food. It's more fun to eat! Don't forget presentation, too! Use pretty napkins, bright colored plates, and fun garnishes. Try different varieties of vegetables that are different from the norm like purple carrots and yellow tomatoes. A little creativity goes a long way!
5. Be sensitive to texture of the foods and what your child tends to like best. Texture, especially for really young kiddos, can be the difference between a thumbs up or a thumbs down. Children are more sensitive to texture than adults. If they say

they don't like a certain vegetable, it may be a texture issue. Canned, frozen, raw, steamed, and sautéed peas have completely different textures and flavors. So experiment with different preparation techniques to find the best ones for you and your family.

6. Use Stevia liberally, especially at first. If your children, like most, are accustomed to a diet filled with lots of sweets, be sure to include desserts and sweet treats often. This makes the transition easier and they don't feel as much like they're missing out.

7. Plant a garden with your kiddos. Even if it's just a couple pots in a windowsill or on a balcony, including your kids in the growing process of food is both fun and educational. Food kids grow themselves is exciting to them and a great way to get them to eat more vegetables. Fresh grown herbs and vegetables taste better than anything you can buy, too! If you're new to gardening, start with some easy plants like radishes, tomatoes, peppers, basil, chives, dill, and parsley. Growing microgreens are fun and nutritious too. Most kids love sunflower sprouts!

8. Be patient and persevere. Kids will tend to balk at first to the food changes and may refuse to eat. Rest assured, that they will eat when they are hungry. If they don't like the meal prepared, have a couple healthy snack options always available so they can try again on the next meal.

9. If your child goes to school, you'll be packing their lunch everyday since the lunches available at the schools will not have much good food they can eat. When my daughter first started

Plant a Garden with your Kids!

Gardening is a fun and educational adventure you can share with your kids. Most children have an inherent love for playing in the dirt and couple that with the excitement of planting something, watching it grow, learning responsibility by caring for it, and then enjoying the fruits of their labor by eating what they grow, kids naturally are drawn to the whole gardening process. If you don't have space or time for a large garden, try a couple simple pots to start. You never know what seeds you will be planting in their futures along with the seeds you plant in the dirt.

Proverbs 22:6 Teach children how they should live, and they will remember it all their life. (GNT)

going to school, I was appalled at what most schools are feeding our kids. I wanted my daughter to have more nutritious meals for her growing body and mind so I started packing her lunches. I didn't want her to feel left out, however, so I developed a lunch system that made it more fun for her to bring her lunch than eat the school lunch. When it comes to packing lunches, follow these simple guidelines:

- Color and Visual Appeal. I use the *Glad* divided containers with the large-sized silicon baking cups in rainbow colors (see photos on the next page) to pack the lunches in. This gives you added color and appeal before even adding the food. When packing hot lunches, use a fun thermos they like or have picked out. (Note: silicon baking cups can be toxic when heated so we don't use them for cooking… but, they make great "dividers" and are colorful additions to your child's lunchbox.)

- Pack a protein, vegetable/s, and healthy fats in every lunch, then include a healthy dessert.

- Add a "prize"! Fast food restaurants started using this as a marketing technique decades ago and it works. Kids love the "toy" or "prize" even if it's just a trinket. I add a fun prize to my daughter's lunch every day. Sometimes it is a "toy" and sometimes it's a small note I write. It makes lunch fun and gives my daughter something to look forward to. You can find fun prizes online, at Dollar-type stores, at Party stores, and various box stores. I have a drawer in my kitchen designated for prizes that I use in her lunches, and it also comes in handy when other kids are visiting!

Communicate with your child's teacher if he/she is in school.

- Be sure to communicate with your child's teacher and stress the importance of adhering to the Candida Cleanse. Teachers use food regularly in the classrooms in both instruction and prizes. Ask them to let you know when they plan to have food in the classroom so you can provide a suitable substitution. Most teachers are understanding and accommodating as they are becoming more and more used to food-related challenges like nut and dairy allergies. Clear communication is key.

- If your child is attending a birthday party where cake and ice cream will be served, contact the host parent and ask if it would be ok for you to bring a treat for your child. Pumpkin Muffins, Double Chocolate Chip Muffins, and Chocolate Chip Cookies work well in cases like these.

The best gift you can give your kids is the foundation for a healthy childhood which will grow into habits that will last a lifetime. Even when they complain, which they will, know you are doing what is best for them both today and into their tomorrows!

Chapter 5: Adapting Recipes & Common Substitutions

You don't necessarily have to give up all your favorite recipes while on the Candida Cleanse!

When we first started our Candida Cleanse, our guidelines were limited and we didn't have much in the way of recipe books or how-to's. I looked online but each website had conflicting reports on what to eat and how to go about eliminating candida. I chose to follow the specific instructions given to me by my healthcare provider as outlined in this book. I admit, it was a bit daunting and overwhelming at first since I didn't even know where to start on planning and preparing meals. So, I started with our family favorites and then set out on a mission to figure out if and how to adapt them to our new protocol. Many of the recipes in this book are the results of our experimentation with adapting age-old favorites.

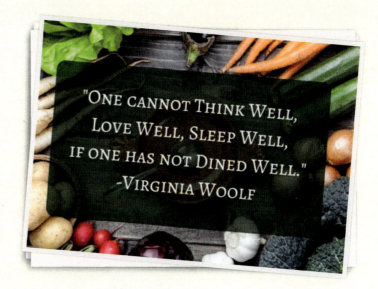

Here are our simple tips on how to convert your recipes to Candida Cleanse friendly.

If you have some favorite recipes you would like to still enjoy while on the Candida Cleanse, try the following these tips I used when converting mine.

- Replace any sugar in the recipe with an equivalent sweetness of stevia or Xylitol. This works well for most recipes, with the exception of those recipes that use sugar as a brine or the chemical structure of sugar to create caramelization.

- Replace potatoes with sweet potatoes, Jerusalem artichokes, or jicama.

- Replace pasta/noodles with zucchini, spaghetti squash, kelp noodles, or eggplant. A spiralizer is a handy kitchen tool if you like pasta sauces and still want your "pasta" dishes. You can make "noodles" out of just about any firm vegetable like broccoli, carrots, zucchini, and even beets.

- Replace rice with finely chopped cauliflower.

- Replace soy sauce and/or Worsteshire sauce with coconut aminos.

- Replace salt with Celtic Sea Salt

- Replace flour with almond flour. This works pretty well unless the recipe requires the gluten in the flour for levening.

"The quality of your recipe will only be as good as the quality of the ingredients." -Margaret Dombrowski (Grandma)

- Replace spinach with kale. Spinach, although normally considered healthy, is too cooling to the digestive system and spleen when on a candida cleanse, especially raw spinach. Opt for kale in your recipes instead.

- Fruit is one thing that doesn't really have a good substitution, but you can still use pumpkin, avocado, and zucchini in baked goods and sweet treats.

- Replace chocolate and cocoa powder with stevia-sweetened chocolate or cacao powder/cacao nibs. Cacao is unrefined raw chocolate and is considered a super food because it has such high levels of nutrients like magnesium.

- Replace lemon juice/lime juice with the zest or food-grade essential oils.

- Replace potato chips with homemade sweet potato and/or rutabaga chips (see recipe).

- Replace commercial crackers with homemade almond crackers or cheese chips (see recipe).

- Avoid any and all starches including corn starch, potato starch, tapioca flour, arrowroot powder and agar agar. Either omit completely and have a resulting recipe less thick or add grass-fed organic gelatin and simmer longer to cook down. You can also use egg yolk as a thickener in sauces, using 1 yolk per cup of liquid, being careful not to let the sauce boil after adding the yolks.

- Use good quality homemade vanilla extract made with vodka (see recipe in our Condiments Section for full instructions).

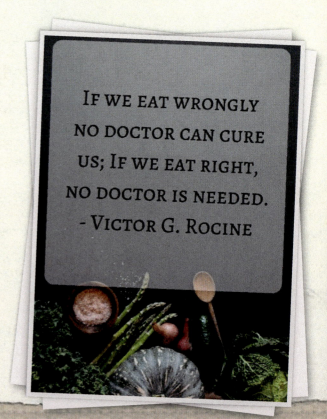

IF WE EAT WRONGLY NO DOCTOR CAN CURE US; IF WE EAT RIGHT, NO DOCTOR IS NEEDED.
- VICTOR G. ROCINE

Feel free to experiment and have fun with your recipes. As long as you are working within the many ingredient choices advocated on the Candida Cleanse, you should be good. And, best of all, there's really no need to count calories during this cleanse!

Chapter 6: Sugar & Candida

Sugar is most commonly the hardest thing to give up when on the Ditch Candida Program. Sugar, which includes honey, agave, fruit sugars, maple syrup, and anything ending in "-ose" is one of Candida's favorite foods. So much so, that your candida can sometimes even control your cravings!

If you find yourself craving sugar… which WILL happen… here are our recommendations to help you get through without sacrificing your progress:

1. Recognize that it is completely normal to be experiencing sugar cravings. Sometimes, just knowing mentally that it's the candida causing the craving… and that if you succumb you are just feeding the "monster", it can help. Sugar is a powerful addiction, however. One that is now being classified along with cocaine on its physical and physiological affects. Cut yourself some slack and know that as you persevere, it WILL get better.

2. Chew on some Cardamom Pods. You can find cardamom at most of your local health food stores in the herb section, or you can purchase them online from great resources like Mountain Rose Herbs. Chewing on the pod can help curb the sugar cravings. I found them very effective.

3. Have plenty of approved snacks and desserts handy that we offer in the Recipe section of this program. That way, when you are faced with those difficult moments, you can satisfy the craving with a "sweet treat" without feeding the candida. Some of our favorites to always have on hand are the Chocolate Chip Cookies, Thin Mint Cookies, and Chocolate Truffles; along with Sweet Tea, and Lemonade.

4. Drink water. If you're having a particularly strong sugar craving, grab a big glass of good ol' H2O. This does several things…. it will fill the stomach and distract the system, it will give you something to orally consume, and it will help hydrate the cells. For an added boost, drink water with your favorite probiotic and prebiotic supplements to further boost the "good bacteria".

5. Hang in there. You got this! Know that you are strong and with time, patience, and perseverance you WILL win this fight!

Chapter 7: Efficiency Tips

We all have the same amount of time in our days. It's how we choose to spend that time that makes all the difference.

One of the most common excuses I hear on why people don't persevere in any program is that they don't have the time. Yes, it's true that you will need to budget some time each day to meal preparation....made much easier for you by our ready-made Menu Plans and Shopping Guides....yet at the same time, there are a few things you can do to make things more efficient and easier should you be on a time crunch.

1. First, having a well-organized kitchen makes a huge difference in efficiency! Keep your counters clear and try to stay ahead of the dirty dishes (yes, I know this can be a challenge… at least is is for me, but worth the effort.)

2. Invest in a few tools that make cooking more efficient like a Crockpot, Power Pressure Cooker, Food Processor, and Mixer. My favorite tool for efficiency is the Power Pressure Cooker. Not only does it save time in cooking, but many dishes can be prepared as "one pot meals" with little or no dishes! So, not only does it save time in the food preparation but in the clean up as well.

3. Plan Ahead. Be sure to reference our Menu Plans to help you with this. Planning ahead will save time in the long run on grocery shopping and cooking time.

4. Pre-prep as much as possible. Taking an hour or two each week to prep for the week makes a HUGE difference. This includes things like full meal preps such as "Salad in a Jar" and "Sweet Potato Quiche", and ingredients prepping like

chopping vegetables, mixing seasonings, making condiments, and marinating meats. To make things easier for you, we include a suggested pre-prep guide with each Menu Plan.

5. Make extras of recipes for left-overs or freeze them in pre-portioned containers for easy dinners when you're more pressed for time.

We know that any program takes some time. We also know that it only takes 21 days to change a habit, and once you get into a routine, you'll be amazed at how smoothly things will go. Just hang in there and do your best. We know you can do this!

Chapter 8: Money Saving Tips

The biggest challenge I hear from people wanting to get healthy is that they just can't afford it. You can! Just follow these tips.

One of the most common excuses people give for not sticking with the Candida Program is that eating healthy is too expensive. Granted, if you're used to eating off the dollar menu every day there may be an adjustment period; yet eating healthy doesn't have to break the bank. Keep in mind, that the health food industry is HUGE business, especially now. Hundreds of companies want you to buy their products and will spend a great deal of money on marketing budgets to convince you that theirs is best. The first rule of thumb when eating healthy on a budget is to become a savvy consumer, not falling for the fancy promises or colorful packaging created by the industry. Place more emphasis on "**ingredients**" rather than convenience. I heard it said once, that the best way to grocery shop when following a healthy lifestyle is to shop the outside perimeter of the grocery store and avoid the center aisles altogether. In this program, you won't be finding much in pre-packaged boxes anyway so you'll find this is an easy transition.

Another great way to save money is to buy in bulk. Even though it may seem counter-intuitive to spend money to save money....it's my favorite money-saving technique. For example, this program allows meat, especially high quality, organically grown cuts. Meat, when purchased from a grocery store, is premium priced....and often hard to find organic. Try buying in bulk instead. You can buy half a beef from a local farmer or butcher and save significantly per pound, plus you get the added bonus of usually getting the bones for making stocks and broth! You also get the advantage of speaking the the farmer who

raised the animal so you know how they were raised and how they were treated. Most local farmers will have pasture-raised animals instead of the large feed-lot stock found in commercial options.

We also like to buy in bulk for those things we use regularly and store well, such as coconut oil, salt, almonds and other nuts, and almond flour. Buying in bulk may come from specific stores or websites that specialize in larger quantities, or it may come from finding your favorites on sale and stocking up.

When buying produce, try local farmers markets, discount stores, and neighborhood co-ops. And you can't go wrong by planting a garden to grow some great vegetables yourself! Gardening is a fun and rewarding hobby and can be done even in limited space. Whether it's growing microgreens on your kitchen window sill, tomatoes on your porch, or rows of green beans in an outside garden, the effort is worth it in the amazing flavor, sense of accomplishment, and cost savings!

One of our favorite ways to save money is to be organized and follow menu plans, such as the ones we offer in this program. With organization and planning, you have a strategic grocery list which saves you from impulse purchases or buying things that may go to waste and get thrown out. Adjust the menu plans as needed to buy items that are fresh, local, and in-season. In-season produce tends to be higher in nutritional value AND often much more economical than when not in season.

Set up a budget and follow it. It often amazes me how few people I meet actually use a budget. My parents always said that every penny should be allocated somewhere…whether it's to big stuff like "House Payment" or "Grocery Budget" or even little things like "Christmas Fund", "Eating Out", or "Stuff Happens". Dave Ramsey recommends using an envelope system after creating the budget and we love this system. An envelope system is where you take the cash allocation for that budget item and put it in a labelled envelope. Using an envelope system helps with controlling spending habits, knowing what you have to spend including how much is left to get through the rest of the month, and for me it was a fun mental game to see how much I could still have in the envelope at the end of the month to carry over or put in another envelope like "Date Night", or "Vacation Fund". Before using the envelope system with planned budgeting, I never seemed to have enough funds. After implementing this one simple change, I was shocked to see how often I had a surplus! Give it a try and enjoy taking control of your money.

Chapter 9: Eating Out

Cooking at home has its benefits, but sometimes it's nice to eat out once in awhile. Follow our simple tips for stress-free and enjoyable dining... on the go.

Just because you're on the Ditch Candida program, doesn't mean you are confined to your house. Go out and enjoy eating out as much as you want to! You just have to keep in mind the guidelines of what you can eat and choose your restaurant accordingly. For example, there are very few "Fast Food" joints that will have much for you to choose from. Most traditional restaurants will have a wide variety of choices for you to enjoy, without any guilt or "cheating." Here are some tips to help you in your eating out adventures.

Have a small "condiments" bag that you prepare ahead of time and take with you. I usually have it in my purse or car all the time so I'm ready no matter when the situation may arise. In this bag I include a small bottle of liquid stevia or a couple packets of stevia powder, Celtic Sea Salt, and a small bottle of a salad dressing like balasamic vinegar and oil. If you make your own ketchup or find a sugar-free version, you can bring a container of that too. Just make sure you use tight-sealing containers! I also like to include a couple good snack options in my bag, too. That way, if I'm out and about and can't find a good restaurant or just need a little something, I have

goodies on hand. Great options are the "Cinnamon Spiced Nuts", "Thin Mint Cookies", and "Trail Mix."

Choose a restaurant that has items on the menu that work for you. For example, most steakhouses work great so you can get grilled chicken, steak, or seafood with steamed vegetables. I find Mexican or Italian restaurants a bit more challenging to find workable choices. If you opt for

Oriental, order without the rice or noodles and make sure they don't use MSG or sugar in the sauce.

Double check with your server on whether they use Canola Oil. If so, request they use butter when preparing your meal. Restaurants are used to more and more people with allergies and dietary restrictions so they SHOULD accommodate. If not, choose another restaurant. If you're in the mood for a good burger, order it without the bun...or see if they can do a lettuce wrap. I'm seeing more and more restaurants who offer sweet potato fries as an option with the burger too!

Say no to the dessert menu. If you have a sweet craving after your meal or are in the habit of dessert after you eat, take some good dessert-type options with you like one of our cookie recipes or Stevia Sweetened Chocolate.

Chapter 10: Navigating the Holidays

Holidays generally center around food. To stay on track and avoid indulging, follow our tips to navigating the holidays.

Holidays and Birthdays can be a tricky time when you're on the Ditch Candida program, mainly because our culture is so food-centered, especially the processed and sweet treat foods. I'm here to tell you, though, that it IS possible to get through the holidays and not even feel like you're missing out. Be sure to check out our Desserts section, Snacks section, and Beverages section for some great options that are festive, delicious, and work well for everyone. Some of them are so good, no one will even guess that they're....HEALTHY!

For holiday gatherings, if YOU are hosting the event, you have the benefit of coordinating the menu and planning accordingly. Roast turkey or chicken with vegetables is a traditional favorite and you can't go wrong. We have included recipes for some wonderful desserts like Pumpkin Pie, Chocolate Truffles, Cookies, Puddings, and Custards to satisfy even the most discerning sweet tooth.

If you are not hosting, we always recommend eating a good meal before you go, so you won't be as hungry or tempted when you arrive. Communicate with the host/hostess and offer to bring some items that will work for you and your family. Have your "condiments" bag as discussed in "Eating Out" with stevia and salt. Most people are pretty understanding when they know you are avoiding certain foods for health reasons.

For birthdays, we stick with things like the "Zucchini Brownies" recipe with "Homemade Ice Cream". The brownies closely resemble a "cake" and are decadently rich and delicious. "Pumpkin Squares" or "Pumpkin Pie" also make great birthday "cake".

Sweet Potato Quiche

This recipe is great for any meal, not just breakfast but also makes a great snack. Save time by making multiple batches at once and refrigerate or freeze for later use. Quiche reheats very well and is sometimes even better when reheated (please don't use a microwave). Change up your ingredients based on what you have on hand, fresh in the garden, or what sounds best to you. Feel free to be creative and experiment to find your favorites.

Sweet Potatoes make an excellent crust alternative that is grain-free yet adds flavor and more nutrients to the dish. You'll never look at quiche quite the same again after trying this recipe!

Husband Approved

Hubby says: "Definitely a two thumbs up recipe. Filling and satisfying, it gives me the energy I need to get through my morning. I like spicy, so my favorite is when this recipe is made with lots of spice and a good chipotle or jalapeno cheese. Eating healthy shouldn't taste THIS good, should it?"

Kid Approved

Daughter says: "I'm not a big fan of eggs so it's not my favorite, but as far as egg recipes go, this one is ok. I like it best with lots of cheese and bacon or ham….then topped with fresh tomato and cilantro or basil!"

Base Ingredients:
- 1 large sweet potato, peeled and thinly sliced
- 1 medium onion, chopped
- ½ sweet bell pepper, chopped
- Handful of fresh kale, de-stemmed
- 4 large eggs
- 2 Tablespoons milk
- 1 cup shredded cheese (any variety)
- Dash Salt and Pepper (to taste)

Optional Additional Ingredients (Mix & Match)
- Turkey Bacon Crumbles (no nitrates or sugar)
- Turkey or Chicken Sausage (check for no sugar)
- Diced Shallots
- Minced Garlic
- Hot Peppers, diced
- Herbs/Spices

Optional Fresh Toppings (after Baking)
- Diced Fresh Tomatoes
- Fresh herbs (dill, parsley, cilantro, basil, or stinging nettle)
- Sauerkraut
- Salsa (fresh, no sugar)
- Sour cream

1. Preheat oven to 350 degrees.
2. Clean, peel, and slice sweet potato and spread evenly on the bottom of a lightly greased pie pan. Note, if your sweet potato is home grown or organic, you don't have to peel.
3. Bake for 20 minutes.
4. While sweet potato crust is baking, saute onions, peppers, and other optional ingredients until soft. When onions are almost translucent, add the kale to lightly cook down.
5. In a separate bowl, whisk eggs, milk, salt, and pepper.
6. When crust is done, remove from oven and top with onion mixture. Add egg mixture to coat. Top with cheese.
7. Bake for 20-25 minutes until eggs are set. Last 2-3 minutes of baking, switch to broil to toast the cheese on top.
8. Remove from oven and let cool slightly.
9. Slice and serve, topped with optional fresh ingredients.

Almond Flour Pancakes

Fast and easy to make, these almond flour pancakes are a great substitution to the traditional pancakes while on your Candida Cleanse. Almond flour contains no gluten so you won't get the light and fluffy version but the flavor is great and gives you some variety for breakfast other than always turning to eggs. Make a double batch for extras and reheat for a quick snack or meal later. Enjoy!

Basic Ingredients:
- 1 ½ cups fine Almond Flour
- 3 eggs
- 1 cup of milk (or slightly less to desired thickness) Note: Any milk of choice works

Optional Additional Ingredients:
Cinnamon, Nutmeg, Pumpkin Pie Spice, Vanilla, Pumpkin, Stevia

1. Mix all ingredients in a medium bowl using a hand blender or immersion blender until batter is a pourable consistency. (I use my Kitchenaide mixer)
2. While mixture is blending, preheat cast iron griddle or griddle pan.
3. Pour about ¼ - ½ cup batter onto griddle depending on desired pancake size and thickness.
4. Cook for about 2-3 minutes per side until bubbles form and both sides are golden brown.

Note About Toppings:

The trick with pancakes is that so often traditional pancakes are consumed smothered in syrup made with high fructose corn syrup and other sugary ingredients that feed the candida. We don't want to do that!

Instead, try topping your pancakes with our Chocolate Pudding or Hot Fudge recipe to use as a topping instead. Or, whip up a batch of homemade whipped cream made with vanilla and stevia with some toasted nuts of choice. The Pumpkin Spice Syrup makes a delicious alternative too!

Husband Approved

Hubby says: "What a treat to get something that I thought was completely off-limits! I love sugary treats and this was pretty good."

Kid Approved

Daughter says: "This was ok. I liked it and all, but it's not the same as Bisquick."

Breakfast Hash

There's something about a good hash recipe that just screams, "Comfort Food." Maybe it has something to do with my Grandma making hash when I spent time at her house and the house would smell so good.

Traditionally, hash uses potatoes but our version uses sweet potatoes which, in my opinion, makes the outcome even better.

Basic Instructions:
Serves 4
- 4 T (half stick) of butter
- Half red onion, chopped
- 1 c chopped zucchini
- 1 c chopped red pepper
- 1 c chopped yellow squash
- Salt and pepper to taste
- 1 sweet potato, baked until tender (45 minutes at 375 degrees) peeled and diced
- 4 fried eggs
- Hot sauce (no sugar), optional

Melt 2 T of the butter in a large skillet over medium high heat.

Add the onion, zucchini, pepper, and squash. Sprinkle with salt and pepper and cook until the veggies are golden brown, 4-5 minutes.

Remove to a plate.

Add the remaining 2 T butter and sweet potatoes, sauté until golden about 5 minutes.

Add the veggies back in and stir everything together. Add the eggs to the skillet and serve the skillet on the table.

Variations:
- Add crumbled meat of choice such as turkey or chicken sausage, turkey bacon, ground turkey, or ground beef.
- Top with sour cream, crème fraiche, or yogurt.
- Top with fresh herbs like basil, cilantro, parsley, rosemary, or mint.
- Top with shredded cheese of choice like cheddar or pepper jack.

Adapted from Pioneer Woman

Husband Approved

Hubby says: "You don't even miss the potatoes in this version of the traditional hash."

Kid Approved

Daughter says: "Oh, yeah! Love this one. Especially with a little bit of cheese melted on top!"

Devilled Eggs / Egg Salad

Husband Approved

Hubby says: "I've never been a fan but these are pretty good."

Kid Approved

Daughter says: "I could eat these every day. I love it when Mom puts these in my lunch for school…and they're one of my favorites at parties."

Devilled Eggs make a great meal, snack, or party platter dish. Use the same recipe and chop up the eggs to make "Egg Salad" and serve over lettuce wrap. To make the original recipe work for the Ditch Candida Program, we substitute a few things with great alternatives and the resulting recipe is simply delicious….some say even better than the original.

1. Hard cook the number of eggs you are wanting. Quantity may vary depending on personal preference. We tend to make extra since it's so good and makes for a great time-saver too. (Place eggs in saucepan and cover with water. Put pan over medium heat until water boils. Cover, turn off heat, and set timer for 15 minutes. Plunge into cold water with ice cubes at once to arrest further cooking and prevent the yolks from discoloring.)

2. Peel eggs.

3. Cut the eggs in half lengthwise, remove yolks carefully so as not to damage the whites. Crush the yolks without packing them and moisten them pleasantly with crème fraiche or Homemade Mayonnaise. Amount used will vary depending on how many eggs and desired consistency.

4. Season to taste with Dry Mustard, Fresh Dill, Celtic Sea Salt and Pepper

Additional Optional Ingredients: dash of cayenne pepper, anchovy or sardine paste, liverwurst, smoked salmon, diced sautéed mushrooms

Put the fillings back in the whites. You may use a pastry tube for dramatic effect. For improved flavor and texture, remove the eggs from the refrigerator a half an hour before serving.

Optional: Garnish with olives, capers, or diced lacto-fermented pickles.

Inspired by Joy of Cooking

Eggs Chiles Rellanos

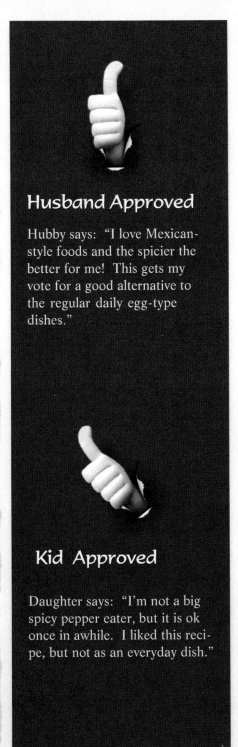

Husband Approved

Hubby says: "I love Mexican-style foods and the spicier the better for me! This gets my vote for a good alternative to the regular daily egg-type dishes."

Kid Approved

Daughter says: "I'm not a big spicy pepper eater, but it is ok once in awhile. I liked this recipe, but not as an everyday dish."

This recipe is fun to make and beautiful on the plate. I like adding some variety to the palate and some heat from the peppers is great for stimulating the digestive system. A little bit of cheese balances out the pepper, making this a great option for any time of day.

Be sure the choose the best possible ingredients and fresh peppers are best.

Base Ingredients:
(Serves 8-10)

- 6 fresh poblano chile peppers or you may use canned roasted green chiles
- 5 large eggs
- 2 c whole milk
- Salt and pepper to taste
- ½ tsp paprika
- ¼ tsp cayenne pepper
- 1 ½ c grated Monterey jack cheese
- Lettuce

Optional Fresh Toppings
- Fresh Salsa (no sugar)
- Fresh Cilantro
- Sauerkraut
- Sour Cream

---

1. Preheat oven to 325 degrees.
2. If using fresh poblanos, begin by roasting the peppers (if using canned, skip this step).

Roast peppers: use tongs to hold peppers over an open flame until the skin is completely charred. If you don't have a gas burner you can grill them or place them under the broiler in the oven. Place charred pepper in a plastic bag and seal to trap in the heat. Leave in the bag for 15 minutes to steam the skin off. Use a knife to scrape the blackened skin off the peppers. You can leave bits behind for flavor. Slice open the peppers and scrape out the seeds. Cut each pepper in half.

3. In a large bowl, combine the eggs, milk, salt and pepper, paprika, and cayenne. Whisk until totally combined. Now to assemble the dish:
4. Arrange half the peppers in a single layer in a 9x13 baking dish. Sprinkle on half the cheese, then layer on the rest of the peppers and the rest of the cheese. Pour the egg mixture evenly over the top. Finally, place the pan into a larger pan and pour hot water into the pan until the water level is even with the level of the eggs. This keeps the eggs from getting over cooked around the edges.
5. Carefully place the pan to the oven and bake for 35-40 minutes or until the eggs are completely set. Watch to make sure the top doesn't get too brown.
6. Let the casserole sit for 10 minutes, then slice it into squares. Top with optional fresh ingredients.

Time Saving Tip: The peppers can be stored in the fridge for 3 days in advance.

Inspired by Pioneer Woman

Eggs en Cocotte

Baked eggs always have "eye appeal" served in little ramekins, casseroles, or cocotte dishes.

Yes, you do need some small casserole or ramekin dishes for this recipe to work well, but it's worth it if you love eggs!

Care must be taken not to overcook them, for the ramekin will retain the heat and continue to cook them after it is removed from the oven. The yolks should be soft, the whites just set. Don't try to hurry baked eggs.

Husband Approved

Hubby says: "This is a great recipe and one that gives eggs a much different look and flavor. I wouldn't want to have it every day, but it is nice as something outside the daily routine."

Basic Instructions:
Preheat oven to 350 degrees. Grease small ramekins with coconut oil.
Break carefully into each one:
- 1 egg

Sprinkle over the top:
- Celtic Salt and pepper
- 1 tsp cream or melted butter

Place ramekin in a pan of hot water. Bake about 6-7 minutes.
You may garnish with:
Tomato sauce
Parsley

Variations:
- You may also garnish with Herbs like fresh parsley, basil, or dill.
- Add spices such as garlic powder, chili powder, taco seasoning, onion powder, smoked paprika, kelp, or ginger
- Top with fresh tomato, salsa (no sugar), sour cream, or crème fraiche.

Kid Approved

Daughter says: "Since I don't like egg yolks much, I liked this ok. It's best when mommy makes it with just the whites and tops it with lots of fresh tomatoes!"

Adapted from Joy of Cooking

Fluffy Omelette Soufflé

Husband Approved

Hubby says: "I liked this one. I'm more of a simple foods, kind of guy and this one is a bit fancier but it's good."

Kid Approved

Daughter says: "The fluffier texture of this recipe made it good and super fun to eat."

This omelette souffle is a fun alternative to the traditional omelette and since it is partially baked, has a different flavor too. Watch it closely so you don't over-cook it and serve immediately. More of a weekend brunch-type of recipe rather than a daily…on-your-way-out-the-door-to-go-to-work type of recipe since it does take a bit more attention. Worth the effort though.

- Combine and beat with a fork:
    - ¼ c milk
    - 4 egg yolks
    - 1 tsp baking powder
- Beat until stiff but not dry:
    - 4-6 egg whites.
- Melt on a low heat in heavy skillet:
    - 1 T butter
- You may add some grated parmesan cheese or chopped parsley, chives, chervil to the egg mixture to the egg mixture before cooking it, or sprinkle these on top before cooking it.
- Fold yolk mixture lightly into egg whites. Pour the batter into the skillet. Cover. As the omelette cooks, slash through it several times with a knife to permit the heat to penetrate from the lower layer. When the omelette is half done, after about 5 minutes, it may be placed onto the center rack uncovered of a 350 degree oven until the top is set.
- Serve quickly after removing from the oven, because it may collapse as it cools.
- Cut omelette into pie shaped segments to serve. Garnish with chopped parsley, shredded cheddar, and chopped crisp turkey bacon.

Inspired by Joy of Cooking

Fluffy Pancakes

Every so often, you just want a good pancake breakfast or snack. This recipe is really good and whips up quickly for easy goodness just about any time.

Ingredients:

- 1 c cooked squash, pureed
- 1 c almond butter
- 5 eggs
- ½ tsp salt
- 1 T cinnamon
- Dash of spice, such as cloves, nutmeg, etc.
- Coconut Oil, Butter, or Ghee for cooking

Husband Approved

Hubby says: "These Pancakes are great as a quick snack when I'm out working. I need 'grab-and-go' snacks that are filling. These fit the bill perfectly."

1. Separate the eggs, putting the whites into one large bowl and the yolks into a separate bowl.
2. Add the remaining ingredients to the egg yolks and mix together.
3. Beat the whites until soft peaks form, and then fold into the yolk mixture.
4. Fry in coconut oil or butter using a griddle or skillet on medium to low heat, as they can burn easily.
5. Serve warm with melted butter and Pumpkin Syrup (recipe in Condiments)

When cold, these pancakes work well to make sandwiches as a bread substitute.

Kid Approved

Daughter says: "It took some getting used to for these pancakes because they have a different texture than what I was used to, but once I got over the change, I really love them."

Inspired by Internal Bliss Cookbook

Fried Eggs

Eggs got some bad publicity for awhile, with so-called experts saying they are high in cholesterol and therefore bad for you. In reality, eggs contain a wide array of nutrients. Eggs are a very good source of inexpensive, high quality protein of which more than half the protein is found in the egg white along with vitamin B2. The whites are rich sources of selenium, vitamin D, B6, B12 and minerals such as zinc, iron and copper.

The yolk contains cholesterol, yet science now shows that the amount of cholesterol you consume is NOT correlated to the amount of cholesterol that builds up in your body. Studies also show, that eating MORE cholesterol from sources like eggs actually can cause your body to produce LESS harmful cholesterol.

Cooking them in healthy fats like coconut oil or butter not only adds to the flavor but makes them even better nutritionally. So enjoy your eggs!

Basic Instructions:
- 1 Egg
- 1 Tablespoon Butter or Coconut Oil
- Celtic Salt and Pepper to taste

Melt butter in a heavy skillet over a medium flame and crack the egg into the pan. Be careful not to break the yolk. Cover with a lid and cook gently for several minutes until the white becomes firm and the yolk somewhat thickened.

If you prefer your eggs with firm yolk, flip egg over with a spatula and cook until desired consistency.

Variations:
- Add spices such as garlic powder, chili powder, taco seasoning, onion powder, smoked paprika, kelp, or ginger
- Top with fresh tomato, sauerkraut, and fresh cilantro (my favorite version)

Adapted from Nourishing Traditions

Husband Approved

Hubby says: "Fried Eggs are a great breakfast but also make a fantastic snack. It's one of the things I don't mind fixing if I am the one to cook. You can't go wrong with fast, easy, and delicious."

Kid Approved

Daughter says: "Fried eggs are yummy when mommy leaves out the yolks. I'm not a big fan of the yolk, but a fried egg white is so good!"

Omelettes

Husband Approved

Hubby says: "Omelettes are one of my favorite egg recipes, especially when it has lots of pepper jack cheese and jalapeño popper dip inside!"

Kid Approved

Daughter says: "Definitely a two thumbs up. I like my omelettes with lots of mushrooms and veggies!"

The basic omelette is a staple in our house. There are so many variations and the combination of eggs, veggies, and cheese are a winner for everyone. I find myself often turning to omelettes when entertaining guests, too since pretty much everyone , regardless of age, can enjoy a good omelette. Vary your ingredients each time you make it for a whole new experience and to keep things interesting.

Base Ingredients:	Sauteed Asparagus
2 eggs or egg whites	Sauteed Broccoli
1 Tblsp Milk, Cream, or Crème Fraiche	Sauteed Mushrooms
Butter	Diced clean meat of choice
Celtic Sea Salt and Pepper to Taste	
	Optional Fresh Toppings (after Baking)
Filling Ingredients (any combinations based on preference):	Fresh herbs (dill, parsley, cilantro, basil, or stinging nettle)
Grated Cheese	Sauerkraut
Cream Cheese	Fresh Tomato
Leftover Jalapeño Popper Dip	Salsa (no sugar)
Sauteed Onions	Sour Cream
Sauteed Bell or Spicy Pepper	Chopped Black Olives

1. In a small bowl, combine Base Ingredients. Whisk briskly with a fork until well mixed and frothy.
2. Melt Butter or Coconut Oil in small saute pan. Gently add egg mixture and heat on low-medium heat until set.
3. Carefully flip omelette and turn off heat to avoid overcooking eggs. Quickly add toppings of choice to half of egg then flip other side of egg over toppings to form omelette.
4. Transfer to a plate and top with fresh toppings of choice.

Pumpkin Muffins

Husband Approved

Hubby says: "These muffins are a surprising treat and very filling. I like them best warm with lots of butter."

Kid Approved

Daughter says: "I love the taste and the texture! You'd never guess these are sugar-free and healthy! The aftertaste takes some getting used to, though, so just one thumb up this time."

Pumpkin makes a great substitute for the fruits that you may be missing on the Candida Cleanse. Since it's a vegetable, it's approved yet works great in recipes we would otherwise be turning to fruit. These Pumpkin Muffins are a great on-the-go breakfast and are a favorite in our house when going on picnics or camping. We use Duck Eggs for this recipe since the yolks are big, rich, and make delicious muffins. Regular Chicken Eggs work great too!

Ingredients:

3 Eggs
1 (12 oz) can pumpkin puree (check ingredients and make sure it's pumpkin ONLY)
¼ cup coconut oil or butter (softened)
3/4 cup almond flour or more if needed
1 teaspoon baking soda
1 teaspoon vanilla
1-2 Tablespoons Pumpkin Pie Spice (or cinnamon)
8-10 drops liquid Stevia (or to taste)

1. Preheat oven to 400 degrees
2. Line muffin tin with paper muffin cups.
3. Thoroughly mix all ingredients until smooth and well incorporated. If batter is too thick, add a little almond milk but don't let it get runny at all. If it is too thin, add more almond flour.
4. Using a ¼ cup measure, scoop batter into muffin cups. Batter will be thick.
5. Bake for 13-18 minutes until lightly browned and set in the middle.
6. Remove from oven and let cool slightly on a cooling rack.

Optional Variations:
- Scoop half the mixture into the muffin cups, then add a dollop of softened cream cheese to the center of each muffin. Top with remaining batter, then bake as directed above.
- Finely grind toasted almonds and/or pecans mixed with some melted butter to make a crumble topping. Sprinkle on each muffin before baking.

Classic Scrambled Eggs

A common choice in our house is the classic scrambled egg. You can't go wrong with this recipe, and with so many different variations on additions, it'll never get old. Always use the best eggs you can find, as it really does make a difference! Farm fresh is worth it, if you have access to a friend or neighbor with chickens. An easy recipe for young cooks, this is a great one to teach your kids to prepare, too!

Basic Instructions:

For best results, eggs should not be below room temperature. To achieve more fluffiness, beaten whites may be added to whole eggs in the proportion of one additional white to three whole eggs.

2 servings

Option 1:
Melt in a skillet over low heat: 1 to 2 tablespoons of butter. Have ready by the time the butter is hot, and add to skillet, well beaten with a fork or whisk:
- 3 eggs
- ¼ tsp salt
- 1/8 tsp paprika
- 2 T milk or cream

As the eggs heat through, increase the heat somewhat, and with a spoon or spatula, shove the eggs about gently but with accelerating speed, turning them if necessary, until they have thickened but are still soft.

Option 2:
A slower but quite foolproof alternative. Melt in a double boiler: 1 Tablespoon butter. Have ready:
The seasoned egg mixture shown above.
When the butter is hot, pour in the egg mixture. Stir repeatedly with a wooden spoon until eggs have thickened into soft creamy curds.

Variations:

Small amounts of the following may be stirred into the egg mixture before scrambling: grated or crumbled cheese, tomatoes, basil, cultured sour cream and chives, capers, chopped onions, chopped bell pepper, crisp turkey bacon bits, sautéed mushrooms.

Adapted from Joy of Cooking

Husband Approved

Hubby says: "Who doesn't like scrambled eggs? I especially love them with lots of toppings and cheese."

Kid Approved

Daughter says: "I like scrambled eggs, but since eggs aren't my favorite, I enjoy them if we don't eat them too often."

Huevos Rancheros

Also called "Cowboy Eggs", this recipe makes a great breakfast, lunch, or dinner. Perfect for those who love southwestern food, Huevos Rancheros is delicious, quick to make, and loaded with protein for lots of energy. Feel free to experiment with some of the suggested variations to find your favorite.

Sauce Ingredients:
These eggs can be baked in the following sauce, or poached or sautéed with the sauce poured over afterward.

Heat in skillet:
- 1/4 c coconut or avocado oil

And saute in it for 5 minutes:
- 1 crushed clove of garlic

Add, sautéing until soft:
- 2 medium sized finely chopped onions
- 1 large finely chopped green pepper

Add:
- 1 cup peeled, seeded, and chopped fresh tomatoes
- ½ tsp salt
- ¼ tsp black pepper
- 2 tsp chili powder
- ¼ tsp oregano
- 1/8 tsp powdered cumin

Simmer, covered, until thick and well blended. Season to taste. The sauce should be very hot and well flavored.

Pour it over:
8 poached or sautéed eggs, allowing 2 eggs per serving.

Or, to bake, preheat oven to 450 degrees. Pour the sauce into a heat proof dish or 4 individual casseroles and nest uncooked eggs in the same.

Garnish with:
Strips of red pimiento.
Sprinkle with a little grated cheese.
Bake until eggs are set.

Variations:
- Add diced and de-seeded fresh jalapeno pepper to the sauce
- Use organic, canned diced tomato if fresh isn't available (check for no sugar added)

Optional Fresh Toppings (after Cooking)
Fresh herbs (parsley, cilantro, basil), Sauerkraut, Sour cream

Husband Approved

Hubby says: "I love the flavors of Southwest Cuisine, and this is a winner. My favorite version is with lots of extra spicy because I like it HOT."

Kid Approved

Daughter says: "This is yummy, especially when mom makes it the way I like it with just egg whites and lots of sauce."

Frittata

Another one of our favorite Egg Recipes is Frittata. Super easy with tons of variations depending on veggie additions, different cheeses, and meat options. Experiment to find your favorites.

Ingredients:

12 large eggs
Celtic Sea salt and pepper to taste
¼ cup grated parmesan
½ cup grated cheddar
Several dashes of hot sauce (optional)
2 T butter
1 medium onion, sliced
1 sweet potato, baked until tender (20 min in power pressure cooker)
2 cups torn kale leaves
2 large jars roasted red peppers, thinly sliced
¼ c green olives, chopped

Husband Approved

Hubby says: "Love this one and it makes a really great lunch in a thermos while I'm on the go working."

1. Prepare the oven to 375 degrees.
2. In a large bowl, whisk the eggs with salt pepper.
3. Add the grated cheeses and stir to mix them in with the eggs. Stir in the hot sauce, if using. Set it aside.
4. In a large oven proof, non-stick skillet, melt the butter over medium high heat. Add the onion and cook for several minutes, until onion is soft and golden. Add the sweet potato, sprinkle with salt and pepper, and stir. Cook with the onion for a couple of minutes. Add the kale and stir, cook for a minute or so. Finally, add the roasted the red peppers and olives.
5. Stir them in, and arrange all the veggies evenly in the pan. Slowly pour the egg mixture over the veggies, making sure it's evenly distributed around the edges. Keep the frittata on the burner for about 45 seconds to set, then slide skillet into the oven.
6. Bake 10-12 minutes, or until eggs set. Keep an eye on it, though, and make sure it doesn't get too brown on top.

Variations: Substitute mushrooms, spinach, bell peppers, asparagus, etc. Experiment with other cheeses such as pepper jack, goat cheese, Fontina, etc. Add cooked crumbled turkey or chicken sausage, or crisp turkey bacon.

Kid Approved

Daughter says: "Yummy recipe. I especially like it with lots of cheese and mushrooms."

Inspired by Pioneer Woman

Poached Eggs & Veggies

We like this recipe as a breakfast, lunch, or dinner. Fast and easy to prepare, it is light and satisfying. If you're new to poaching eggs, having a very large slotted spoon really helps when pulling the perfectly cooked eggs out of the boiling water. Top with fresh herbs for a different flavor, or sprinkle with some smoked paprika.

Farm fresh eggs are best, especially with poached eggs. You can see the difference in the yolk color and taste the difference too.

Base Ingredients:
- 1 T butter or olive oil
- ½ medium onion, cut into chunks
- ½ zucchini, cut into chunks
- ½ yellow squash, cut into chunks
- Salt and pepper to taste
- 1 tomato, sliced thickly
- 1 tsp vinegar
- 2 large eggs
- 1 thin slice of cheese of your choice

Optional Fresh Toppings (after Baking)
- Fresh herbs (dill, parsley, cilantro, basil, or stinging nettle)
- Sauerkraut

Husband Approved

Hubby says: "I enjoy these eggs as a dinner rather than breakfast, when you want a simple meal that isn't to heavy when you are getting dinner late. I don't care for fresh tomatoes, but the gentle cooked tomato in this recipe is good."

Kid Approved

Daughter says: "The veggies are the best part of this recipe, especially with some fresh basil or cilantro."

1. Bring a medium saucepan of water to a gentle boil over medium heat. Melt the butter or heat olive oil in a large skillet over medium heat.
2. Add the onion. Cook 2-3 minutes until soft. Add zucchini and squash and sprinkle with salt and pepper. Cook for 3-4 minutes until veggies are cooked but still somewhat tender. Remove them from heat and set aside.
3. In a grill pan or skillet, grill or sauté the tomato slices a few minutes to soften and give them slight color. Remove tomato and set aside.
4. To poach the eggs, add the vinegar to the pan of boiling water. Use a wooden spoon to stir the water in a circular whirlpool. Once the whirl pool is swirling, crack in one of the eggs. The egg will swirl around itself and begin to set. Leave in the water 1 minute or longer if you would like a more set yolk. Then remove it from the pan with a slotted spoon and set it on a plate while you poach the second egg. You can do both at once if you're feeling adventurous.
5. To assemble the dish, pile the veggies in a bowl and top with tomato slices. Add the eggs and serve with cheese. Sprinkle with a little salt and pepper.

Inspired by Pioneer Woman

Homemade Broth

Many of the soup, stew, and chili recipes offered here use a base of broth or stock. Although you can buy it commercially, making your own is so easy, much more economical, and you can control the ingredients as well as how it is handled. Homemade broth tends to be more nutritious and especially flavorful.

We have a full online video course on making broth in our Living Foods Academy, which will take you step-by-step through making various types of broth using the stockpot, slow cooker, and pressure cooker. We also show you how to preserve your broth so you can make big batches and then freeze, dehydrate, or can it for later use. As an added bonus, we also share our technique for making Perpetual Bone Broth. Be sure to check out the full course at www.HealthyHomesteadLiving.com to learn about making broth.

The easiest way to make broth is with a slow cooker. Here are the basic instructions:

Making Nourishing Broth
(Slow Cooker Method)

The crockpot and the electric pressure cooker are our favorite methods of preparing broth. The key to good broth is a long, slow simmer…the longer the better…at very low heat to avoid scorching. With a crockpot, we can safely get a good slow simmer over a 12 hour period (or more) without hassle or worry. The crockpot is a fairly common household appliance these days, so it negates the need to purchase extra equipment to make your broth. Be sure to start with a clean crockpot, check carefully for cracks or blemishes, and find a safe place to situate your unit during the long cooking process.

Ingredients for Bone Broths

1. First, you will need **bones**. Best will be a variety of bones from a quality and organically raised animal, fish, or fowl. Broth is economical to make so it is recommended to get the best quality bones you can find. If possible, include feet, neck, and bones with tendons for the best broth.

2. Broth also contains a combination of **vegetables and herbs**. The classic combination, called a *mirepoix* in French cuisine, includes carrots, celery, and onions. You can add anything else that might be in your garden or maybe wilting in your refrigerator (broth is a great use for those veggies a little past their prime) such as:

    a. Root vegetables like beets, turnips, parsnips, jicama, celeriac
    b. Vegetables such as leek, tomato, peppers
    c. Sea Vegetables such as kombu, wakame, kelp
    d. Herbs such as parsley, rosemary, thyme, sage, cilantro, bay leaf, mint, oregano
    e. Spices and aromatics such as peppercorns, garlic, horseradish, ginger, turmeric
    f. Other additions such as mushrooms, lemon and/or lime wedges

The combination of vegetables, herbs, aromatics, and spices will affect the flavor of your final broth. Feel free to experiment and find the ingredients that work best for you. We don't recommend adding starchy vegetables such as potatoes or corn to your broth as they may adversely affect the final broth. Save those ingredients for your recipe after the broth has been made. Also, don't add salt to your broth. Salt can be added later in your final recipe when you can better control the final flavor.

3. All good broth will require the addition of small amounts of **vinegar**. The vinegar helps extract minerals from the bones. Any good vinegar will do, and the vinegar doesn't need to be raw or contain the "mother" since you will be heating the broth enough to negate the benefits of raw. Apple cider vinegar is the most common choice, yet wine vinegar, white vinegar, kombucha vinegar, or other vinegar you may have on hand will work fine.

4. You will want to use clean, filtered **water** for your broth. Try to avoid water that may be contaminated with any chemicals like fluoride or chlorine, often found in most city tap water.

**If using a whole chicken, frozen is acceptable. Cooked bones, leftover from previous recipes (like a good rotisserie chicken) may also be used. When using cooked bones, be sure to add a chicken foot or other additional bones for added nutrient value.

- Place bones, vegetables, herbs, spices, and vinegar in the crockpot. (Frozen whole chicken is acceptable with the crockpot method. If making broth with large vertebrate bones such as beef, first roast the bones for 30 minutes at 350°, turning once.)

- Fill with filtered water to cover the bones. Careful not to over-fill the crockpot.

- Place the lid on the crockpot.

- Plug in and set crockpot to the lowest possible setting or longest cooking time depending on your unit.

- Cook for 6-24 hours.

- Unplug crockpot and cautiously remove lid, facing lid away from you to direct steam away from your body.

- Carefully strain off broth, remove meat (if applicable). Broth and meat will be HOT!

- Allow broth to cool to room temperature or use in your favorite recipe.

- If not using right away, store strained broth as desired (information on freezing, dehydrating, or canning can be found in our online course at www.healthyhomesteadliving.com).

Note: Normally in our Ditch Candida program, we want to avoid Apple Cider Vinegar. Making broth is one small exception, however. Since we are only using 2 Tablespoons of vinegar for the process of making at least 2-3 quarts of broth, the amounts are not enough to cause problems or feed the candida. The benefits of the broth will far outweigh the ACV in the ingredients.

Bacon Butternut Squash Soup

Butternut squash has a deep, rich flavor that makes a great soup. Winter squashes like butternut are loaded with nutrients, are easy to grow, economical to purchase, and store very well for several months. This recipe is loaded with creamy flavor... and topped with bacon makes a wonderful breakfast, lunch, dinner, or snack.

Ingredients:
- 1 large butternut squash, peeled; de-seeded; cut into large chunks
- 3 whole carrots, peeled and cut into large chunks
- 1 ½ T coconut oil, melted
- ½ lb turkey bacon (nitrite/nitrate free)
- 1 small onion, chopped
- 2 cups chicken stock/broth (homemade is best)
- 1 cup whole milk
- 1 tsp Celtic Sea salt
- 1 T cinnamon
- 1 T nutmeg

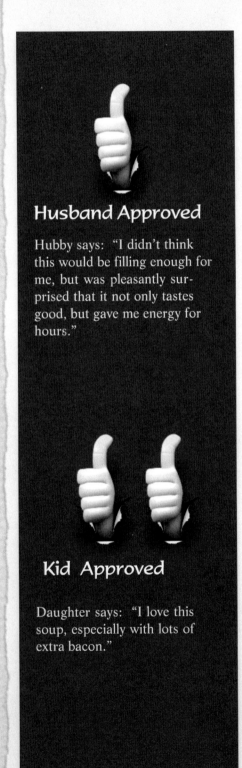

Husband Approved

Hubby says: "I didn't think this would be filling enough for me, but was pleasantly surprised that it not only tastes good, but gave me energy for hours."

Kid Approved

Daughter says: "I love this soup, especially with lots of extra bacon."

1. Preheat oven and baking dish to 350°.
2. Toss squash and carrots with coconut oil and roast uncovered for 35 minutes or until tender.
3. In large stock pot or Dutch Oven, cook bacon until crisp. Remove bacon and set aside for garnish (try not to snitch too many bites while cooking the recipe; you may need to set the bacon aside out of site if your family members happen to come into the kitchen while cooking….yes, I speak from experience.)
4. Add the onion and saute in the bacon fat until tender.
5. Add the roasted squash and carrots, chicken broth, and milk and bring to a boil, stirring often.
6. Remove from heat. Using an immersion blender, blend the soup until smooth. You can also transfer to a regular blender and work in batches until all the soup is smooth and blended.
7. Season with salt, cinnamon, and nutmeg.
8. Serve in large bowls, garnished with bacon.

Note: This soup freezes very well for fast and easy meals at a later date.

Bacon Vegetable Soup

Husband Approved

Hubby says: "A simple soup, but one with lots of flavor. The bacon is what makes it good, at least for me!"

Kid Approved

Daughter says: "I love this soup. Bacon is so good and makes it super yummy!"

Some soups, like this one, call for wine in the original recipe. In experimenting to find the best candida fighting recipes, we simply omitted the wine…and sometimes added balsamic vinegar instead. The results? Delicious!

Ingredients: (serves 8)

1 lb turkey bacon, cut into small pieces (no sugar or nitrates/nitrites)
1 medium onion, finely chopped
2 carrots, peeled and grated
2 celery sticks, finely chopped
1 red bell pepper, finely chopped
1 (28 oz) can chopped tomatoes (or 2 cups fresh)
2 quarts beef broth (homemade is best)
2 T balsamic vinegar
2 T fresh parsley
Celtic Sea salt and pepper to taste

1. In a stockpot, cook the bacon over medium heat, stirring often, until the fat is rendered, about 15 minutes.
2. Add the onion, carrots, celery, and bell pepper and saute until the vegetables are softened, about 5 minutes.
3. Add the tomatoes, balsamic vinegar, and broth and return to a simmer.
4. Season with salt and pepper.
5. Serve garnished with fresh parsley.

Variations:
Add mushrooms with the vegetables.
Top with extra bacon and goat cheese (or any cheese of your choice)

Inspired by Nourishing Broths

Bouillabaisse (Fish Stew)

Not a beginners recipe as it uses some unusual ingredients, but we had to include it in the program because it is so delicious and worth the extra work once in awhile, especially if you want something a little more "fancy". Use fresh fish for best results. Traditional Bouillabaisse uses fresh Mediterranean fish but you can use one or a combination of red snapper, halibut, scallops, shrimp, clams, perch, and lobster.

1. Heat in large casserole:
   - ¼ cup coconut oil
2. Add:
   - ¼ cup finely chopped onion
   - 4 finely julienned leeks
   - 4 medium sized skinned and de-seeded tomatoes or 2 cans diced tomatoes, drained
3. Combine and add to mixture:
   - 5 minced cloves of garlic
   - 1 T finely chopped fresh fennel
   - 1 tsp saffron
   - 2 crushed bay leaves
   - 1 tsp orange zest
   - 2 T tomato paste
   - 1/8 tsp celery seed
   - 3 T chopped parsley
   - 1 tsp freshly ground white pepper
   - 2 tsp Celtic Sea salt
4. Cook until vegetables are transparent and soft.
5. Add:
   - 4 lbs fresh fish (see list above for suggestions)
   - 4 cups fish broth (may substitute chicken broth if you must)
6. Bring to rapid boil, keep heat high and continue boiling for 15-20 minutes.
7. Season to taste.

Husband Approved

Hubby says: "This is a delicious stew and reminiscent of my days in the military when we were stationed abroad."

Kid Approved

Daughter says: "I like this soup with lots of shrimp."

Inspired by Joy of Cooking

Cabbage Soup

Husband Approved

Hubby says: "Warm and hearty, this soup makes a nice, simple breakfast, especially served with a fried egg."

Surprisingly simple and easy, this soup is especially good for those days when you're feeling a bit under the weather. Simple, nourishing, and delicious it is quick to prepare and tastes great even as leftovers. You can make it in a slow cooker or power pressure cooker, too so dinner is ready when you get home or better yet…breakfast is ready when you wake up.

1. Saute in skillet over medium heat:
   - 2 T butter
   - 1 large minced onion
2. Grate, shred, and add:
   - 1 small head green cabbage
3. Saute lightly for one minute to barely soften cabbage then add:
   - 4 cups (1 quart) beef bone broth
   - ¼ tsp paprika
   - ½ tsp parsley
   - Celtic Sea salt and pepper to taste

Optional toppings:
- Sour cream
- Fresh parsley
- Shredded fresh parmesan cheese

Kid Approved

Daughter says: "I love cabbage so this soup is super good. I like it topped with some parmesan cheese."

Cheesy Cauliflower Soup

Husband Approved

Hubby says: "Cheesy goodness. I like this recipe with broccoli instead of cauliflower. Both are good."

Kid Approved

Daughter says: "One of my favorites! I love this soup, especially with lots of bacon on top."

A variation on the classic cheesy soup, this is a common favorite in our house. Rich and filling and so very delicious, we love enjoying this soup all year. It's one of my favorite breakfasts, reheats very well, and stores great frozen if you want to make it ahead of time.

Ingredients: (serves 10)

1/2 lb turkey bacon, cut into small pieces (no sugar or nitrates/nitrites)
1 large onion, finely chopped
1 cauliflower head, cut into small florets
½ tsp **Cajon Seasoning** (see Condiments Section for recipe)
½ tsp black pepper
8 cups (2 quarts) chicken broth (homemade is best)
4 T butter (½ stick)
1 cups organic whole milk
1 cup half and half
¼ cup sour cream
3 cups grated Monterey Jack cheese
2 T minced parsley
Celtic Sea salt

1. In a large pot, fry the turkey bacon pieces over medium-high heat until crisp. Remove the bacon to some paper towel to drain and set aside.
2. Add the onion to the pot and cook, stirring frequently until translucent.
3. Add the cauliflower, Cajun seasoning, and pepper and cook another 3-4 minutes until cauliflower starts to brown.
4. Pour in the broth, stir, reduce heat to simmer, and cook another 5 minutes.
5. Using an immersion blender, puree the soup to desired consistency…or you can carefully transfer to a blender and blend until smooth.
6. In a separate saucepan, melt butter on medium heat. Turn to low and add milk and half-and-half. Careful not to overheat.
7. Add milk to puree and heat while stirring to mix well.
8. Add the sour cream and cheese and stir until cheese is melted and soup is thickened.
9. Season to taste, and serve topped with parsley and turkey bacon.

Inspired by Pioneer Woman

Clam Bisque

This soup contains clams and therefore one we no longer make for ourselves since we switched to the Theologenic Lifestyle; however if you like clams and still enjoy them from time to time, you'll love this recipe. Start to finish, this soup takes less than 30 minutes to prepare, especially if you have an immersion blender to puree the vegetables. If you use a blender, use caution in transferring the hot soup to the blender to avoid scalding and you may want to blend in batches. Personally, I like using the immersion blender since it makes preparing this recipe a snap.

Try topping this soup with a little fresh grated Parmesan cheese for some added flavor, or garnish with fresh parsley, mint, dill, or basil.

Husband Approved

Hubby says: "This soup makes a great breakfast or light dinner. Creamy and delicious."

Ingredients: (serves 4)

- ½ cup chopped onion
- ¼ cup chopped celery
- ¼ cup chopped carrot
- 1 cup diced peeled sweet potato
- 1 garlic clove, peeled & chopped
- 2 ½ T coconut oil
- 2 T tomato paste
- 1 lb clam meat, divided
- 1/½ cups chicken broth
- 2 T white balsamic vinegar
- 1 bay leaf
- ½ tsp oregano
- 1 tsp dried thyme
- 1 cup cream
- Celtic Sea salt and pepper

1. In a medium saucepan, heat coconut oil and saute onion, celery, carrot, sweet potato and garlic until soft.
2. Add tomato paste and stir well. Add half of the clam meat, chicken broth, balsamic vinegar, bay leaf, oregano, and thyme; simmer 15 minutes.
3. Reduce heat to low and stir in cream. Heat for an additional 5 minutes but careful not to boil as cream will start to curdle. Remove bay leaf and remove from heat.
4. Let mixture cool slightly. Use an immersion blender or transfer to a Vitamix or other blender and puree until smooth.
5. Add remaining clam meat and pulse blender a few more times to mix and chop.
6. Season to taste with salt and pepper.

Kid Approved

Daughter says: "This is one of my favorite breakfasts and is such a treat when mom fixes it. I love it topped with lots of parmesan cheese."

Inspired by Vitamix

Clam Chowder

I used to love clam chowder. To me it's one of those comfort foods. Most clam chowder recipes use potatoes, though. When I first started on my Ditch Candida journey, I omitted clam chowder out of my menu planning for that very reason. However, one day, when I was especially wanting to savor that delicious spoonful of clammy goodness, I whipped up a batch and substituted sweet potatoes for the regular potatoes. Bam! So good! Here is the recipe I used before switching to a Theologenic Lifestyle and omitting clams. Feel free to adjust according to your preferences.

1. Cook until crisp in large skillet:
   - 6 slices of turkey bacon, cut into pieces then set aside.
2. Reserve about 1 T bacon grease and add:
   - 1 cup diced peeled sweet potatoes
   - ½ cup chopped celery
   - ¼ cup chopped onion
   - ¼ tsp Celtic Sea Salt
   - 1/8 tsp dried thyme leaves, crushed
   - 1/8 tsp pepper
3. Add reserved liquid from:
   - 2 (6 ½ oz) cans minced clams
4. Bring to a boil. Reduce heat to low, cover and simmer 10 minutes or until vegetables are crisp tender.
5. Gently stir in:
   - 3 cups whole organic milk
   - Clams
6. Heat on low, being careful not to overheat or boil. Add:
   - 2 egg yolks
7. Remove from heat and stir constantly until heated through and thickened somewhat.
8. Serve sprinkled with reserved bacon bits.

Husband Approved

Hubby says: "Creamy and delicious. The perfect evening meal or light lunch."

Kid Approved

Daughter says: "I love soups and this one is delicious, especially with lots of bacon."

Inspired by Grandma Margaret and Joy of Cooking

Classic Tomato Soup

Ingredients: (serves 8)

- 2 T coconut oil
- 1 T unsalted butter
- 1 large white onion, finely chopped
- 1 large clove garlic, smashed and peeled
- 3 cups chicken broth (homemade is best)
- 28-oz. can whole peeled plum tomatoes, puréed (include the juice)
- 1-1/2 tsp. xylitol
- 1 sprig fresh thyme
- Celtic Sea salt and freshly ground black pepper
- 3 T thinly sliced fresh basil, chives, or dill, (or a mixture of all three)

Optional topping:

Combine ½ cup sour cream with ¼ cup crumbled goat cheese. Add 1 T grated Parmesan, 1 T chives, and 1 T olive oil. Mix thoroughly and season to taste with salt and pepper

Husband Approved

Hubby says: "I can live without tomatoes as they're not my favorite vegetable. This soup has good flavor though, so I can see where it'd be really good if you like tomatoes."

Kid Approved

Daughter says: "Perfect combined with Cauliflower Grilled Cheese."

1. In a 5- to 6-quart Dutch oven, heat the coconut oil and butter over medium-low heat until the butter melts. Add the onion and garlic and cook, stirring occasionally, until soft but not browned, about 8 minutes.
2. Add the broth, tomatoes, xylitol, thyme, and 1/4 tsp. each salt and pepper. Bring to a simmer over medium-high heat while stirring the mixture to make sure that nothing is sticking to the bottom of the pan. Reduce the heat to low, cover, and simmer for 40 minutes.
3. Discard the thyme sprig. Let cool briefly and then purée in two or three batches in a blender or food processor, or use an immersion blender. Rinse the pot and return the soup to the pot. Season to taste with salt and pepper. Reheat if necessary. Serve warm but not hot, garnished with the herbs or dolloped with the garnish above.

Inspired by Grandma Margaret

Cock-a-Leekie Soup

It may have a funny name, but this soup is a nice light soup that works well for those days when your digestive system may need a little rest. Since there's not much to it, you get a filling and nourishing soup without much stress to your gut. For the full benefits, be sure to use homemade bone broth. Any broth will work, but the traditional version uses a strong chicken or "cock" broth…thus the name. Make it in the pressure cooker for a super fast one pot dish.

1. Place in a large kettle or pressure cooker:
   - 6 leeks, well washed to remove sand, cut in half, then cut into 1/8 inch slices
   - 3 cups water
   - 1 ½ tsp Celtic Sea salt
2. Bring to boil and simmer for 5-7 minutes. If using pressure cooker, use saute setting on your machine.
3. Add:
   - 2 T butter
   - 1 ½ cups strong chicken broth
   - 1 T gelatin (optional)
4. Bring to boil then reduce heat to simmer about 15 minutes or if using pressure cooker, set to high pressure for 5 minutes and then quick release.
5. Stir in:
   - ½ cup cream
6. Serve right away.

Husband Approved

Hubby says: "I generally like a heartier soup, but this one is good in its simplicity."

Kid Approved

Daughter says: "I especially like it when mom gives me this soup when I'm sick. It tastes good and feels good too."

Inspired by Joy of Cooking

Cream of Watercress or Purslane Soup

A more unusual recipe in our program, I had to include it since it's so good and uses basically a healthy weed. If you have a yard or live in the country and have space, consider planting some purslane. It's a delicious "weed" that is loaded with nutrients and makes a great "greens" addition to any salad or dish using greens. For this soup, you can also substitute watercress, which is more commonly found in grocery stores. A more "peppery" flavored green, watercress gives this soup a full flavor and a fun variety to the typical dish one would usually think to prepare. Have some fun and try something new.

1. Saute until just wilted:
   - 1 cup chopped watercress or purslane
   - 1 T butter
2. Add and cook gently about 3 minutes:
   - ¼ cup white balsamic vinegar
   - Dash of smoked paprika
   - Celtic Sea salt and pepper to taste
3. Reduce heat to very low and add:
   - 3 cups light cream
4. Heat but do not boil. Serve at once.

Husband Approved

Hubby says: "This was unique but surprisingly good."

Kid Approved

Daughter says: "This is super creamy and I enjoyed it. Mom serves it with some smoked fish which is really delicious together."

Inspired by Joy of Cooking

Garden Vegetable Soup

Husband Approved

Hubby says: "I didn't think I would like this one since it has so many vegetables, but it is a winner in my book. It makes a great soup all year round, even in the hot summer months...and is sometimes even better in the summer when the vegetables are freshest."

Kid Approved

Daughter says: "I love this soup. It's a good one for taking to school for lunch since it's so filling."

This recipe is one of those where you pretty much just can throw in whatever vegetables you have on hand and it will turn out amazing. Whatever you might be picking fresh from your garden or available at the farmer's market will be delicious. We sometimes call it Kitchen Sink Veggie Soup, since it seems to have all the best vegetables in it. This is one of those recipes that always tastes good and even my hubby, who says he's not a big vegetable eater...loves this one!

1. Combine the following ingredients and simmer about 20 minutes:
   - 4 cups (1 quart) chicken or turkey broth
   - 1 medium zucchini, cut into ½ inch slices
   - 1 carrot, cut into slices
   - 1 rib celery, cut into slices
   - 1 chopped leek or sweet onion (or both)
   - 1 cup green beans (fresh or canned)
   - 3 T fresh parsley, or 1 T dried parsley
   - 1 tsp minced garlic
   - ¾ tsp pepper
   - ½ tsp dried oregano
2. Add the following ingredients and simmer an additional 10 minutes:
   - 2 cups cooked chicken or turkey (optional)
   - 1 cup chopped broccoli (fresh or frozen)
   - ½ cup fresh or frozen peas
   - Celtic Sea Salt to taste.

Optional additional ingredients:
- Cubed Butternut Squash
- Cubed Turnips
- Cubed Sweet Potatoes
- Diced Jerusalem Artichoke
- Diced Tomato

Optional additional toppings after cooking:
- Shredded Cheese
- Microgreens
- Sauerkraut or Lacto-Fermented Vegetables

Gazpacho Soup

Husband Approved

Hubby says: "I don't care for tomatoes, and normally prefer soups hot, but this would be a great hit for those who like tomatoes and cucumbers."

Kid Approved

Daughter says: "I love this soup, especially when mom puts in extra cucumbers."

I was told this soup originated in Spain where they chilled this soup deep in caves, then served with fresh vegetables. Whatever its origins, this soup is especially good in the summer when the ingredients are fresh. Served cold, it is refreshing as well as nourishing and makes a wonderful treat after a busy day out in the sun.

1. Peel and seed:
   - 2 large ripe tomatoes
   - 1 large sweet green pepper
2. Add them to a food processor or mixer with:
   - 1 clove garlic
   - ½ cup or more of fresh mixed herbs like chives, parsley, basil, & tarragon
3. Pulse to chop. Do not over-mix.
4. Gradually stir in:
   - ½ cup olive oil
   - Zest from one lemon
   - 3 cups chilled beef stock, strained
5. Add:
   - 1 peeled, thinly sliced sweet onion
   - 1 cup peeled, seeded, diced cucumber
   - 1 ½ tsp Celtic Sea salt or to taste
   - ½ tsp paprika
6. Chill at least 2 hours before serving.

Inspired by Joy of Cooking

Green Chili Chicken Stew

I first tried this recipe at a friend's house who graciously was respectful of my desires to stay within the guidelines of what I needed to do to quickly get my candida overgrowth back into balance. She made this recipe and I had to share it with you since it is so very delicious.

Even though you are avoiding certain foods, you don't have to avoid life and not socialize. You'll find your good friends will support you whole-heartedly…and who knows? Maybe you will be a blessing to them to help them eat healthier too!

Husband Approved

Hubby says: "I like taking this recipe for lunches when I'm working. It's delicious, hearty, and gives me energy."

Ingredients:
(4 servings)

- 2 T coconut oil
- ½ cup zucchini, sliced
- ½ cup yellow squash, sliced
- ½ cup chopped onion
- 2 stalks celery, sliced
- 2 cloves garlic, minced
- 4 cups chicken broth
- 8 oz shredded cooked chicken
- 1 (8 oz) can green chilies
- 1 tsp oregano
- ½ tsp Celtic Sea salt
- ¼ tsp pepper
- 3-4 drops Lime Essential Oil
- Avocado slices
- Fresh Cilantro

1. In a large heavy pan or Dutch oven, heat oil over medium heat. Add the zucchini, squash, onion, celery, and garlic; cook, stirring occasionally, until they begin to soften, about 5 minutes.
2. Add chicken broth and bring to boil.
3. Reduce heat and add chicken, green chilies, dried oregano, salt and pepper.
4. Simmer stew on low for 15-20 minutes.
5. Serve with a drop of lime essential oil, and topped with avocado slices and fresh cilantro.

Kid Approved

Daughter says: "I like this stew with extra lime and lots of fresh cilantro."

Inspired by Bobi Spilker

Hungarian Mushroom Soup

Husband Approved

Hubby says: "I didn't think I would like this recipe the first time I tried, it...especially since I'm not usually a big soup fan, but this one is really good and very filling."

Kid Approved

Daughter says: "I love this soup. It's one of my favorites."

I first had this recipe at a Soup Cook-off Contest at the local farmer's market. My vote went to the Shiitake Mushroom Farm who made this incredibly delicious soup. Easy to make, incredibly nutritious, reheats very well for amazing leftovers the next day, and is economical too. We recommend using smoked Hungarian paprika rather than regular paprika for extra flavor.

1. Melt butter in a large pot over medium heat. Saute 4 cups chopped onions until translucent.
2. Add 4 lbs fresh sliced mushrooms (especially good with shiitake) and saute about another 5 minutes or so.
3. Stir in:
   - 4 tsp dried dill
   - 2 T paprika
   - 2 T coconut aminos
   - 4 cups (1 quart) chicken broth (homemade is best)
4. Reduce heat to low, cover, and simmer for about 15 minutes.
5. Add:
   - 2 cups whole organic milk
6. Stir well to blend, cover and simmer another 10 minutes on low heat, stirring occasionally.
7. Stir in:
   - 2 tsp Celtic Sea Salt
   - Pepper to taste
   - 2 tsp lemon zest (or zest from 1 large organic lemon)
   - ¼ chopped fresh parsley
   - 1 cup sour cream.
8. Remove from heat. Mix thoroughly until all ingredients are well blended. DO NOT BOIL.

Inspired by Ozark Shiitake Farms

Lemon Chicken & Kale Soup

I love this soup. It's another great recipe with tons of flavor and so good for you on many levels. If you make your own chicken broth, this recipe is a great use for the chicken meat and broth you get from the broth-making process.

Best of all, this soup freezes really well. Store in pint jars for the perfect single-serving breakfast, lunch, or dinner. Just warm and serve!

Husband Approved

Hubby says: "Another great soup with lots of flavor and very filling. It's a great soup for those cold winter days or when you're not feeling so great and need some soothing fare that's easy on the stomach."

Kid Approved

Daughter says: "This is super yummy, especially with cheese on top."

Ingredients: (serves 2)

3 T coconut oil
1 medium onion, finely diced
4 cloves garlic, minced
2 stalks celery, minced
5 cups homemade or salt free chicken or vegetable broth
1 teaspoon balsamic vinegar
1/2 teaspoon Dijon mustard
1 cup cooked pastured chicken, cubed or shredded
2 bunches kale, cut into 1-inch pieces
Zest of one lemon
Celtic Sea sea salt, to taste
Freshly ground black pepper, to taste
Freshly grated Parmesan cheese, for serving

1. Heat the coconut oil over medium heat in a large saucepan.
2. Add the onion, garlic, and celery, along with the black pepper and a tiny pinch of the sea salt. Saute until onions and celery are very tender.
3. Add chicken, Dijon, and kale, along with the zest of a lemon, and saute an additional 5 minutes.
4. Add chicken broth and balsamic, and reduce heat to low. Simmer, covered, for 35 minutes, before serving topped with a little parmesan cheese.

Inspired by Dr. Steven Gundry

No Bean Chili

Some days just call out for the warm comfort of a bowl of chili. We love using the Power Pressure Cooker for this recipe to save time and dirty dishes. Best served in the fall and winter months.

Husband Approved

Hubby says: "This is my all-time favorite recipe on the Ditch Candida program. I don't even miss the beans. Throw it in a Thermos and it makes a great on-the-go lunch, too!"

Kid Approved

Daughter says: "I like this chili even better than the way Mom used to make it. Two thumbs up!"

Ingredients:
- 1-2 lbs ground beef (grass fed if possible)
- 1 medium onion, diced
- 1 bell pepper, chopped
- 4-5 jalapeno peppers, de-seeded and de-veined and chopped (optional)
- 2 quarts canned tomatoes (or 4 cans diced organic tomatoes)
- ¼ cup homemade chili seasoning (see recipe in Condiments section)
- Celtic Salt to taste

*For extra "heat" add Cayenne Pepper to taste

Optional Toppings:
Shredded cheese
Sour Cream

1. Brown ground beef in heavy skillet with onions and peppers until beef is brown and veggies are soft. Drain grease.
2. Add remaining ingredients and simmer 20-25 minutes.

***or, transfer all ingredients to Slow Cooker or Power Pressure Cooker and heat until ready to serve.

Quick Lobster Chowder

We live in the heart of the country, about as far from the sea as you can get, so fresh seafood is a rare treat. Luckily, we can get a hint of seafood delights with the convenience of canned or frozen varieties. Use fresh if you have access where you live for an even better resulting chowder.

Note: Omit this recipe for Theologenic Lifestyle, as Lobster is not considered a "clean" meat in Leviticus.

1. Saute in a saucepan about 5 minutes:
   - 2 T butter
   - ¼ cup finely diced onion
   - ½ cup finely diced celery
2. Add:
   - 1 ½ cups water or fish stock
   - 1 small bay leaf
   - 1 package frozen mixed vegetables, defrosted
3. Cover and bring to a boil. Watch carefully as you don't want to overcook the vegetables. Cook until barely tender, about 5 minutes. Remove the bay leaf.
4. Add:
   - 1 can chopped mushrooms, drained
   - 1 cup tomato sauce
   - 2 cups milk
   - 1 cup canned lobster
5. Heat slowly but do not boil.
6. Season to taste.
7. Serve topped with choice of cheese

Husband Approved

Hubby says: "This is a good soup, made best by lots of cheese on top."

Kid Approved

Daughter says: "I really enjoy creamy soups and this one is really good. I especially like it topped with fresh grated parmesan cheese."

Inspired by Joy of Cooking

Quick Vegetable Soup

Some days you just want something super quick and easy yet nourishing too. This is one of those great "go-to" recipes for days you didn't plan ahead or forgot to pull something out of the freezer. Made with staple vegetables and ingredients, this takes about 20 minutes in the pressure cooker.

1. Place in a large kettle or pressure cooker:
   - 2 T butter or coconut oil
   - 1 large sweet green pepper
2. Saute briefly in the fat:
   - ¼ cup diced carrots
   - ¼ cup diced onions
   - ½ cup diced celery
3. Add:
   - 1 quart (4 cups) broth
   - 1 cup canned tomatoes
   - ½ cup pared, diced turnips
   - ½ cup chopped cabbage
   - 1 T chopped parsley
   - ½ tsp Celtic Sea salt
   - 1/8 tsp pepper
4. Cover and cook about 35 minutes on the stovetop or 15 minutes in the pressure cooker. Quick release pressure after cycle is complete.
5. Add:
   - 2-3 leaves chopped, de-stemmed kale
6. Stir, let stand for 5 minutes to wilt kale leaves.

Husband Approved

Hubby says: "This soup is really good and a great way to eat a bunch of different vegetables."

Kid Approved

Daughter says: "I really like vegetable soups and this one is good. I like it topped with a little cheese."

Inspired by Joy of Cooking

Reuben Soup

I love a good Reuben! Maybe it's my Germanic and Polish ancestry coming through... When I first tried this soup, I was in heaven. All those great Reuben flavors in a SOUP! You can't get much better than this...that is, if you like Reuben's!

Use lacto-fermented sauerkraut instead of canned or bagged as lacto-fermented has the added benefit of gut-healing probiotics. We add the sauerkraut at the end and don't cook it so we don't risk harming the beneficial living bacteria that are so good for us.

This recipe makes a big batch, but it reheats very well and makes great leftovers.

Ingredients:
(8-10 servings)

- 1 large onion, chopped
- 4 stalks celery, chopped
- 1 red bell pepper, chopped
- 1 cup butter
- 2 cloves garlic, minced
- ½ tsp tarragon
- ½ tsp caraway seeds
- ¼ cup almond flour
- 4 cups beef stock
- 1 quart half and half
- 1 lb cooked corned beef, chopped
- 1 cup lacto-fermented sauerkraut
- 1 tsp Celtic Sea salt
- Freshly ground black pepper
- 2 ½ cups shredded Swiss Cheese

1. Cook and stir onion, celery, red bell pepper, butter, garlic, tarragon, and caraway seeds in a large stock pot over medium heat until vegetables are tender, about 6-8 minutes.
2. Stir almond flour into vegetable mixture. Cook on low until almond flour is lightly browned, stirring constantly, about 10 minutes.
3. Stir in beef stock, half-and-half, corned beef, salt and pepper into the vegetable mixture. Reduce heat to low and simmer until soup is heated through and slightly thickened, about 30 minutes.
4. Ladle soup into bowls. Add sauerkraut and top with Swiss Cheese.

Inspired by Shannon A.

Sausage and Kale Soup

When I first saw this recipe, I passed on it...thinking it wouldn't be something my family would like....although now in retrospect, I'm not sure why. But then our neighbor gave us a package of home-grown sausage so I thought I'd give it a try. Wow, was I wrong in my initial assumption! Both Hubby and Daughter LOVED it and I have to say it ranks up there as one of my very favorite soups now. After our first experiment, this recipe has become a regular "go-to" in our repertoire.

Husband Approved

Hubby says: "Definitely a two thumbs up recipe. I'm not usually a big fan of soups, but this one gets my vote as one I'd eat over and over. Delicious and filling with just a little bit of kick."

Base Ingredients:	Variations
1 ½ lb Italian Sausage or Breakfast Sausage (use turkey or chicken sausage if Theologenic) 1 large Onion, chopped 4 cups whole Milk 1 cup Cream 1 quart (4 cups) Chicken Broth 2-3 cups diced Butternut Squash 1-2 bunches Kale; stalks removed, torn into bite-sized pieces ½ tsp dried Oregano ½ tsp Red Pepper Flakes Celtic Salt and Pepper to taste	• Add 2 Tblsp. Pesto to soup after cooking. • Omit Sausage for a Meat-Free soup • Add chopped Collard or Mustard Greens along with the Kale • Stir in 1 cup Parmesan cheese into the soup just before serving. Note: This recipe works very well in the Power Pressure Cooker as a one-pot meal for fast prep and quick dinner.

Kid Approved

Daughter says: "I love soup and this one is really good. The colors of the soup with the green makes it fun to eat, too. One thumb up since it's a little spicy after you swallow it."

1. In large pot over medium-high heat (or with the "Saute" function on your Power Pressure Cooker), saute onions and sausage until sausage is totally cooked (5-7 minutes). Drain off the excess fat, then pour the sausage mixture onto a rimmed baking sheet lined with paper towels in order to remove as much fat as possible. Set aside.
2. Wipe the pot clean, then pour in the milk, cream, broth, herbs, butternut squash, and kale. Return sausage/onion mixture to the pot.
3. *If using a Pressure Cooker omit adding the milk and cream, attach the lid and pressure cook on high for 15 minutes. Allow the pressure to release, then add milk and cream. Heat gently.
   * If making on the stovetop, heat on low but do no boil, covered, and simmer for 10 minutes.
4. Stir gently and enjoy.

Recipe adapted from Ree Drummond, Pioneer Woman Cooks Dinnertime Cookbook

Spicy Beef & Kale Soup

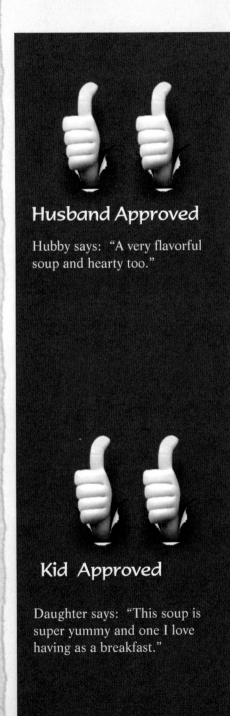

Husband Approved

Hubby says: "A very flavorful soup and hearty too."

Kid Approved

Daughter says: "This soup is super yummy and one I love having as a breakfast."

When I first saw the ingredients list for this recipe, I knew it was going to be a winner. I mean, really! Mushrooms, beef, and kale? Yum! Easy to make and reheats well too. You'll want to have on hand some of our Homemade "Soy" Sauce to make it when on the Ditch Candida program.

Ingredients:
- 2 quarts homemade beef broth
- 2/3 cup coconut oil
- 1 large peeled and sliced onion
- 1 lb cremini mushrooms, sliced
- 2 finely minced cloves garlic
- 3 de-seeded and thinly sliced jalapeno peppers
- 1 lb beef steak, thinly sliced
- Homemade "Soy" Sauce
- Fish sauce
- 4 large Kale leaves, stemmed and chopped
- 1 bunch green onions, chopped
- Celtic Sea salt to taste

1. In a large saucepan, heat the broth to a simmer.
2. Meanwhile, melt 1/3 cup coconut oil in a large skillet over medium heat. Add the onions, mushrooms, garlic and jalapenos and saute until softened and lightly browned. Add to onion mixture to the broth.
3. Melt the remaining 1/3 cup coconut oil in the saucepan with the remaining clove of garlic. Add the steak and stir-fry until the meat is lightly pink. Pour into broth mixture.
4. Season with salt, pepper, "soy" sauce, and fish sauce and simmer for 10-15 minutes for flavors to blend. Ad the kale and cook until the kale turns an intense shade of green.
5. Serve hot, garnished with green onions.

Pressure Cooker Method:
1. Set pressure cooker to Saute and add 1/3 cup oil, onions, mushrooms, garlic, jalapenos and saute until soft.
2. Add the steak and continue to cook until steak is pink.
3. Pour in the broth and seasonings.
4. Set cooker for 15 minutes on high pressure. Release steam and add kale.
5. Serve hot, garnished with green onions.

Spicy Chicken & Shrimp Soup

Husband Approved

Hubby says: "Delicious and satisfying with just the right amount of spice and heat."

Kid Approved

Daughter says: "I love chicken, shrimp, pesto, and most of the flavors used in this recipe, but don't care for spicy. I especially love this recipe when mom leaves out the jalapeno's."

This soup is so nourishing and good for the digestive system, it's one of our go-to recipes when someone is feeling under the weather. The ginger and peppers, along with the benefits of broth are warming and healing. The recipe makes enough for up to 8 servings so enjoy as leftovers, freeze for future use, or half the recipe if you don't need that much.

Note: Omit the shrimp if following the Theologenic Lifestyle as shrimp is not considered a "clean" meat in Leviticus.

Ingredients: (serves 8)

- 2 cups thinly sliced green cabbage
- Zest from one lemon or lime
- 2 quarts chicken broth
- ¼ cup coconut oil
- 1 lb cremini mushrooms
- 1 clove garlic
- 3 fresh jalapeno peppers, chopped
- 1/3 cup grated fresh ginger
- ½ cup Homemade Pesto
- 2 cups frozen peeled cooked shrimp
- 2 cups diced cooked chicken
- 1 cup whole milk
- 1 bunch fresh cilantro, chopped
- Coconut Aminos
- Fish Sauce
- Celtic Sea salt and Pepper

1. In a large bowl, combine cabbage and zest and set aside.
2. In a large saucepan or stockpot, bring broth to a simmer over medium-high heat.
3. While broth is heating, melt coconut oil in a large saute pan over medium heat. Add mushrooms and garlic and cook until softened and fragrant, about 10 minutes.
4. Add the peppers and ginger and cook another minute or so, then transfer mixture to the broth.
5. Stir in pesto and shrimp and return broth to a simmer.
6. Add chicken, cabbage, milk, and cilantro and cook on low to heat through. Don't boil or milk may start to curdle.
7. Season with coconut aminos, fish sauce, salt and pepper.
8. Ladle into bowls and serve with additional cilantro as garnish.

Inspired by Nourishing Broths

Sweet Potato Soup with Seared Tomatillos

This recipe uses a delightful blend of two unique yet flavorful vegetables. It takes a little more time to prepare, but well worth the efforts. You do need a good blender for this recipe to get the best results. Choose fresh produce whenever possible. This soup doesn't freeze as well as others due to the delicate nature of the ingredients so enjoy it fresh.

Ingredients: (serves 4)

- 4 T coconut oil
- 1 lb smoked beef bones
- 1 lb onions, peeled and diced
- 3 jalapeno peppers, seeded & diced
- 2 bay leaves
- 1 cinnamon stick
- 3 cloves garlic, peeled & sliced
- ¼ lb poblano peppers, diced
- 1 T coriander seed
- 2 lbs sweet potatoes, peeled/diced
- 8 cups chicken broth
- 1 tsp Celtic Sea salt
- ½ tsp pepper
- 1 ½ lbs small tomatillos (husks removed & cut into small wedges)
- Zest from 2 limes
- 1 cup fresh cilantro, chopped

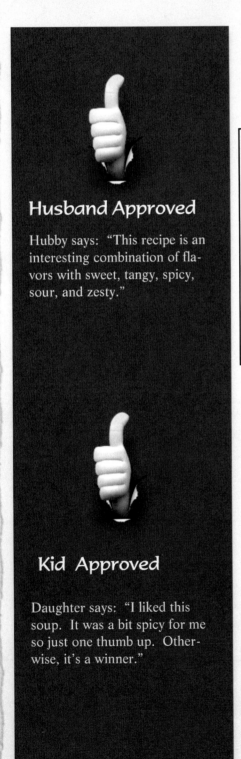

Husband Approved

Hubby says: "This recipe is an interesting combination of flavors with sweet, tangy, spicy, sour, and zesty."

Kid Approved

Daughter says: "I liked this soup. It was a bit spicy for me so just one thumb up. Otherwise, it's a winner."

1. Add 2 T coconut oil to a large stockpot and heat on medium-high heat to melt. Add bones and render for 3 minutes.
2. Add onions, 1 jalapeno, bay leaves cinnamon stick, garlic and poblano and heat for 5 minutes, stirring frequently.
3. Add the coriander and cook another minute.
4. Add sweet potatoes and broth and bring to a boil. Reduce heat and simmer, uncovered for 25-30 minutes or until potatoes are tender.
5. Remove bay leaves, cinnamon stick, and pork bones or ham. Set bones/ham aside. Let soup cool for about 30 minutes.
6. Using an immersion blender, blend soup until soup; or blend in blender in batches.
7. Meanwhile, heat a saute pan until very hot. Toss the tomatillos with 2 T coconut oil and add to the pan to sear. Cook for 1 minute.
8. Add the remaining 2 jalapeños and cook for 30 seconds. Transfer tomatillos and jalapeños to soup. Remove meat from pork bones and add to soup or return ham to the pot.
9. Top with lime zest and cilantro. Season with salt and pepper.

Inspired by Vitamix Cookbook

Taco Soup

Husband Approved

Hubby says: "Excellent version of a classic dish."

Kid Approved

Daughter says: "This soup is so good I have dreams about it."

I came up with this one in desperation when I was looking for something fast and easy to whip up after a long day away from the kitchen one time. I grabbed what I had on hand and threw it in the Pressure Cooker, with amazing results. Now, I get requests to make this one on a regular basis. You can make it on the stovetop, too, if you don't have a Power Pressure Cooker…yet.

Ingredients:
2 lbs ground beef (or whatever leftover meat you might have…chicken, pork loin, or stew beef works great too)
2 quarts of bone broth (beef, but chicken works fine too)
1 finely chopped onion
1 chopped bell pepper
1 quart diced organic tomatoes
¼ cup Homemade Taco Seasoning or to taste
Celtic Sea salt to taste

1. Brown ground beef, with peppers and onions, then drain off the grease. If using leftover chicken or pork loin, dice or shred and throw into the pressure cooker or pot
2. Add remaining ingredients, stir.
3. If using the pressure cooker, set timer to 20 minutes. If using a stockpot on the stove, bring to a low simmer. Reduce heat and cook about 30 minutes or until flavors have blended and vegetables are soft.
4. Salt to taste.

This recipe reheats very well and works well in a thermos for a meal on the go.

Variations:
- Top with shredded cheese.
- Top with sour cream
- Add a little cayenne pepper for some extra heat.
- Add diced and seeded jalapeno pepper.

Tomato Basil Parmesan Soup

The flavors of tomato and basil are just meant to go together…then add parmesan to the mix and you have pure heaven. This recipe is so good and is super fast and easy, especially when using the power pressure cooker. You don't get this kind of goodness from a jar or can!

1. In a large stockpot or power pressure cooker, melt:
   - 3 T butter
2. Add and cook about 5 minutes or until tender:
   - 1 diced carrot
   - 2 stalks celery, diced
   - 1 onion, diced
   - 2 cloves garlic, minced
3. Add:
   - 3 lbs diced tomatoes
   - 1 quart chicken broth
   - 1 T tomato paste
   - ¼ cup fresh basil
   - ½ tsp Celtic Sea salt
   - ½ tsp pepper
4. If using a stockpot, cover and simmer 20 minutes. If using a pressure cooker, cook for 5 minutes on high pressure then allow cooker to sit 5 minutes, followed by a quick release.
5. Use an immersion blender to puree the mixture until it is smooth.
6. Add:
   - 1 cup cream
   - ½ cup shredded fresh parmesan cheese
7. Stir to combine. Garnish with additional basil and parmesan if preferred.

Husband Approved

Hubby says: "Nice and creamy with a great blend of cheesy and savory."

Kid Approved

Daughter says: "I loved this soup, and it was good cold, too."

Inspired by Michael Elliott

Tomato Bouillon Soup

This is a light and flavorful soup that is wonderful either hot or cold. We especially like it cold in the summer when lots of fresh tomatoes are coming in from the garden. Best served as a side dish rather than the main course, we love this soup with fried or poached eggs or a salad.

1. Bring to a boil and simmer 5 minutes:
   - 3 cups strained tomato juice or diced fresh tomatoes
   - 2 cups chicken or vegetable broth
   - ½ small bay leaf
   - 1-2 stalks chopped celery with the leaves
   - 2 T chopped fennel
   - 2 whole cloves
   - 1 T fresh basil
   - 1 small onion, chopped and lightly sauteed
2. Strain and season to taste with:
   - Celtic Sea salt
   - Ground black pepper
3. Serve hot or cold, topped with:
   - Sour cream

Husband Approved

Hubby says: "I don't care for tomatoes, but this was good topped with sour cream and cheese."

Kid Approved

Daughter says: "I like this soup better warm than cold but it's good either way."

Inspired by Joy of Cooking

Winter Squash Soup

Husband Approved

Hubby says: "Chicken, shrimp, AND bacon? If you're a meat lover like me, you'll love this one and not even really notice you're getting healthy ingredients like vegetables and broth."

Kid Approved

Daughter says: "I eat the shrimp out first since that's my favorite part. This soup is like something we had at a fancy restaurant once."

I never ate much squash growing up. I'm not sure why, but as a result I didn't really tend to gravitate to many squash recipes. As I was looking for a more varied diet on the Ditch Candida program, I found myself more and more intrigued by these delicious vegetables. Loaded with nutrients and flavor, economical, easy to store, easy to grow, and with over 1000 varieties, I am developing a secret love for squash. This soup is a wonderful blend of flavors and the ginger adds extra candida-fighting power.

1. Place in a large kettle or pressure cooker:
   - 4 cups (1 quart) chicken or turkey broth
   - 1/3 cup diced cooked chicken breasts
   - 1 cup shelled, cleaned shrimp (omit if following Theologenic Lifestyle)
   - 1 lb seeded winter squash cut into 1 inch squares (butternut, acorn, pumpkin, or cushaw as some examples)
   - 1 small diced leek or onion
   - 1 diced bamboo shoot (optional but great if you can find)
   - ¼ tsp grated fresh ginger
   - 1 lb sliced and cleaned fresh mushrooms of choice
2. Bring soup to boil, cover and lower heat to simmer for 20 minutes or if using a pressure cooker, set to high pressure for 10 minutes and quick release.
3. Before serving, add:
   - 1/3 cup diced, cooked turkey sausage (no sugar or nitrates/nitrites)

Inspired by Joy of Cooking

Antipasto Mediterranean

Husband Approved

Hubby says: "This was surprisingly good. I normally don't like olives but I enjoyed this dish."

Kid Approved

Daughter says: "Yummy. I liked this with lots of mushrooms."

Mediterranean cooking is so light and refreshing, with perfect blends of vegetables, oils, and spices. This is a cold dish rather than a warm one so makes a great lunch, especially when on the go or on a picnic. The original recipe, found in a book about Biblical Diets, suggests eating the dish with wooden picks rather than forks. My daughter loves to eat it with her fingers. Whatever your method of eating it, I'm sure you'll enjoy the flavors.

1. Combine in a heavy skillet over medium heat:
   - ¼ cup balsamic vinegar
   - ¼ cup coconut oil
   - 12-18 drops liquid stevia
   - 1 T Celtic Sea salt
   - ½ tsp oregano
   - ¼ cup water
   - ¼ tsp black pepper
   - 2 large carrots, peeled and cut into ½ inch pieces
2. Simmer, covered, for about 2 minutes then add:
   - 2 ribs celery, cut into 1 inch pieces
   - 1 small head of cauliflower, broken into bite-sized pieces
3. Simmer, covered, for an additional 2-3 minutes longer, then add:
   - 1 sweet bell pepper, sliced lengthwise
   - 1 lb button mushrooms, or sliced mushrooms
   - 1 (4 oz) jar black olives, drained
   - 1 (4 oz) jar green olives, drained
   - 1 tsp onion powder
4. Simmer, covered, for another 5 minutes or so or until mushrooms are tender.
5. Cool. Chill, covered, for 24 hours. Drain off excess juice and serve.

Inspired by What Would Jesus Eat Cookbook

Beef & Eggplant Casserole

This recipe makes a great buffet or potluck dish, and gives a delicious alternative for you and your family. Or, make it during the week and have leftovers to enjoy. It freezes well and reheats well.

Husband Approved

Hubby says: "I was surprised with the flavor and texture of this dish. Much better than I expected for a guy who doesn't really like vegetables."

Kid Approved

Daughter says: "This is so good, especially with lots of cheese."

Ingredients: (serves 12)

- 8-10 large eggplants
- ½ cup or more melted coconut oil
- 4 lbs ground beef (or lamb)
- 3 medium onions, minced
- 2 cans tomatoes, drained & chopped
- 1 cup beef stock
- 1 tsp cinnamon
- Celtic Sea salt and pepper
- 2 cups fresh grated cheddar or parmesan cheese

1. Cut ends off eggplants and peel (or leave peels on if from your garden and organic). Cut into 3/8 inch lengthwise slices. Salt and set aside, covered with a towel, for about 1 hour.
2. Rinse slices well, dry off, and place on cookie sheets brushed with coconut oil. Generously brush top sides with coconut oil and grill under broiler until lightly browned.
3. Meanwhile, cook the beef in a large pan until crumbly and brown. Drain the grease and return to the pan.
4. Add onions, tomatoes, stock, and cinnamon. Bring to boil.
5. Reduce heat to simmer and cook uncovered until most of the liquid has evaporated.
6. Oil a large 9 x 13 baking pan that is at least 2 inches deep. Arrange a layer of eggplant on the bottom, then a thin layer of meat. Repeat for at least two more layers to give at least three layers of eggplant but four is better.
7. Sprinkle cheese on top.
8. Bake at 350 degrees for 1 hour.

Inspired by Nourishing Traditions

Butternut Squash Mac 'n Cheese

Who doesn't love a good mac and cheese? Simply the best comfort food ever! You can still have this classic dish, with a few substitutions...and you may not even miss that there isn't any pasta in the dish!

This dish reheats very well so you can make it ahead on a prep day, or enjoy as leftovers.

If you desire meat with your mac 'n cheese, try adding some tuna, canned organic chicken, grilled chicken breast, or cooked ground beef.

Husband Approved

Hubby says: "I like this recipe even better the second day as leftovers. Very good, especially with some chicken added."

Kid Approved

Daughter says: "So cheesy and delicious. I'll have seconds please."

Ingredients:
(4-6 servings)

- 1 head of cauliflower, riced
- 1 tsp coconut oil
- 1 medium onion
- 2 medium red bell peppers, chopped
- 3 cups cubed butternut squash
- 1 ¾ cups organic chicken broth
- 1 cup whole milk
- 2 T Greek yogurt
- 1 cup shredded Swiss cheese
- 1 cup shredded sharp cheddar
- Celtic Sea salt and pepper
- Chopped fresh parsley (optional)

1. Preheat oven to 375°.
2. Coarse chop cauliflower in a food processor to make large "rice".
3. Heat oil in a large skillet and add onion and bell peppers. Cook, stirring frequently, for 4-6 minutes or until onion is translucent. Set aside.
4. Combine squash, broth and milk in medium saucepan. Bring to boil over medium high heat. Reduce heat to medium; gently boil for 20-25 minutes or until squash is tender.
5. Place squash mixer in a blender and blend until smooth or puree using an immersion blender.
6. Combine squash mixture, cauliflower, onion mixture, yogurt, and cheeses. Season with salt and pepper. Mix well.
7. Place mixture in a 9 x 13 glass baking dish that has been lightly greased with butter.
8. Bake for 25-30 minutes or until sauce is bubbling.
9. Garnish with parsley.

Inspired by Beach Body

Cauliflower Grilled Cheese

You don't even miss the bread with these delicious "sandwiches". Feel free to mix and match your cheeses to personal preferences and serve with a bowl of **Tomato Basil Parmesan** soup for that classic Grilled Cheese with Tomato Soup flair.

Ingredients: (makes 3-4 sandwiches)

1 head of cauliflower (to make about 4 cups of "rice" cauliflower)
2 eggs, lightly beaten
½ cup finely grated parmesan
½ tsp oregano
1 ½ cups shredded white cheddar cheese
Celtic Sea salt and pepper to taste

Husband Approved

Hubby says: "Filled with cheesy goodness, these are great for those packed lunches on the go."

Kid Approved

Daughter says: "So good. I love these on their own or dipped in tomato soup."

1. Cut cauliflower into florets and place in a food processor. Process until the texture resembles rice. If you don't have a food processor, you can grate the cauliflower with a cheese grater, but it takes a little longer.
2. In a medium bowl, combine cauliflower rice with eggs, parmesan, and oregano. Mix until evenly combined and season with salt and pepper.
3. Heat a large skillet over medium heat and add a little coconut oil or butter to lightly grease the pan.
4. Scoop the cauliflower mixture into a "patty", then carefully place on one side of the pan. Repeat the process with a second "patty" on the other side of the pan. (These are your "bread" slices)
5. Press down on both sides with a spatula to form patties into "bread" shape and cook until golden underneath (about 5 minutes). Flip and cook until the other sides are golden (about another 3 minutes).
6. Top one cauliflower slice with cheese then place the other cauliflower slice on top. Lower heat to low to avoid burning and heat until cheese is melted.
7. Repeat with remaining ingredients.

Inspired by Delish.com

Cobb Salad

You can't go wrong with a classic Cobb Salad. This recipe can be made into a "Salad-in-a-Jar" recipe by assembling the ingredients ahead of time for a meal in a hurry. I especially love this recipe when the tomatoes are ripe from the garden.

Ingredients: (serves 6)

2 boneless, skinless chicken breasts, sliced in half down the middle
2 heads of romaine lettuce, chopped
1 bunch mixed greens
6 hard boiled eggs, peeled and sliced
2 avocados, pitted, peeled, and diced
1 lb bacon, cooked crisp and chopped
2 cups red grape tomatoes
1/3 cup crumbled blue cheese
Celtic Sea Salt and Pepper to taste
Blue Cheese Dressing (see recipe in Condiments section)

Husband Approved

Hubby says: "I'm a take-it-or-leave-it kind of guy when it comes to salads. This one is really good with great flavors."

1. Heat a grill pan or skillet over medium-high heat and drizzle with coconut oil or butter.
2. Sprinkle the chicken with salt and pepper and cook until done in the middle, about 3 minutes per side.
3. Let the chicken cool, then dice and set aside.
4. Meanwhile, wash and dry lettuce. Cook eggs and bacon if not already done.
5. Assemble the salad. Start with lettuce then top with chicken, eggs, avocado, tomatoes, bacon, and blue cheese. Top with dressing.

Note: Most ingredients can be prepared ahead of time and stored separately in the fridge.

Variations:
- Use Feta cheese instead.
- Substitute cooked and cooled shrimp for the chicken.
- Add a little salsa with fresh cilantro for a southern flair.

Kid Approved

Daughter says: "I love salads and this one has so many great flavors. I especially like it with feta and extra bacon."

Creamy Italian Eggplant

Husband Approved

Hubby says: "Another great dish with an Italian flare."

Kid Approved

Daughter says: "This recipe is especially good when mom pairs it with kelp noodles and tops it with lots of cheese."

Serve this flavorful sauce over cauliflower "rice", kelp noodles, or spaghetti squash. Eggplant is a fun vegetable that when baked, almost gets a "meaty" texture, giving you some good vegetable-centered dishes without sacrificing flavor. Eggplants are in the nightshade family of vegetables and are cousins to tomatoes, peppers, and potatoes.

1. Preheat oven to 350°.
2. Peel, cube, and salt, tossing with your hands until well coated:
   - 1 ½ lbs eggplant
3. Set eggplant aside and allow to drain for about 30 minutes. Meanwhile, in a large saucepan, heat:
   - 1 T butter or coconut oil
   - ½ cup diced onion
4. Cook until onions are soft then add:
   - 1 clove minced garlic
   - 1 can crushed tomatoes
   - 1 can diced tomatoes
   - 3-4 chopped kale leaves
   - 2 T fresh chopped parsley
   - 2 tsp dried basil
   - 1 tsp oregano
   - 1 bay leaf
5. Simmer, covered, over low heat for about 30 minutes.
6. Pat eggplant dry, then heat 1 T butter or coconut oil in a separate saucepan and saute eggplant until slightly browned.
7. Grease a 9x13 baking dish with coconut oil, then add eggplant.
8. Remove bay leaf from sauce then pour sauce over eggplant.
9. Top with:
   - Sliced black olives (optional)
   - ½ cup fresh grated parmesan cheese
10. Bake uncovered 30 minutes

Inspired by Kristen Feola, Daniel Fast

Greek Style Stuffed Peppers

I first had this recipe when on a Daniel Fast years before my candida diagnosis. If you're not familiar with a Daniel Fast, it's a time of prayer, cleansing, and eating the way God instructed us in the book of Daniel. Daniel Fasting is similar to the Ditch Candida program in that it focuses on vegetables and eliminates all sugar and processed foods. Now I know why I felt so much better every time I went through the fast!

Ingredients:
- 1 T Coconut Oil
- ½ chopped onion
- ½ cup chopped zucchini
- 1 minced glove garlic
- 1 8 ounce can tomato sauce
- 3 chopped canned artichokes, drained
- ½ cup chopped black olives
- 1 small bunch chopped fresh kale leaves
- 1 tsp oregano
- 1 tsp parsley
- ½ tsp Celtic Sea salt
- 6 medium bell peppers (green, orange, red, yellow, and/or purple)

1. Preheat oven to 350°. Prepare pot of boiling water.
2. Place artichokes in a food processor and pulse until artichokes are well chopped. Set aside.
3. Heat coconut oil over medium heat in a skillet. Add onion and zucchini, and cook 3-5 minutes until veggies are softened.
4. Lower heat, and add garlic. Then add tomato sauce, artichokes, olives, kale, oregano, parsley, and salt. Cook 15 minutes, or until sauce is thickened.
5. While sauce is cooking, prepare peppers. Cut in half lengthwise and remove stems and seeds. Drop peppers in boiling water for 5 minutes to blanch.
6. Drain peppers in colander and place in a large baking dish, cut side up. Spoon mixture evenly into pepper halves. Add hot water from boiling pot to baking dish to a depth of about ½ inch.
7. Bake uncovered for 20 minutes.

Husband Approved

Hubby says: "Stuffed peppers are like comfort food and this recipe is so good. I like a little pepper jack cheese sprinkled on top, too."

Kid Approved

Daughter says: "The olives in this meal make it really good. I especially like it with orange peppers."

Grilled Antipasta

Sometimes you are in the mood for something light and simple. This recipe is very versatile in that it make the perfect light and easy dinner yet also works well for lunches, snacks, or as a side dish.

Ingredients: (3-4 servings)

1 small eggplant
1 medium zucchini, sliced
1 medium yellow squash, sliced
1 chopped green bell pepper
Drizzle of coconut oil
1 T Italian Seasoning
1 can artichoke hearts
8 oz mozzarella cheese, shredded
Celtic Sea salt

1. Cut eggplant crosswise into ½ inch slices. Sprinkle sides with Celtic Sea salt and layer on paper towels. Let stand for 30 minutes to "sweat".
2. Rinse eggplant with water and let dry. Arrange in a single layer on a lightly greased grill pan or grill basket.
3. Add zucchini, squash, and green peppers. Lightly brush with melted coconut oil then sprinkle with Italian seasoning.
4. Cook covered, with grill lid, over medium high heat 12-15 minutes or until slightly browned and tender.
5. Meanwhile, add artichoke hearts to a small saucepan and heat gently. Drain.
6. Place grilled vegetables on a platter, top with artichoke hearts, and sprinkle with cheese.

Variations:
- Add sliced black olives before serving.
- Add Homemade Breakfast Sausage
- Use shredded Swiss cheese, pepper jack, or other cheese of choice instead of the mozzarella

Inspired by In the Kitchen with MRC

Husband Approved

Hubby says: "I am learning to like vegetables more and more. This is one of those recipes I never would have even considered trying before this program...but was surprised that I quite enjoyed it!...especially with some sausage to spice it up!"

Kid Approved

Daughter says: "So many fun and pretty colors in this dish make it yummy AND fun to eat."

Mushroom Risotto

This is one of those recipes that makes a great meal OR side dish, depending on your mood. We use cauliflower as a delicious and fun "rice" substitute for our risotto. Use a food processor to make your cauliflower "rice" quickly and easily. I find this recipe makes great leftovers and is good both warm and cold. Throw it in a thermos for a healthy lunch on the go.

Husband Approved

Hubby says: "I especially like this one with lots of parmesan, served with grilled steak."

Ingredients:
- 4 ½ cups "riced" cauliflower
- 3 T coconut oil or butter
- 1 lb mushrooms, sliced (portabello, crimini, or shiitake)
- 1 lb white mushrooms, thinly sliced
- 2 shallots
- ¼ cup organic vegetable or chicken broth
- 3 T finely chopped chives
- 1/3 cup fresh grated parmesan cheese
- 4 T butter
- Celtic Sea salt
- Freshly ground black pepper

Kid Approved

Daughter says: "Mushrooms are so yummy and this is super good, especially with lots of parmesan."

1. Place cauliflower in food processor and pulse to make "rice" or use a cheese grater if you don't have a food processor.
2. Heat 2 T butter or oil to a saucepan over medium heat and add mushrooms. Cook, stirring frequently until soft.
3. Remove mushrooms and their liquid and set aside.
4. Add 1 T butter or oil to the heated pan and stir in the shallots. Cook about 1 minute or until fragrant.
5. Add cauliflower, stirring to coat with oil/butter then add broth. Cook another 5 minutes or so until broth is absorbed.
6. Remove from heat.
7. Stir in mushrooms with their liquid, 4 T butter, chives, and parmesan cheese.
8. Season with salt and pepper to taste.

Inspired by Maria Emmerich

No Rice Sushi

Sushi makes a great light meal or snack and the nori (sea vegetable) used to make sushi is not only delicious but very nutritious too. We can still enjoy a good sushi on the Ditch Candida program…just without the rice.

Husband Approved

Hubby says: "I like my sushi with chicken added, but it's good just about any way it's served."

Kid Approved

Daughter says: "The cream cheese and cucumbers makes this really good."

Base Ingredients:
  5 sheets of Nori (Sushi SeaVegetable)
  1 carrot, thinly sliced lengthwise
  1 cucumber, thinly sliced lengthwise
  Cream cheese, softened
  Meat of choice such as fish, chicken, etc. (optional)

Optional Additional Ingredients (Mix & Match)
  Guacamole
  Fresh herbs
  Kimchi

1. Put a piece of Nori on waxed paper or sushi mat (if you have one).
2. Carefully spread cream cheese on nori (careful not to tear nori)
3. Spread guacamole, if using, onto nori.
4. Place pieces of vegetable across the end of the nori sheet closest to you.
5. Add optional meat or other toppings of choice.
6. Starting with the end closest to you with the vegetables, carefully roll nori tightly to form a log.
7. Repeat the process with additional sheets and ingredients.
8. Carefully slice into 1 inch diameter bites.
9. Serve with kimchi.

Pizza

Pizza was the biggest challenge for our family to give up, so I experimented with multiple variations to come up with a solution that we could enjoy and still get our pizza. To save time, make multiple batches and freeze for future enjoyment.

Husband Approved

Hubby says: "Not exactly the same as traditional, but sure made a great substitute. The crust has a different texture from the almond flour but still really good."

Kid Approved

Daughter says: "Super tasty, especially with lots of cheese and all my favorite toppings."

Ingredients:

(For the Crust)
- 1 cup almond flour
- ¼ tsp Celtic Sea salt
- ½ tsp basil
- ½ tsp oregano
- 1 tsp melted coconut oil
- 1 large egg

(For the Sauce)
- 1 (6 oz) can tomato paste
- 6 oz warm water
- 5 T grated Parmesan Cheese
- 1 tsp minced garlic
- 1 packet stevia
- ¾ tsp onion powder
- ¼ tsp oregano
- ¼ tsp marjoram
- ¼ tsp basil
- ¼ tsp pepper
- 1/8 tsp cayenne pepper
- 1/8 tsp red pepper flakes

Pizza Toppings of Your Choice
Grated Mozzarella or other cheese of choice.

1. Preheat oven to 325°.
2. Line a pizza pan or round baking stone with parchment paper and lightly grease.
3. In a medium mixing bowl, combine sauce ingredients and combine until well mixed. Allow sauce mixture to sit for about 30 minutes to fully blend flavors.
4. Meanwhile, in a separate bowl, combine crust ingredients and combine until well mixed.
5. Spread dough/batter onto parchment paper until it is about 8-10 inches in diameter and about ¼ inch thick. Remember, the consistency of this dough is not going to be like traditional pizza dough; it's more like crisp-bread or flatbread.
6. Bake for 10 minutes. While baking, saute any toppings if needed.
7. Remove crust from oven and add sauce, cheese, and toppings. Bake for another 15-20 minutes or until desired doneness.

Inspired by Grandma Margaret

Ratatouille

Husband Approved

Hubby says: "I didn't think I would like this one since it has so many vegetables, but it is a winner in my book."

Kid Approved

Daughter says: "I love this dish and it's fun helping mom make it too."

Made famous by the Disney film by the same name, Ratatouille is a wonderful all-veggie dish with classic flavors and lots of beautiful colors and textures. It's a great way to get your kids to eat their vegetables. Makes great left-overs too. Top with crème fraiche, sour cream, or shredded fresh parmesan cheese.

1. Peel, slice, and salt to get rid of excess moisture:
   - 2 ½ cups diced eggplant
2. Heat in a deep skillet and saute until golden:
   - 1/3 cup coconut oil
   - ¾ cup thinly sliced yellow onions
   - 2 cloves of garlic
3. Add:
   - ½ cup whole pitted black olives
   - 4 julienned green peppers, seeds and membrane removed
   - 3 cups zucchini, cut into ½ inch slices
   - 2 cans diced tomatoes
4. Drain and blot the eggplant to remove moisture then add to skillet.
5. Add:
   - ½ tsp oregano
   - 2 tsp chopped fresh basil
6. Simmer covered over very low heat about 45 minutes then remove lid and simmer an additional 15 minutes to reduce liquid.
7. Serve hot or cold.

Inspired by Grandma Margaret and Joy of Cooking

Stuffed Acorn Squash

Squash is such an unsung hero in the vegetable world. There's so much you can do with squash and they come in a wide range of colors and flavors. Acorn squash has a nice nutty flavor that makes a filling meal. Try this recipe with other varieties of winter squash for a varied flavor.

Ingredients:
- 2 small acorn squash, halved and seeded
- ¼ cup water
- ½ cup diced onion
- ½ cup diced carrot
- ½ cup diced red bell pepper
- ½ cup thickly sliced zucchini
- ½ tsp minced garlic

1. Preheat oven to 350° and coat baking dish with coconut oil.
2. Steam acorn squash by placing cut side down on baking dish with ¼ cup water in oven for 10-15 minutes.
3. While acorn squash is cooking, lightly steam-fry remaining ingredients, a few minutes only, stirring frequently. Don't overcook.
4. Spoon vegetables into squash halves.
5. Bake 20-25 minutes until squash is tender.

Variations:
- Top with shredded cheese.
- Use Butternut Squash or other winter squash varieties.
- Add bacon.

Husband Approved

Hubby says: "This is a hearty meal that is really good. I liked it topped with spicy cheese and some Cajun seasoning."

Kid Approved

Daughter says: "This is fun to eat since you get to scoop the veggies out of the squash shell. Yummy too."

Tuscan Style Eggplant

Eggplant is one of those vegetables I didn't really eat very often until I started the Ditch Candida program...but now it's a regular on our table. Lots of nutrients and a simple flavor that blends well with the recipe ingredients. This dish has a delightful Italian flair.

Ingredients:

- 1 medium to large eggplant, sliced and peeled (if not organic)
- ½ tsp Celtic Sea Salt
- ¼ tsp pepper
- 2 T. Coconut Oil, melted
- 1-2 bunches kale, de-stemmed and leafed to bite-size pieces
- 1 cup sliced fresh mushrooms
- 1 can organic diced tomatoes
- ½ tsp basil
- ¼ tsp oregano
- 4-5 oz grated mozzarella cheese

1. Peel and Slice Eggplant in generous ½ - ¾ inch slices. Season with salt and pepper and coat with melted coconut oil.
2. Preheat grill pan or heavy skillet and heat eggplant until cooked through, flipping once during cooking.
3. While eggplant is cooking, add remaining ingredients (except cheese) to bowl and mix gently. Pour tomato mixture over eggplant.
4. Cover and cook 4-5 minutes until heated and bubbly.
5. Remove pan from heat, top with cheese, cover and let stand 2-3 minutes until cheese melts.

Husband Approved

Hubby says: "This recipe made me feel like we were eating out at a fancy Italian restaurant. Very good, especially for a meat-free dinner."

Kid Approved

Daughter says: "I love this one when the eggplants are fresh from the garden. Mom sends me out to pick some, along with fresh tomatoes, and she makes this dish."

Inspired by a recipe given to me by my sister, Amanda Plaster

Vegetable Lasagne

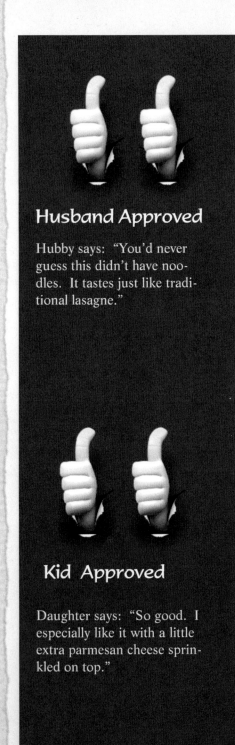

Husband Approved

Hubby says: "You'd never guess this didn't have noodles. It tastes just like traditional lasagne."

Kid Approved

Daughter says: "So good. I especially like it with a little extra parmesan cheese sprinkled on top."

We love Italian cuisine at our house and starting the Ditch Candida program, I especially missed my noodles. This recipe makes a wonderful alternative because the vegetables fill in the texture of the noodles in lasagne and you don't even miss them. If you have a smaller family, this dish makes great left-overs too and reheats very well. In fact, I even sometimes think it tastes better the second day.

1. Preheat oven to 375°.
2. In a heavy skillet, melt ½ T coconut oil or butter over medium heat until melted. Add 1 diced **onion** and saute until tender.
3. Add 2 minced cloves of **garlic** and saute about 2 more minutes.
4. Add, bring to boil, then reduce heat to simmer:
   - 1 quart or 3 cans diced strained tomatoes
   - ½ tsp red pepper flakes
   - ½ tsp Celtic Sea salt
5. Simmer tomato sauce for about 10 minutes to fully blend flavors.
6. While sauce is cooking, slice long-wise into ½ inch strips, then set aside:
   - 1 large zucchini (may substitute eggplant)
   - 1 large yellow summer squash
7. In a bowl combine:
   - 1 large pastured egg
   - 1 container ricotta or cottage cheese
   - ¼ cup fresh basil, chopped (or 1 T dried Italian herbs)
8. Place 1/3 of the cooked tomato sauce in the bottom of a large baking dish. Layer ½ zucchini on top of tomato sauce, then top with ½ of the cheese mixture.
9. Layer another 1/3 tomato sauce, remaining zucchini, and remaining cheese mixture.
10. Top with:
    - 4 cups baby kale
    - ½ cup shredded raw parmesan cheese
    - ½ cup shredded mozzarella cheese
    - Remaining Tomato Sauce
11. Bake for 30-40 minutes until bubbly and cheese is slightly browned. Remove from oven and let sit about 10 minutes before serving.

Inspired by Food Babe

Baked Cinnamon "Apples"

Cushaw squash is a versatile and wonderful variety that tastes like a cross between apples and pumpkin….which makes it a great substitute for any recipe calling for baked apples. Try the recipe below and enjoy plain, or add to Grandma's No Roll Pie Crust for a pretty amazing "Apple" Pie knock off. Cushaw may not be found at your local grocery store, so try the farmers markets or grow your own. They're super easy to grow, super delicious, and high in vitamins.

Ingredients:
- 4 cups cubed cushaw squash, peeled
- 4 T butter
- 6-9 drops liquid stevia or 1 stevia packet
- 2 T cream
- 1 tsp pumpkin pie spice

1. Heat butter in a medium skillet.
2. Add cushaw squash and cover.
3. Simmer, stirring occasionally for 5 minutes.
4. Add stevia and pumpkin pie spice, simmer 2-3 more minutes or until tender.
5. Add cream and cook for 2 minutes more to heat through.

Serve topped with optional chopped nuts and homemade whipped cream.

Variation:
Double or triple above recipe and bake it in the oven in a large baking dish at 400° for 20 minutes.

Husband Approved

Hubby says: "This really does taste a lot like apples. Tasty."

Kid Approved

Daughter says: "Anything with cinnamon has to be good and this was super yummy."

Inspired by Wellness Mama

Baked Onions with Pecans

Onions are such a versatile vegetable, and one that is delicious served so many ways. For this recipe, choose large sweet onions for best results. Onions are a warming food, so eat liberally in the winter months especially.

Ingredients:

- 4 large onions, peeled
- 1 cup chicken stock or broth
- 3 T butter
- 1 tsp grated lemon rind
- ¼ tsp paprika
- ½ cup pecans, finely chopped
- 1 T Xylitol or stevia equivalent

1. Preheat oven to 350°.
2. Cut onions in half along the equator and place cut side up in a buttered glass baking dish.
3. Mix stock, butter, lemon rind, paprika, and sweetener of choice in a small saucepan and heat gently until well blended.
4. Pour over onions.
5. Bake, covered, for about 50 minutes, basting occasionally (stir sauce over onions), until onions are just tender.
6. Remove cover, sprinkle with pecans, and bake another 10-15 minutes until lightly browned.

Husband Approved

Hubby says: "I love onions, and this recipe is simply delicious. The flavor of the onions is so good with the crunchy pecans."

Kid Approved

Daughter says: "This is good. I wouldn't want to eat it every day, but once in awhile is good."

Inspired by Nourishing Traditions

Baked Portobello Mushrooms

I have a fascination for mushrooms. Technically a fungus, mushrooms are incredibly nutrient dense, delicious, and beneficial. Many varieties of mushrooms are now being classified as "super-foods." When selecting mushrooms at the store, look for firm and plump caps of good color and texture. Avoid mushy, shriveled, or dark spotted caps. Store mushrooms in the refrigerator in a paper bag (never plastic, or they get soggy).

Ingredients: (4 servings)

4 large portobello mushrooms, cleaned, stemmed
¼ cup coconut oil
2 garlic cloves, minced
2 T balsamic vinegar
½ cup fresh thyme leaves, chopped (or 1 T dry)
Celtic Sea salt and pepper to taste

Husband Approved

Hubby says: "Mushrooms and garlic are a great combination and especially are good with a grilled steak."

1. Preheat oven to 350°.
2. Make several shallow cuts in the center of each mushroom where the stem was attached.
3. Meanwhile, heat coconut in a small saucepan until melted. Add garlic and heat for about 8-10 minutes on medium heat stirring frequently. Remove from heat and strain out garlic pieces, reserving the oil.
4. Combine garlic-flavored oil with balsamic vinegar, thyme, salt and pepper in a small bowl and mix well.
5. Arrange mushrooms, cut side down, on a baking pan lined with parchment paper.
6. Drizzle the oil mixture over the mushrooms and bake for 15 minutes; turn mushrooms over and bake for 10-15 minutes longer or until tender.

Variation: You can also use smaller portobello mushrooms and slice; then follow the recipe otherwise, reducing baking time by about 5 minutes.

Kid Approved

Daughter says: "I like to eat these with my fingers. Mushrooms have such a fun texture."

Inspired by What Would Jesus Eat

Baked Summer Squash

Even if you don't think you like to garden, it's worth planting a few things in the summer. There's nothing like picking something fresh and enjoying the flavor…along with the satisfaction that comes from growing it yourself. Summer squash is one of those great beginner-type plants that will give you a bountiful return for minimal efforts. Just plant the seed in decent soil after frost, water once in awhile, watch for bugs, and enjoy a beautiful harvest. This recipe is especially good when the zucchini and summer squash are fresh picked!

1. Preheat oven to 350°.
2. Cut into strips and place in a greased baking dish:
   - 3 cups summer squash (leave skins on if you grew it yourself or if organic, otherwise peel and slice.
3. Cover it with:
   - ¼ cup milk
4. Dot with:
   - 2 T chilled butter, cut into small pieces
5. Sprinkle with:
   - 1 tsp Celtic Sea salt
   - ¼ tsp paprika
   - Dash of nutmeg
6. Cover the dish and bake for about ½ hour or until tender.
7. Optional: Top with crisp crumbled bacon and/or shredded cheese

Husband Approved

Hubby says: "I don't normally love squash since it's a texture thing for me, but the flavor of this is really good."

Kid Approved

Daughter says: "I love this one when mom uses several kids of summer squash so it's colorful as well as delicious."

Inspired by Joy of Cooking

Baked Sweet Potato

Husband Approved

Hubby says: "Baked sweet potatoes are a real treat and make great lunches too."

Kid Approved

Daughter says: "If I had a choice, I'd go with regular baked potatoes, but I really like these too, especially with lots of butter."

I didn't really fix sweet potatoes much before the Ditch Candida program, but now I love them and turn to them often. A favorite in our house is a Baked Sweet Potato. They even make a great light meal by themselves. If you have a Power Pressure Cooker, Baked Sweet Potatoes are perfectly cooked and ready to eat in about 30 minutes. Easy peasey!

Ingredients:
  Organic Sweet Potatoes, washed
  Butter
  Celtic Sea Salt

Power Pressure Cooker Method:
1. Place about an inch of hot water in the bottom of your pressure cooker and add the steamer basket insert.
2. Add sweet potatoes and secure lid, using pressure cook setting.
3. Cook 25 minutes at high pressure then allow the pressure to release naturally for an additional 5-10 minutes.
4. Release any remaining pressure, carefully remove lid, and transfer sweet potatoes to plate.
5. Serve with butter and salt to taste.

Oven Method:
1. Preheat oven to 400°.
2. Arrange sweet potatoes in a deep baker and prick each potato with a fork.
3. Bake until tender, about 45 minutes to 1 hour.
4. Serve with butter and salt to taste.

Caprese Salad

This recipe just screams summer sunshine! If you can find good, fresh tomatoes out of season…you'll feel like it's summer when you take a bite. Or, enjoy this delight all summer long when the tomatoes are fresh from the vine.

Husband Approved

Hubby says: "I don't like raw tomatoes, so this is not my cup of tea, but if you do like tomatoes, I would think it would be a winner."

Ingredients:

- 1-2 Sliced or Diced Fresh Tomatoes (per serving)
- Sliced Mozzarella Cheese (fresh is great but in a pinch we've used sliced string cheese)
- Fresh Basil (or dry if you must)
- Drizzle Olive Oil
- Celtic Sea Salt to taste

Variations:

- Add sauerkraut
- Substitute fresh Cilantro for the Basil
- Substitute other healthy oil of choice or omit altogether

Combine all ingredients artfully on a plate and enjoy.

Kid Approved

Daughter says: "I love it when Mom fixes this one, especially when the tomatoes and basil are fresh from the garden and we make our own mozzarella.!"

Cauliflower Couscous

Husband Approved

Hubby says: "The flavors in this recipe are really good. After my cancer surgery I have texture challenges with some foods so this one gave me some texture trouble. But I liked it."

Kid Approved

Daughter says: "Yummy. I like this one with extra parsley and mint."

This recipe takes only about 20 minutes to prepare and makes a great breakfast, lunch , or dinner side dish. You can make it ahead of time as it stores very well. Fresh herbs really do make a difference but use the dried versions if you must.

Ingredients: (4-6 servings)

2 tsp coconut oil
2 tsp cumin
½ tsp turmeric
1 small yellow or red onion, finely minced
1 cup water
1 large or 2 small head of cauliflower, finely "riced"
1 red bell pepper, finely chopped
4 T fresh parsley, minced
1 T fresh mint, minced (optional)
2 drops of Lime Essential Oil (food grade only)
7-8 sun-dried tomatoes, finely chopped
2 cloves garlic, minced
Celtic Sea salt

1. In a skillet, heat melt oil then add cumin and turmeric. Stir to combine.
2. Keeping the heat low, add onion and soften slightly.
3. Add water and bring to a low simmer.
4. Add cauliflower, pepper, garlic, and tomatoes and heat until "al dente", cauliflower is softened but still firm. Water should be mostly absorbed at this point. If not, drain.
5. Add herbs, lime, and salt to taste.

Inspired by pH Miracle

Cauliflower Mashed "Taters"

If you are looking for a delicious alternative to mashed potatoes, you can always go with mashed sweet potatoes instead...or try this recipe. Cauliflower makes a pretty good alternative!

Ingredients: (serves 4)

1 head of cauliflower, cut into florets
2 T butter
¼ cup sour cream
¼ cup grated parmesan cheese
Celtic Sea salt and pepper to taste

1. Place cauliflower into steamer basket over about an inch of water in a pan. Cover and steam for about 5 minutes or until cauliflower is soft.
2. Transfer steamed cauliflower to a medium bowl and add sour cream, butter, and cheese.
3. Using a blender, potato masher, or mixer, blend until smooth like mashed potatoes.
4. Season with salt and pepper to taste.

Husband Approved

Hubby says: "Personally I love sweet potatoes, so that's hard to top...but this is good too."

Kid Approved

Daughter says: "I could eat this as a meal or a snack just by itself."

Inspired by Gundry MD

Fried Green Tomatoes

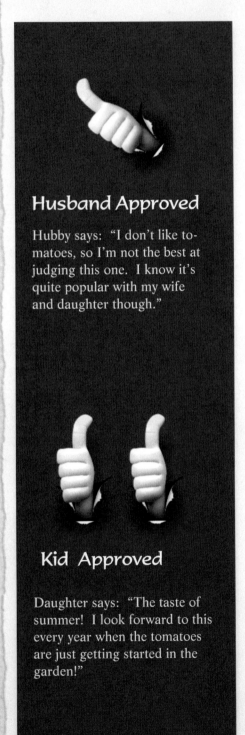

Husband Approved

Hubby says: "I don't like tomatoes, so I'm not the best at judging this one. I know it's quite popular with my wife and daughter though."

Kid Approved

Daughter says: "The taste of summer! I look forward to this every year when the tomatoes are just getting started in the garden!"

Tomatoes are the number one thing that is grown in American gardens…and for a good reason! There is just no comparison between store-bought and home-grown. If you are blessed with a tomato plant or can get them fresh…use them. If not, check out the local farmer's markets in your area. It's so worth it!

1. Heat 3-4 T coconut oil and 2 T butter in a heavy skillet.
2. Slice Green Tomatoes into thick rounds.
3. Dredge tomato slices first in:
   - 2 eggs, whipped well with a fork, poured in shallow platter
4. Then quickly coated with:
   - 1 cup almond flour mixed with **Homemade Seasoned Salt**
5. Transfer to skillet and fry for 1-2 minutes until brown then flip and cook other side.
6. Transfer to a plate and serve.

Optional toppings:
- Fresh grated Parmesan cheese
- Fresh basil
- Fresh cilantro

Italian Mushrooms

Mushrooms make a great quick snack. Saute them plain with a little butter then salt to taste, or try adding some additional flavors like what we offer in this recipe. Don't use canned mushrooms as the texture is just not as good as fresh. Any mushroom variety will do, but we especially like shiitake if they are available.

Ingredients:
- 1 lb mushrooms, sliced
- 2 T coconut oil or butter
- 1 T basil
- ½ tsp garlic powder
- Celtic Sea salt and Pepper to taste

1. Heat oil or butter in a skillet over medium heat.
2. Add mushrooms and saute until mushrooms are slightly browned.
3. Top with seasonings and stir to coat.

Variations and serving ideas:
Serve alone as a snack.
Serve as a side dish.
Serve over eggs or as a filler for omelettes.
Mix with softened cream cheese and sour cream for a mushroom dip.
Serve as a topping for steak.

Husband Approved

Hubby says: "This recipe makes a great snack, but is also really good as a topping on eggs."

Kid Approved

Daughter says: "I love mushrooms and this recipe is really good, especially when mom serves them with sauerkraut and fresh tomatoes."

Kale with Tomatoes & Onions

Husband Approved

Hubby says: "Who knew I would give a kale recipe two thumbs up? Surprisingly tasty."

Kid Approved

Daughter says: "This is super yummy, and I especially like it when mom puts a little feta cheese on top of the kale and tomatoes."

I first tried this recipe when on a Daniel Fast years before learning about Candida. Now, I realize why I felt so much better when on the Daniel Fast...since we would cut out all processed foods, sugars, and heavy carbs during the fast. Sound familiar?

The flavors of this recipe blend so nicely and it's one of those you can make quickly. We like making this one as a breakfast dish for that very reason.

Ingredients: (4-6 servings)

- 6 cups (4 oz) of curly kale, stems removed and coarsely chopped
- 1 T coconut oil
- 1 small thinly sliced sweet onion
- 2 cloves garlic, minced
- 3 cups chopped tomatoes, unpeeled, unseeded
- 1 tsp dried basil
- 1 tsp dried oregano
- ½ tsp Celtic Sea salt

1. In a large skillet, heat oil over medium heat. Add onions and garlic.
2. Put tomatoes in a large bowl, and squeeze with your hands so that some juice is extracted. Pour tomatoes with their juice into the skillet with onions and garlic. Cook about 15 minutes until onions are tender.
3. Stir in kale, basil, oregano, and salt. Cover, simmer 5-7 minutes or until kale is softened and bright green.
4. Serve immediately.

Inspired by Ultimate Guide to the Daniel Fast, Kristen Feola

Mashed Sweet

I used to think that sweet potato[es]... ar, and marshmallows so they didn['t]... Then, I realized how good they are mashed with... Now, we have mashed sweet potatoes regularly and someti[mes]... a meal of them.

Ingredients:

Sweet Potatoes, preferably organic, washed
Butter
Celtic Sea Salt

Stovetop Method:

1. Bring a pot of water to boil over high heat.
2. Meanwhile prepare sweet potatoes. You can either leave the skins on or peel them, depending on personal preference. Cut sweet potatoes into cubes or large diced chunks. Number of sweet potatoes depends on how many people and size of potatoes. Generally 1 per person is sufficient.
3. Add sweet potatoes to boiling water, reduce heat to medium-low and simmer for 40-45 minutes until soft.
4. Strain.
5. Mash with a potato masher, forks, or blender.
6. Add butter and salt to taste.

Pressure Cooker Method:

1. Add about an inch of HOT water to the bottom of the pressure cooker pan. Insert steamer basket so contents sit off the bottom of the unit.
2. Place whole sweet potatoes into the pressure cooker.
3. Make sure pressure valve is closed and lock the lid.
4. Set cooker to high pressure for 25 minutes.
5. Release pressure, remove lid, and remove sweet potatoes to a large bowl.
6. If desired, remove skins (they peel right off) and mash.
7. Season with butter and salt to taste.

Husband Approved

Hubby says: "This is one of my favorites on the whole program and I love taking mashed or baked sweet potatoes for lunch when I'm at work."

Kid Approved

Daughter says: "I'm not a huge sweet potato fan, but I like it once in awhile."

Oven Roasted Broccoli

My friend Christina first made this recipe for me and I had no idea prior to this, that broccoli could taste so amazing. Granted, I've always loved broccoli, but usually just steamed or sauteed it. Roasting, with the added flavors of lemon and garlic, make this one of those dishes that you just can't seem to stop eating once you take your first bite…. Or at least that was what happens to me every time I make it. Be sure to preheat the dish along with the oven for best results.

Ingredients:
2-3 bunches of fresh broccoli, washed and cut up into bite-sized pieces
2 cloves minced garlic
Zest from 2 lemons
2-3 T coconut oil, melted
Celtic Sea salt to taste

1. Preheat oven and baking dish to 425°.
2. Place all the ingredients in a large bowl and mix with your hands until all the broccoli is coated evenly with the seasoning and oil.
3. Carefully remove baking dish from the oven and pour broccoli mixture onto dish. You may hear a bit of sizzle.
4. Roast for 20 minutes or until broccoli is cooked and crispy on the edges.
5. Serve immediately…if it makes it as far as the table. :-)

Husband Approved

Hubby says: "The texture of this is what makes it so good. Broccoli is usually soft when steamed or baked, but roasted gives it a nice crisp."

Kid Approved

Daughter says: "I love broccoli and this is so good."

Inspired by Christina Cooper

Roasted Root Vegetables

Roasted Vegetables are so crazy delicious. There's something about roasting that really brings out the flavor. Spicy vegetables like radishes and turnips are almost magically transformed to become almost sweet. We encourage you to experiment and find which ones you like best and which toppings. A few great options include: Turnips, Carrots, Radish, Kohlrabi, Beet, Rutabaga, etc.

Note: This recipe also works well with Winter Squashes, like Butternut, Acorn, and Pumpkin, and you can also use the same technique with Broccoli, Cauliflower, Brussels Sprouts, and Kale.

Base Ingredients:
- 3-4 Cups diced, sliced, or chunks of Root Vegetable of Choice
- 1-2 Tblsp Coconut Oil
- Celtic Salt and Pepper to taste

Variations:
- Combine various Root Vegetables together in one dish.
- Top with Toasted Pecans, Toasted Slivered Almonds, or Toasted Walnuts
- Top with Fresh Herbs after roasting, such as Cilantro, Basil, Parsley, and Mint.
- Add Garlic to mixture before roasting.

1. Preheat oven to 425° F. Place baking sheet or roasting pan in oven to preheat with the oven.
2. Prepare vegetables according to serving preference (dice, slice, or chop). Try keeping pieces relatively uniform for even cooking.
3. Place in large mixing bowl and add oil and seasoning of choice.
4. Gently mix with your hands to coat all vegetables evenly.
5. Carefully remove roasting pan from oven and add vegetables. You may hear a light "sizzle". Spread vegetables evenly in pan.
6. Roast 20 minutes until thoroughly cooked.

Note: Roasted Vegetables can be made ahead of time on prep days then frozen or refrigerated for time saving during the week. Simply pull out and reheat when needed.

Husband Approved

Hubby says: "Texture is a big deal for me and there's something about the texture and flavor of roasted vegetables that makes me want to go back for seconds....and sometimes thirds!"

Kid Approved

Daughter says: "My very favorite roasted vegetable is radish! I don't really like raw radishes, but roasted radishes are such a treat!"

Sweet Potato Fries

"French Fries", (which aren't even really French), are a traditional American fare that many of us may have consumed regularly before the Ditch Candida program. You can still enjoy this great side or snack, but with our own Ditch Candida spin on it. Simply replace the regular potato with sweet potatoes, use a healthier oil, bake them, and voila….your very own fries. Personally, I think they're even better than the ones we used to eat!

Ingredients:
2-3 large sweet potatoes, washed, peeled, and cut into strips (fries)
¼ cup melted coconut oil
Spices of choice:
(experiment to find your favorites: Celtic Sea Salt, pepper, garlic powder, basil, oregano, rosemary, thyme, sage, cinnamon)

Husband Approved

Hubby says: "Who said eating healthy had to be bland and boring? I'm improving my health AND getting to eat delicious foods that I love…like fries."

1. Preheat oven to 400°.
2. Melt oil and add spices of choice. I generally just use salt.
3. Slice sweet potatoes and place on a large baking sheet.
4. Pour oil over fries and toss with hands to evenly coat.
5. Bake for 25-30 minutes or more until slightly browned and tender.
6. Serve with **Homemade Ketchup**.

Note: You can sometimes find Sweet Potato Fries in the frozen section of Health Food Stores. Watch the ingredients carefully. Although they may be more convenient than making your own, many times you will still see some form of sugar in the ingredients list.

Also, if ordering Sweet Potato Fries at a restaurant, ask what kind of oil they use to make them and if there is any sugar added. If they use Canola oil, order something else as Canola is highly toxic to the body.

Kid Approved

Daughter says: "Oh yeah! These are so good, and I love them dipped in ketchup."

Inspired by Grandma Margaret and Wellness Mama

Tomatoes & Okra Creole

Husband Approved

Hubby says: "Tomatoes are not my favorite, but this is pretty good."

Kid Approved

Daughter says: "I love okra, even raw out of the garden. This recipe is super duper good."

I love to garden, and it's so satisfying when you can enjoy the bounty of your labors with delicious recipes like this one. In the heat of late summer when the tomatoes and okra are coming in from the garden daily, this recipe is a favorite. Also good any time of year with the wonders of our modern grocery stores, you'll be sure to enjoy this combination of flavors and textures.

Ingredients:
(4-6 servings)

- 4 cups sliced okra
- 1 cup chopped onion
- 1/3 cup chopped bell pepper
- 2 cups chopped tomatoes
- ½ tsp Celtic Sea salt
- 1/8 tsp pepper
- 1/8 tsp curry powder
- 1/8 tsp thyme

1. Wash okra, cut off stem ends, slice, and set aside.
2. Chop onion and bell pepper, steam fry in a large skillet with about 1 T coconut oil or butter and cook until lightly transparent.
3. Add okra and tomatoes. Stir in mixture of salt, pepper, curry powder, and thyme.
4. Simmer, covered, 30-40 minutes or until okra is tender.

Inspired by pH Miracle Diet

Buffalo Chicken Salad

If you like Buffalo Chicken, this is a great recipe for you to enjoy. Topped with homemade Blue Cheese Dressing (see recipe in our Condiments section), you will feel like you're indulging. This recipe offers the perfect combination of spice, crunch, tangy, and sweet.

You can make the dressing and the chicken ahead of time so assembling the salad is quick and easy when in a rush.

Ingredients: (2-3 servings)

1 boneless, skinless, chicken breast
1 T butter
1 T coconut oil
Celtic Sea salt and Black Pepper
½ cup Louisiana Hot Sauce
6 cups chopped salad greens
½ cup **Blue Cheese Dressing**
½ cup Blue Cheese Crumbles

Husband Approved

Hubby says: "I love this recipe with lots of Buffalo Chicken and less lettuce. Delicious any way you make it."

Kid Approved

Daughter says: "This salad is fun to eat. Lots of flavors and the crunch of the lettuce."

1. Using a sharp knife, carefully slice through the middle of the chicken breast horizontally, making two thin cutlets.
2. Heat butter and coconut oil over medium high heat and add chicken to the pan. Sprinkle with salt and pepper and cook on both sides until chicken is golden and done in the middle, about 3-4 minutes per side.
3. Reduce heat to low and pour the hot sauce over the chicken. Turn the chicken over to coat thoroughly in the sauce, then turn off the heat. Keep the chicken warm in the pan.
4. Meanwhile, assemble salad. Place salad greens in a large bowl. Drizzle with dressing and toss to coat.
5. Slice chicken into thin slices or bite-sized pieces. Add to the salad.
6. Top with additional crumbled blue cheese

Inspired by Renee Drummond

Chicken a la King

I remember having this dish when I was a kid and it was a favorite for both me and my sister. With a few small tweaks, this recipe is a delicious Ditch Candida version. Reheats well too!

1. Saute in a saucepan about 5 minutes then set aside:
   - 1 T butter
   - ½ cup cleaned and diced fresh mushrooms
2. Melt:
   - 3 T butter
3. Stir in and make a paste:
   - 3 T almond flour
4. Add and heat but don't boil:
   - 1 ½ cups chicken broth or cream
5. When sauce is smooth, add:
   - 1 cup cooked diced chicken
   - ¼ cup chopped pimiento
   - Sauteed mushrooms
6. Reduce heat to low. Pour some sauce over:
   - 1 beaten egg yolk
7. Return mixture to the pan and stir until it thickens slightly. Careful not to boil.
8. Add:
   - ¼ cup blanched slivered toasted almonds
   - Celtic Sea salt and pepper to taste.

Serve with **Cauliflower Fried "Rice"**

Husband Approved

Hubby says: "This is as good as going out to an Oriental restaurant."

Kid Approved

Daughter says: "The mushrooms and almonds make this super good."

Inspired by Joy of Cooking

Chicken & Bacon Cas[serole]

I threw this recipe together one time when I found myself suddenly hosting a large family get-together and needed to provide the main dish. I needed something that could easily feed a crowd yet please even the pickiest eaters. The results were so popular that I now get requests to bring it to family events. If you can, grill the chicken breasts outside instead of pan-frying for even more flavor. Super simple and always a hit.

1. Preheat oven to 350°
2. Saute in a large saucepan or grill pan until cooked:
   - 4 T butter
   - 5-6 boneless diced chicken breasts
   - Sprinkle of **Homemade Seasoned Salt**
3. Meanwhile, prepare until crispy:
   - 1 package turkey bacon
4. Transfer chicken to 9x12 baking dish. Top with:
   - 2 cups shredded cheddar cheese
   - Crumbled cooked bacon
5. Bake for 15-20 minutes or until cheese is melted and bubbly.

Husband Approved

Hubby says: "You had me at 'Bacon'."

Kid Approved

Daughter says: "One of my favorite chicken meals, especially with some steamed broccoli."

Chicken Caesar Salad

Caesar salad is a versatile and delicious choice for a meal anytime of the day or as a side dish or snack. Our recipe for the dressing can be found in the Condiment Section and takes just minutes to make. For time savings, make the dressing and grill the chicken ahead of time on your prep day. Try some of our suggested variations to keep things interesting.

Ingredients: (serves 8)

1 batch of **Caesar Dressing** (see Condiments Section)
2 grilled chicken breasts, diced
3 romaine lettuce hearts
Fresh grated parmesan cheese
Fresh ground black pepper to taste

Husband Approved

Hubby says: "Great salad and best when the chicken is grilled."

1. Make Caesar Dressing if you haven't made it ahead of time.
2. Prepare grilled chicken breasts if you haven't made them ahead of time.
3. Clean and course chop romaine lettuce and put in salad bowl.
4. Top with chicken and cheese.
5. Drizzle with dressing.
6. Toss to combine. Add pepper to taste.

Variations:
Use shrimp instead of chicken.
Add bacon.
Add mixed greens and/or kale.
Top with **Chipotle Flank Steak**.

Kid Approved

Daughter says: "Delicious. I love this salad with extra chicken and parmesan."

Inspired by Pioneer Woman

Turkey or Chicken Divan

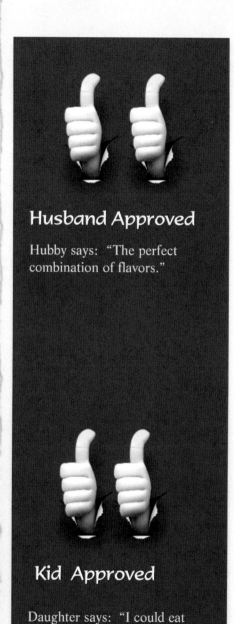

Husband Approved

Hubby says: "The perfect combination of flavors."

Kid Approved

Daughter says: "I could eat this every week, especially topped with bacon!"

I came up with this recipe one night when I was in the mood for cheesy broccoli and thought I'd throw in some leftover turkey. Equally good with chicken, it's best with white meat. You can also use boneless, skinless, chicken breasts.

1. Preheat oven to 400°
2. Saute in a large saucepan until soft:
   - 4 T butter
   - ½ cup minced onion
3. Add:
   - 2 tsp Celtic Sea salt
   - 1 tsp dry mustard
   - 1 cup milk
4. Stir until well mixed then add:
   - 3 cups grated fresh parmesan cheese
5. Heat on low and stir constantly until cheese is melted and thick sauce has formed. Set aside.
6. Meanwhile, butter a 9x12 baking dish and line with:
   - Sliced cooked chicken or turkey, or cooked boneless chicken breasts
7. Top with:
   - 1 bag frozen broccoli or asparagus
8. Cover with cheese sauce and sprinkle with a little additional grated fresh parmesan cheese (or 4 cheese blend).
9. Bake uncovered about 10 minutes or until heated through and sauce is bubbling.
10. Remove from oven and let rest for 2-3 minutes before serving.

Variations:
- Use cheddar cheese instead of parmesan
- Use diced cooked chicken breast rather than whole
- Top with crumbled turkey bacon

Chicken Lettuce Wrap

Husband Approved

Hubby says: "Tastes just like the version we like from our favorite Thai restaurant."

Kid Approved

Daughter says: "This is really good, but messy to eat in the lettuce wrap. I liked mine made into a salad so I could eat it easier with a fork."

This is another great Pressure Cooker recipe, but if you don't have a pressure cooker, you can use the stovetop...it just takes a little longer. I love this recipe as a simple, light meal. We like this one for dinner so we get some good protein and veggies but not too heavy before bed. Garlic and ginger are natural candida fighters which makes it a great choice regardless of the time of day you enjoy it.

Ingredients:
- ½ lb ground chicken
- 2 T chicken broth
- 2 ½ tsp minced fresh garlic
- 1 T balsamic vinegar
- 1/3 cup diced onion
- ¼ tsp ginger
- 2 T coconut aminos
- ¼ cup drained canned water chestnuts
- Pinch ground allspice
- 4 romaine lettuce leaves
- ¼ cup scallions

1. Place all ingredients except for lettuce and scallions in your pressure cooker pot.
2. Seal the lid and cook on high pressure for 10 minutes, then quick release the steam.
3. Use a potato masher or wooden spoons and break up the meat, stirring until well combined.
4. Roll meat topped with scallions into lettuce leaves.

If making on the stovetop, combine all ingredients except lettuce and scallions in large heavy skillet and cook on high heat until meat is cooked and flavors well combined. Serve as directed above.

Variation: You can use ground turkey instead of the ground chicken

Inspired by Instant Pot recipes by Michael Elliott

Chicken Paprika

Husband Approved

Hubby says: "I enjoy this chicken. The meat is so tender and not dry like some other recipe preparations."

Kid Approved

Daughter says: "Such good chicken and the meat just falls off the bone."

This is another great quick and easy one-pot power pressure cooker recipe. You can make it on the stovetop, but it's so much faster in the pressure cooker and the chicken comes out so very tender and flavorful. Adjust the amount of paprika to your personal flavor preference. We especially like using smoked paprika for extra flavor. The paprika gives the sauce a beautiful reddish color.

1. Saute in heavy skillet or pressure cooker until soft:
   - 1 ½ T butter
   - 1 ½ T coconut oil
   - 1 cup finely chopped onions
   - 1 T paprika
2. Add:
   - ½ tsp Celtic Sea salt
   - 2 cups chicken broth
3. Bring to boil then add:
   - 2 ½ lbs whole chicken, cut into pieces
4. Cover and simmer about 1 hour or if using a pressure cooker, cook on high pressure for 35 minutes and allow pressure to equalize naturally.
5. Stir in:
   - 1 cup sour cream
6. Stir until sauce has thickened.

Inspired by Joy of Cooking

Chicken Taco Salad

This is a very versatile recipe with so many uses. Serve it as a salad, in a lettuce wrap, as a pizza topping,….the possibilities are endless. It also freezes very well, so make a double batch and store it for future quick dinners when you don't have time to cook.

Ingredients: (serves 6)

6 boneless, skinless organic chicken breasts
¼ cup Homemade Taco Seasoning (see Condiments section)
2 T chili powder
2 (8 oz) cans tomato sauce
Celtic Sea salt (optional)
¼ cup coconut oil
Several dashes hot sauce (no sugar)

Husband Approved

Hubby says: "So delicious and I especially like it on homemade taco pizza."

1. Coat both sides of the chicken with the taco seasoning and chili powder. Rub it into the meat so the chicken is totally coated. Add salt if desired.
2. Heat a large skillet over medium heat and add the coconut oil. Working in batches if needed, cook the chicken breasts on both sides until they're deep golden on the outside and done in the middle, about 4 minutes per side.
3. Set the chicken aside to cool slightly.
4. In the same skillet, combine the tomato sauce and 1 cup of hot water, stirring and scraping the bottom of the skillet to loosen all the flavorful bits.
5. Bring the sauce to a gentle boil, then reduce heat to simmer for a few minutes while you shred the chicken.
6. Use two forks to completely shred chicken, then transfer chicken to the sauce.
7. Stir to coat and simmer about 5 more minutes.
8. Serve with your favorite taco toppings such as lettuce, fresh tomato, cheese, sour cream, Homemade Guacamole, onions, black olives, etc.

Kid Approved

Daughter says: "I love this recipe, especially as a salad topped with lots of cheese, sour cream, and mom's homemade guacamole."

Inspired by Renee Drummond

Chicken Fried "Rice"

In our house, we're big fans of international cuisine and a big challenge for my husband was not having rice. Cauliflower make an excellent rice substitute. Simple chop the cauliflower fine until it resembles rice then cook according to various recipe instructions. A food processor makes short order of the work.

Note: This recipe uses Coconut Aminos as a "Soy Sauce" substitute. Where coconut is not generally recommended other than coconut oil, small quantities of coconut aminos may be used occasionally, just be sure to use in moderation and no more than once or twice per week.

Husband Approved

Hubby says: "I'm not a big fan of Cauliflower, so was skeptical about this at first. I was surprised at how good it turned out and satisfied my craving for some Oriental Rice."

Base Ingredients:
- 1/3 cup Chopped Onion
- 1 clove Garlic
- 2 Tblsp Butter or Coconut Oil
- 4 cups "Riced" Cauliflower
- 2 Tblsp Coconut Aminos
- 1 tsp Fish Sauce
- 2 Tblsp minced fresh Parsley or 1 Tblsp dried Parsley
- 1/8 tsp Pepper
- 1 Egg, lightly beaten
- Diced Chicken from 1-2 Cooked Breasts

Variations:
- Substitute Chicken with your chunks or strips of Beef
- Add chopped carrots and/or peas

Kid Approved

Daughter says: "You'd never guess this is almost all vegetables! So good and fun to eat too."

1. Make Cauliflower "rice" by chopping or place in food processor.
2. In skillet, saute butter or coconut oil with onions and garlic until tender.
3. Stir in the Cauliflower, Coconut Aminos, Parsley, and pepper.
4. Cook over medium to low heat for about 5 minutes, stirring occasionally.
5. Make a well in the center and add the egg. Cook and stir until egg is completely set.

Recipe Adapted from MindBodyHealth.com

Chop Chop Chicken Salad

I love this salad, especially in the spring with the radishes and zucchini are fresh from the garden. Make the chicken breasts ahead of time on prep day…or make this as a "Salad-in-a-Jar" for fast and easy meals.

Ingredients: (serves 8)

- 1 cup walnut halves
- 1 carrot, quartered
- 6 large radishes
- 1 medium zucchini, cut into 1 ½ inch sections
- 2 cooked, boneless, skinless chicken breasts, cut into quarters
- 2 cups chopped lettuce
- 1 cup **Blue Cheese Dressings** (see Condiments Section for recipe)
- ½ tsp Celtic Sea salt
- ¼ tsp pepper

Husband Approved

Hubby says: "For a salad, this is really good. I liked the walnuts. They add just the right amount of flavor and crunch."

1. In a Vitamix or powerful blender, add walnuts and secure lid.
2. Pulse 2-3 times on medium intensity.
3. Add carrots, radishes, and zucchini and pulse 3-4 more times.
4. Add chicken and pulse another 3-4 times.
5. Pour contents into a large bowl. Add lettuce and dressing. Stir to mix well.
6. Salt and pepper to taste.

Variations:
- Add sauerkraut and/or lacto-fermented pickles.
- Add feta, goat, or grated Parmesan cheese.
- Serve in a lettuce wrap rather than as a salad.

Kid Approved

Daughter says: "This is super good, especially when mom adds a little feta cheese."

Inspired by Vitamix Cookbook

Curried Barbecue Chicken

Husband Approved

Hubby says: "You had me at 'Barbeque'."

Kid Approved

Daughter says: "I like this one with bone chicken where I can eat the leg meat."

Summer or winter, we love to grill. One of the great things about living where we do in the Ozarks of Missouri is that we still get nice days even in January. This recipe takes pre-planning as you have to marinate the chicken overnight, but it's worth it! Delicious flavor and marinating helps keep the chicken from drying out too much during cooking. Remember to grill low and slow for best results.

1. Combine in large bowl:
   - 1 ½ cups plain, unsweetened yogurt
   - Zest from 2 limes
   - 2 crushed cloves garlic
   - 2 tsp finely chopped ginger
   - 1 ½ tsp paprika
   - 2 tsp ground coriander
   - 1 tsp ground cayenne pepper
   - 1 tsp ground curry
   - 1 tsp Celtic Sea salt
2. Mix thoroughly then add:
   - Chicken pieces from 1-2 chickens or 5-6 boneless chicken breasts
3. Stir to fully coat chicken. Cover with a tight fitting lid and refrigerate overnight.
4. Grill or broil chicken until meat is completely cooked.

Inspired by Joy of Cooking

Grilled Chicken and Beef Burrito Bowl

One of my favorite things when eating out used to be the Burrito Bowls. Southern cuisine at its finest, in my opinion. This recipe takes the flavors and charm of the traditional burrito bowl…but with a few twists to make it Ditch Candida friendly. You can make the Cauliflower "Rice" and cook the Beef and Chicken ahead of time for a faster meal.

Ingredients: (serves 8)

- 2 cups Cauliflower Fried "Rice" (made with zest from 2 limes and 1/3 cup fresh cilantro)
- 1 lb grass fed sirloin steak, cut into small cubes
- 1 lb boneless, skinless chicken breasts, cut into bite-sized pieces
- ½ tsp Celtic Sea salt
- ½ tsp black pepper
- 1 tsp cumin
- 1 tsp chili powder
- 4 T melted coconut oil
- 4 T (½ stick) butter
- 1 medium onion, diced
- 1 zucchini, diced
- 1 yellow squash, diced
- 1 red bell pepper, diced
- 1 yellow bell pepper, diced
- 1 jalapeno pepper, finely diced
- ½ cup shredded lettuce
- Shredded cheese
- Sour cream

1. Make the Cauliflower "Rice" by chopping cauliflower in a food processor until resembles rice. Saute in coconut oil or butter with lime zest until 'el dente' in texture. Add cilantro and set aside.
2. Meanwhile, in a small bowl, mix together the salt, pepper, cumin and chili powder until blended.
3. Add chicken and beef to two separate bowls. Sprinkle half the seasoning over the chicken and half over the beef. Toss to coat.
4. In a large skillet, heat ½ the coconut oil and ½ the butter until melted. Add the beef and cook until done. Remove the beef and keep warm. Add the chicken to the same pan and cook until done. Remove the chicken and keep warm.
5. To the same pan, add the remaining butter and coconut oil. Toss in all the vegetables and saute for a few minutes until golden and cooked.
6. To assemble burrito bowl, add cauliflower rice to the bottom. Top with meat, then veggies, then toppings of choice such as lettuce, shredded cheese, sour cream, Pico, or guacamole.

Inspired by Pioneer Woman

Husband Approved

Hubby says: "Excellent flavor and very filling. You even forget that you're eating so many vegetables with this dish."

Kid Approved

Daughter says: "I like this as long as it's not too spicy, so it's best when mom serves it with lots of lettuce and sour cream on top."

Italian Turkey Meatballs

Meatballs are a versatile dish since there are so many things you can do with them. Serve them over vegetable "noodles", in a soup, as an appetizer, as a main dish, or even as a snack. This recipe is a great make-ahead dish as they freeze and reheat well. Double the below recipe and preserve some for future "grab and go" meals.

Ingredients: (serves 6)

1 lb ground turkey
8 oz fresh grated parmesan cheese
1 ½ T garlic powder
1 ½ T **Italian Seasoning** (see Condiments section)
1 tsp pepper
3 T parsley flakes
1 lb fresh mushrooms, sliced

1. Mix all ingredients except mushrooms in a large bowl.
2. Using your hands, roll mixture into 2 inch balls.
3. Heat a large skillet on medium-high heat and add 2 T coconut oil.
4. Brown meatballs until fully cooked, turning to cook all sides.
5. Add sliced mushrooms and cook until mushrooms are tender.

Husband Approved

Hubby says: "An Italian spin on the classic 'Swedish' meatball. These are delicious!"

Kid Approved

Daughter says: "The first time I tried these I didn't know if I liked them or not, but the second time I thought they were delicious. Maybe mom made them with more parmesan... Yum!"

Inspired by In the Kitchen with MRC

Quick Chicken Creole

Husband Approved

Hubby says: "I enjoyed the flavors of this recipe, with a touch of spice but not too strong."

Kid Approved

Daughter says: "Don't leave out the shrimp! It's super good."

If you're in the mood for some deep south cooking, this recipe is an excellent choice. Classic Creole flavors come together in this dish to make a delicious breakfast, lunch, or dinner. Throw it in a thermos for an easy on-the-go meal or take it to your next potluck.

1. Saute in a large saucepan until golden:
   - 3 T butter
   - 2 T minced onion
   - 1 minced clove garlic
   - ¼ tsp Celtic Sea salt
   - ¼ tsp paprika
2. Add and bring to low boil:
   - ½ cup tomato puree or strained tomatoes
   - 1 cup chicken broth
3. Add:
   - 1 lemon zest
   - ½ tsp horseradish
   - 2 cups diced cooked chicken meat
   - 1 cup cooked, peeled shrimp (optional)
   - ½ cup sliced fresh mushrooms
   - ½ cup chopped pimiento
4. Heat until fully cooked and mushrooms are tender. Add:
   - Celtic Sea salt (or Cajun Seasoning) and pepper to taste.
5. Serve with **Cauliflower Fried "Rice"**

Inspired by Joy of Cooking

Southern Chicken Salad

Chicken salad sandwiches are so refreshing and make great lunches when on the go. In the Ditch Candida Program, we can still enjoy this southern classic by converting a few ingredients and wrapping in lettuce. Or, just put the chicken salad in a bowl and eat it straight. The original recipe for this version came from a dear friend from Texas.

1. In a bowl, combine:
   - 1 can organic canned chicken, drained
   - 1-2 T homemade mayo or crème fraiche
   - 2 T finely chopped lacto-fermented dill pickles
   - Pinch of smoked paprika
   - Cajun seasoning to taste
2. Mix well until chicken is well crumbled.
3. Serve in lettuce wrap.

Variations:
- Add a dash of hot sauce (no sugar version)
- Add sauerkraut
- Serve in a bowl and top with fresh cilantro, grated cheese, fresh dill, or fresh parsley
- Add finely chopped raw onion (especially good with sweet red onion)
- Add diced sweet bell pepper
- Add chopped celery

Husband Approved

Hubby says: "I wouldn't want to eat this one every day since I don't like mayo much, but I thought it was surprisingly good."

Kid Approved

Daughter says: "Yes please! I love this one and it's especially good on picnics. Food always tastes so much better outside. Why is that?"

Inspired by Heidi A.

Stuffed Chicken Breasts

This recipe is another one of those quick and easy recipes that is a great option for those busy moments when you don't have much time to spend in the kitchen. Following the classic Chicken Cordon Bleu style, the flavors of chicken, ham, and cheese in this recipe go so very well together. Also reheats well, so make extras and have them available as leftovers. The recipe below is for each individual serving, so adjust according to how many you need or want to make. You can also omit the sauce and just serve the chicken with the ham and cheese.

1. Layer **1 boneless, skinless chicken breast** between two layers of plastic wrap and beat with a meat cleaver or rolling pin until thin.
2. In a medium skillet, heat until melted:
   - 1 ½ - 2 T butter
3. Add chicken and cook until no longer pink, about 2-3 minutes per side.
4. Layer on one side of chicken:
   - 1 thin slice of ham (omit on Theologenic Diet)
   - 1 thin slice of Swiss cheese
5. Fold chicken over so cheese and ham are in the center of the chicken sides.
6. Remove chicken from the pan, but keep warm.
7. Add to the hot pan with drippings:
   - 1 T finely minced shallots
   - 3 diced mushroom caps
8. When mushrooms have cooked about 3 minutes and are slightly soft, add:
   - ¼ cup chicken broth
   - 2 T freshly skinned and seeded, chopped tomato
9. Simmer another 3 minutes or so. Add:
   - 2 T heavy cream
10. Return chicken to skillet with sauce and heat on low until warmed. Careful not to allow sauce to boil or cream will curdle. When heated through, add:
    - 1 T chopped fresh parsley
    - Celtic Sea salt and pepper to taste
11. Serve immediately.

Inspired by Grandma Margaret and Joy of Cooking

Husband Approved

Hubby says: "This recipe is really good, but since I don't care for tomatoes, I like it served plain without the sauce."

Kid Approved

Daughter says: "Chicken AND ham? Awesome and so good. I love the sauce too."

Turkey/Chicken Casserole

This is a great recipe for leftover turkey or chicken. We like to make a roast bird then make this recipe the next day with what is left. Simple and easy, and very good. Be sure to watch the mixture after adding the egg yolk to avoid curdling of the eggs. Egg yolks work pretty well as a sauce thickener substitute.

1. Saute in a saucepan until golden:
   - 3 T butter
   - ½ cup diced celery
   - 1/3 cup thinly sliced onions
   - 1/3 cup thinly sliced bell pepper, seeds and membrane removed
2. Gradually stir in:
   - 1 ½ cups turkey or chicken broth
3. Heat to low simmer but not boiling. Add turkey/chicken meat.
4. Remove the pan from heat. Pour some sauce over:
   - 2 beaten egg yolks
5. Return mixture to the pan and stir until it thickens slightly. Careful not to boil.
6. Add:
   - Minced chives or parsley
   - Celtic Sea salt and pepper to taste.
7. Serve with **Cauliflower Fried "Rice"**

Husband Approved

Hubby says: "A delicious way to enjoy leftovers."

Kid Approved

Daughter says: "Very good, especially with lots of dark meat."

Inspired by Joy of Cooking

Tuscan Style Chicken

The original recipe called for a little white wine added to the tomato mixture while it simmers, but you don't really miss it with the aromatic herbs like oregano and basil. The results are super fast and easy, but will seem like you've made a fancy Italian dinner.

Ingredients:

1 lb boneless chicken breast cutlets
½ tsp Celtic Sea Salt
¼ tsp pepper
2 T. Coconut Oil, melted
1-2 bunches kale, de-stemmed and leafed to bite-size pieces
1 cup sliced fresh mushrooms
1 can organic diced tomatoes
½ tsp basil
¼ tsp oregano
4-5 oz grated mozzarella cheese

1. Season both sides of chicken with salt and pepper.
2. Preheat grill pan or heavy skillet with coconut oil or butter and heat chicken until cooked through, flipping once during cooking.
3. While chicken is cooking, add remaining ingredients (except cheese) to bowl and mix gently. If serving several kids, remove chicken from pan and cut into bite-sized pieces then return to pan. For adults, keep chicken breasts whole. Pour tomato mixture over chicken.
4. Cover and cook 4-5 minutes until heated and bubbly.
5. Remove pan from heat, top with cheese, cover and let stand 2-3 minutes until cheese melts.

Variations: Try different kinds of cheese like pepper jack or Monterey jack. Use fresh diced tomatoes when in season.

Inspired by a recipe given to me by my sister, Amanda Plaster

Husband Approved

Hubby says: "This recipe made me feel like we were eating out at a fancy Italian restaurant."

Kid Approved

Daughter says: "What's not to love about this recipe? Chicken, veggies, and cheese. So good!"

Beef Goulash

My dad used to make this over a campfire when I was a kid. I still remember the smell of the dish mixed with campfire smoke and woods. So good. This is one of those simple recipes that works well in a Dutch oven over a fire, in a stockpot, or in your pressure cooker.

This makes 2 lbs of meat, so use the leftovers to make soups or stews.

1. Melt in a heavy pot or pressure cooker pot:
   - ¼ cup butter, coconut oil, or bacon drippings
2. Add and cook until well browned:
   - 2 lb stew beef, cut into cubes
3. Add and saute until soft:
   - 1 ½ cup chopped onions
4. Once meat is brown and onions are soft, add:
   - 1 cup beef broth
   - 1 diced bell pepper, any color, seeds and membrane removed
   - 1 tsp Celtic Sea salt
   - 2 tsp smoked paprika
5. Cover and simmer 1 ½ hours or pressure cook on high for 35 minutes.

Variations:
- Add a can of diced tomatoes
- Add a can of chopped green chile peppers
- Top with spicy cheese
- Add a diced, de-seeded jalapeno pepper

Husband Approved

Hubby says: "I like it spicy so this is a great recipe, especially with added peppers and cheese."

Kid Approved

Daughter says: "I like this recipe topped with parmesan cheese and served with green beans."

Inspired by Joy of Cooking

Beef Stroganoff

Husband Approved

Hubby says: "Love this recipe. It's a family favorite."

Kid Approved

Daughter says: "Yum! I love this recipe served with zucchini noodles."

Stroganoff was a favorite of my hubby, but for years I would make it with processed canned soups…not realizing that it is just as easy and so much more delicious to make it from scratch. This recipe is another one of those we often serve; partly because it's so easy and partly because everyone love it so much.

Traditional Stroganoff is often served over noodles. Our version is great with kelp noodles, spiralized veggie noodles, or with baked sweet potatoes.

1. Sauté in a heavy skillet:
   - 1 T butter
   - 1 small grated onion
2. Add and sauté until evenly browned:
   - 1 ½ lb fillet of beef, stew beef, or sirloin…thinly sliced
3. In a separate skillet, heat and saute:
   - 2 T butter
   - ¾ lb fresh mushrooms, sliced
4. Combine the mushrooms and beef and season with:
   - ½ tsp basil
   - Dash of nutmeg
   - Salt and Pepper to taste
5. Reduce heat to low and add:
   - 3 T white balsamic vinegar
   - 1 cup cultured cream, crème fraiche, or sour cream

Inspired by Joy of Cooking

Boiled Beef

Boiled Beef is popular in many ethnic dishes. We find it flavorful, easy to make, and wholesome. Be sure to choose good quality beef from organically raised cows. It really does make a huge difference. This recipe makes large batch, so if you're serving just a few people, you'll have plenty of leftovers. Use leftovers in soups and stews or reheat as is.

1. Bring to a boil in a heavy pot:
   - 6 cups of water
2. Add and bring to boil:
   - 3 lb lean stewing beef in one piece or roast
3. Skim if necessary any impurities that may have risen during boiling then add:
   - 1 onion
   - 3 cloves
   - 1 bay leaf
   - ½ cup sliced carrots
   - ½ cup sliced celery with leaves
   - 1 sliced turnip
   - 1 tsp Celtic Sea salt
4. Cover and simmer until the meat is tender (about 3-4 hours) or if using pressure cooker, cook on high pressure for 45 minutes.
5. In a separate stockpot, sauté:
   - ¼ cup butter
   - ¼ cup chopped onions
6. Stir in slowly, 2 cups of the stock made from the boiled beef. Season the stock with:
   - 2 T horseradish
   - Celtic Sea salt
7. Reduce heat to low and add:
   - 2 egg yolks
8. Stir briskly until sauce has thickened. Don't allow to boil or overheat.
9. Cut meat into slices against the grain and top with sauce and fresh parsley.

Inspired by Joy of Cooking

Husband Approved

Hubby says: "The texture of the beef is very tender and has great flavor. I like this server with baked sweet potatoes."

Kid Approved

Daughter says: "I like this recipe with fresh sauerkraut."

Chipotle Flank Steak

Flank steak is one of the cheaper cuts so you can still enjoy a tasty steak for dinner or in your salad with this recipe. Normally a "tougher" cut, marinating in yogurt and mustard help to 'soften' the fibers of the meat and the results are a flavorful and tender dish. You can substitute a can of chipotle peppers for the chili powder if you like a deep chipotle flavor.

Ingredients: (serves 4)

3 Tablespoons extra virgin olive oil
Zest of one lime
1 T **Homemade Dijon mustard**
1 garlic clove, minced
1 tsp ground cumin
1 T chili powder
1 cup plain goat's milk yogurt
1 grass-fed flank steak (about 1 ¼ pounds)
Celtic Sea salt to taste

1. Combine all ingredients except the steak and sea salt in a reseal- able zip top plastic bag. Seal bag and shake to mix well.
2. Add steak and press air out of the bag, making sure the meat is well coated in marinade. Let marinate AT LEAST one hour, or as long as 8.
3. Preheat a grill or skillet over high heat.
4. Remove steak from marinade, pat dry, and sprinkle with salt.
5. Grill to desired doneness — medium rare is about 4 minutes per side — and let rest for 5 minutes before serving.
6. Slice steak against the grain into thin, diagonal slices. Serve 4 oz of meat per person.

Suggested sides: Cauliflower Mashed Potatoes, Cauliflower Rice, Sauteed Asparagus, Oven Roasted Vegetables

Note: This steak is good hot or cold, so leftovers make a great salad topping. Or, dehydrate the leftover slices to make a delicious jerky.
Inspired by Gundry MD

Husband Approved

Hubby says: "Good both hot and cold, this one is a winner for sure."

Kid Approved

Daughter says: "I especially like this cold on a salad with feta cheese."

Corned Beef & Cabbage

Corned beef and cabbage was a dish my grandmother would serve regularly when we visited. Even now, whenever I prepare it or enjoy the flavors, it brings back memories of Grandma's kitchen. Corned Beef is generally made with some sugar as a curing agent, so be sure to rinse thoroughly before cooking.

1. Wash under running water to remove surface brine:
   - Corned Beef Brisket
2. Cover with boiling water and simmer, allowing 1 hour per pound on the stovetop or 20 minutes per pound if using a pressure cooker.
3. Meanwhile, prepare until crispy:
   - 2-3 slices of bacon per person
4. Reserve drippings and set aside. In heavy skillet, add 1-2 T bacon drippings. Steam/saute until wilted:
   - 1 small head of cabbage, coarse shredded
5. When cabbage is soft, remove from heat and top with crumbled bacon.
6. When meat is done, carefully remove from pot and slice thinly against the grain. Serve with cooked cabbage and bacon.

Husband Approved

Hubby says: "The perfect blend of flavors and textures...especially with lots of bacon."

Kid Approved

Daughter says: "I like this recipe in the winter when it's cold outside. My favorite is when mom adds extra bacon."

Inspired by Joy of Cooking

Green Pepper Steak

Who needs Chinese take-out when you can make this recipe and enjoy delicious Oriental cuisine without the MSG or preservatives notorious to the fare? You'll need to whip up a batch of our Homemade "Soy" Sauce and the meat needs time to marinate so make the beef the day before or add it to your prep day then freeze for later quick meals.

Serve over Cauliflower "Rice".

A winner every time.

1. Cut into ½ inch strips and trim the fat from:
   - 2 lb round steak, ½ inch thick
2. Combine:
   - ¼ cup **Homemade "Soy" Sauce** (see condiments section for recipe)
   - 1 cup beef broth
   - 2 cloves of garlic, mashed
   - ½ tsp ginger
3. Pour the marinade over the meat and refrigerate covered 2-12 hours.
4. Drain meat, discarding garlic and reserving ½ cup of the marinade for the sauce.
5. Dry meat strips on paper toweling. In a large skillet, saute meat until light brown in:
   - 3 T coconut oil
6. Add reserved marinade and 1 cup hot water. Cover and simmer about 45 minutes.
7. Add:
   - 3 large green bell peppers, cut into ½ inch chunks with veins and seeds removed
   - 1 cup sliced water chestnuts
8. Simmer an additional 15 minutes until peppers are tender.
9. Reduce heat to low and add:
   - 2 egg yolks
10. Heat while stirring constantly until sauce has thickened slightly. Serve immediately over cauliflower "rice".

Inspired by Joy of Cooking

Husband Approved

Hubby says: "The sauce is what makes this recipe so good....well, that and fresh green peppers from the garden."

Kid Approved

Daughter says: "Green peppers aren't my favorite, but this is good. Sometimes, mom makes it for me with Red or Orange peppers instead and that's even better."

Meatball Bombers

This recipe is adapted from Grandma Margaret's Special Meatball Bomber recipe. Every Christmas, Grandma would make these with her special homemade sauce. If I close my eyes, I can still remember the incredible smells and tastes.

Most meatballs call for breading of some kind to help hold them together. We substitute egg and parmesan cheese, giving them great flavor that I think are even better than the traditional variety you may be used to.

This recipe freezes well for make-ahead meatballs and quick future recipes.

Husband Approved

Hubby says: "Best meatballs ever!"

Ingredients:
- 3 lb. Ground Beef
- 2 eggs
- ¼ cup milk
- 1 onion, chopped fine
- 1 bell pepper, chopped fine
- 1/3 cup parmesan cheese, grated
- 1/3 cup Romano cheese, grated
- ½ tsp oregano
- 1 T parsley flakes
- 1 T garlic powder
- 1 T onion powder
- Celtic Sea salt
- Fresh ground black pepper

1. Add all ingredients to a large mixing bowl.
2. Mix well by hand to fully incorporate all the ingredients.
3. Form into balls the size of large walnuts.
4. Freeze for later use…or carefully pan fry, turning gently until all sides are brown, then add to sauce of choice and simmer 1 hour. We recommend making with **Grandma's Special Spaghetti Sauce** (found in the condiments section).

Kid Approved

Daughter says: "You don't even miss the noodles when you have these meatballs."

Inspired by Grandma Margaret

Meatloaf

Would you believe meatloaf can still be on the menu? Yep! And it's super delish too! We just substitute a couple ingredients and voila! Since the recipe takes about 2 hours start to finish, you can make the meatloaf ahead of time and either freeze it or refrigerate until ready to serve.

Husband Approved

Hubby says: "Meatloaf makes a great meal any time of day and the leftovers are sometimes even better than the first go-round."

Ingredients: (serves 8)

2 lbs grass-fed ground beef (or other ground red meat or turkey)
1 onion, diced
2 cloves garlic, minced
1 carrot, finely diced
1 stalk celery, finely diced
4 T coconut oil
1 tsp fresh or dried thyme
1 tsp dried chili flakes

1½ cups almond meal (not almond flour…meal is courser)
2 eggs
1 T fish sauce
4 T **Homemade Ketchup** (see condiments section)

1. Preheat oven to 350 degrees.
2. Sauté onions, carrots, and celery in coconut oil for five minutes. Add garlic and continue cooking until veggies are soft.
3. Mix in chili flakes, thyme, and salt. Remove from heat and set aside.
4. In a large bowl, whisk the eggs and combine almond meal.
5. Using your hands, mix ground meat, sautéed vegetables, soaked eggs and almond meal, and fish sauce. Place mixture into an oiled, glass loaf pan. Bake for about 1½ hours. If desired, cover the top of the meatloaf with homemade ketchup for the last 15 minutes of baking.

Kid Approved

Daughter says: "This is really good with mashed sweet potatoes or cauliflower mashed taters."

Inspired by The Whole Journey

No-Bun Hamburgers

Hamburgers are about as traditional and American as we can get, and they're a favorite in our house…mostly because they taste so good! On the Ditch Candida program, we can still enjoy this classic…just without the bun and watching the ingredients on any condiments we may use. Check out the Condiments Recipes section for quick and easy homemade **Ketchup**, **Mustard, Mayo**, **Barbeque Sauce,** and **Relish.** Or try adding fresh lettuce, raw onion, dehydrated onion chips, fresh tomato, sauerkraut, or lacto-fermented dill pickles to your burgers.

Husband Approved

Hubby says: "What's not to like about this one, other than we get to eat it with a fork instead of with our hands?"

Ingredients:
  1 lb ground beef, preferably organic grass-fed
  1 small onion, diced
  1 T garlic powder
  1 egg
  Celtic Sea Salt and Pepper to taste

Optional additional ingredients:
  ½ cup finely grated raw carrots
  ½ cup chopped raw mushrooms
  2 T beef broth
  1 tsp anchovy paste
  Dash hot sauce
  Or top with cheese after cooking for a cheeseburger

1. Place all above ingredients in a large bowl and mix well with your hands until well combined.
2. Shape lightly into patties, keeping each burger to 6 oz or less.
3. Cook according to desired method. You may saute, broil, or grill using an outdoor grill or indoors on a grill pan.

Notes: You may pre-make the patties, then store between wax or parchment paper in the fridge or freezer for time savings.

Kid Approved

Daughter says: "This is another one of my favorites, especially with fresh tomatoes from the garden."

Inspired by Grandma Margaret.

Pepper Steak

We don't always grow our own beef, but when we don't we buy half a beef from a neighbor who grass feeds. What a huge difference a good grass fed organic beef makes! Not only is the flavor far superior, we're saving money and supporting the local economy. Win-win-win. Give it a try and experience the difference yourself!

Ingredients: (4 servings)

4 small 1" thick beef tenderloin steaks, rib eye, or T-bone steaks
1 T of dried green peppercorns, crushed
1 tsp balsamic vinegar
1 tsp coconut oil
2 T butter
4 shallots or 1 bunch of green onions, finely chopped
2 cups beef broth
1 T beef gelatin
Celtic Sea salt

Husband Approved

Hubby says: "You had me at steak…then add pepper? Yep, this is a true winner in my book."

1. Crush the peppercorns and mix them with the balsamic vinegar. Rub into the steaks and marinate for several hours.
2. Brush a heavy skillet with coconut oil and heat to medium high. Pat the steaks dry, leaving as much pepper adhering to the steaks as possible.
3. Cook steaks over medium high heat about 5 minutes per side or until cooked to your desired doneness. Transfer to a heated plate and keep warm in the oven while making the sauce.
4. Pour out any grease from the pan. Add butter and gently saute the shallots or green onions. Add stock and gelatin and bring to a rapid boil until sauce is reduced to about 2/3 cup.
5. Transfer steaks to individual plates and spoon a little sauce over each.

Kid Approved

Daughter says: "I don't like spicy so the pepper in this is a bit strong, but other than that it's really good."

Inspired by Nourishing Traditions

Peppery Flank Steak

Husband Approved

Hubby says: "I love pepper flavors and this steak is the perfect combination of pepper and garlic. Paired with a baked sweet potato and I'm in heaven."

Kid Approved

Daughter says: "I don't usually like lots of pepper, but this is a good dinner once in awhile."

Flank steak is a tougher cut so be careful not to overcook. Like prime rib, it does best when cooked medium or medium-rare for tender flavor. It is important to preheat the roasting pan prior to cooking to get the best results.

1. On a large baking sheet, season on both sides with Celtic Sea salt:
   - 1-2 lb flank steak
2. Sprinkle meat evenly with:
   - 1 T crushed or coarsely ground black pepper
   - 1 small bunch of rosemary leaves
   - 6 cloves of garlic, minced
3. Massage spices into the meat with your hands after drizzling with:
   - 4 T melted coconut oil
4. Allow to rest at room temperature for 1 hour for flavors to blend.
5. Meanwhile, preheat oven to 450°. Place a heavy roasting pan or heavy cast iron skillet large enough for the steak into the oven to also preheat. This is an important step to get a nice crust on the steak without overcooking the steak, which would make it tough.
6. Carefully add steak to the preheated roasting pan or skillet and cook for 5 minutes.
7. Flip the steak (it should be well browned on the bottom) and cook an additional 4-5 minutes until juices appear on the surface of the steak.
8. Remove steak and let rest about 10 minutes before carving. Cut into thin slices diagonally and against the grain. Serve.

Philly Cheesesteak

This recipe makes great leftovers, so make plenty and have more for later. I even think the leftovers are sometimes even better. Be sure to get real roast beef and not the sandwich meat version. We want to avoid processed sandwich meats. Plus, the flavor of the real deal is so much better!

Ingredients:
- 4 ounces thinly sliced roast beef
- 2 slices provolone cheese
- 1 large green bell pepper
- 1/3 medium sweet onion
- 3 ounces mushrooms
- 1 T butter
- 1 T coconut oil
- 1/2 tablespoon garlic, minced

Husband Approved

Hubby says: "I especially like this recipe when it's made with the sliced peppers rather than stuffed peppers, yet it is really good either way."

1. Preheat oven to 400*.
2. Slice top off pepper, remove ribs and seeds.
3. Slice onions and mushrooms. Saute over medium heat with butter, coconut oil, minced garlic and a little salt and pepper. Saute until onions and mushroom are nice and caramelized.
4. Add thinly sliced roast beef to the onion/mushroom mixture. Allow to cook 5-10 minutes.
5. Line the inside of the pepper with a slice of provolone cheese. Fill the pepper with meat mixture until it is nearly overflowing. Top the pepper with another slice of provolone cheese.
6. Bake for 15-20 minutes until the cheese on top is golden brown.

Time Saving Variation:
Slice pepper and saute along with onions and mushrooms. Add roast beef and cook until beef is done. Top with cheese and heat until melted.

Kid Approved

Daughter says: "I love this recipe with extra cheese and extra mushrooms."

Pot Roast

I grew up on a farm with lots of beef cattle so just say "Pot Roast" and I start salivating. Tender and juicy, pot roast is almost like comfort food to me. The best part, is left-overs make some fantastic soups…like try adding it to our Hungarian Mushroom Soup for a delicious beef version. You may not have many left-overs, though, as good as this recipe is! You can make it in the oven in a roasting pan, but I recommend using the Crock Pot or Power Pressure Cooker for extra convenience and time savings.

Husband Approved

Hubby says: "Delicious and filling. I like this one with lots of gravy on top and some melted pepperjack cheese."

1. In a roasting pan, Slow Cooker, or Pressure Cooker, combine:
   - 1 beef roast (any cut, but we especially like Chuck Roast)
   - Celtic Sea Salt and Pepper rubbed into beef roast
   - 4 cups (1 quart) beef broth or water (the broth will be extra rich, add nutrients, and make a great au jus or gravy
   - 1 large onion, chopped
   - 2 cloves of garlic, minced
   - 1 T balsamic vinegar (trust me!)
   - 1 sprig fresh rosemary (optional)
2. If you are roasting in the oven preheat to 325°, then when oven is hot, place roasting pan on center rack, covered, and roast for 2 hours and 15 minutes. If using a Slow Cooker, cook on low for 6-8 hours. If using a Power Pressure Cooker, cook on high pressure for 35 minutes then allow pressure to equalize on its own (about another 10 minutes)

Variations:
- Add additional root vegetables like carrots, turnips, parsnips, beets, and rutabaga.
- Add fresh mushrooms
- Add 1 quart of diced tomatoes
- Replace fresh rosemary with fresh thyme
- Double the garlic

Kid Approved

Daughter says: "I remember having this for dinner even before I started going to school. It's so good, especially with a baked sweet potato."

Note: To make a gravy, remove and strain 2-3 cups of the broth after cooking. While still very hot, add 1 egg yolk per cup of liquid used and stir briskly until thick. Serve immediately.

Inspired by a recipe from Grandma Margaret

Shepard's Pie

Shepard's Pie was often served in our home growing up. My mom loved to make this flavorful casserole and it symbolizes 'comfort food' at it's finest for me. Traditionally, Shepard's Pie is served with mashed potatoes. In our version we use sweet potatoes, but you could also substitute **Cauliflower Mashed Taters** if you prefer. Make ahead for time savings up to 2 days ahead of time or freeze. Leftovers are delicious too.

Ingredients: (serves 6)

1 1/2 lb. ground beef
2 lb. sweet potatoes, peeled and roughly chopped
1/2 onion, diced
2 carrots, peeled and diced
2 celery stalks, diced
2 garlic cloves, minced
2 T tomato paste

2 cups beef stock
2 fresh thyme sprigs
2 fresh bay leaves
Fresh parsley
1/4 cup ghee
Cooking fat or coconut oil
Celtic Sea salt and freshly ground black pepper

1. Add the sweet potatoes to a large pot and fill with water.
2. Bring to a boil and allow to cook until the potatoes are soft (about 20 minutes).
3. Drain the potatoes and put them back in the pot. Add the ghee, season to taste with salt and pepper, and mash until smooth.
4. Preheat oven to 375 F.
5. In a large skillet, brown the ground beef until no longer pink, and drain grease if necessary.
6. Add the onions, carrots, celery, garlic, tomato paste, beef stock, thyme sprigs, and bay leaves; season with salt and pepper to taste.
7. Cook over medium heat until everything is cooked and vegetables are soft (10 to 12 minutes).
8. Remove the thyme and bay leaves from the skillet.
9. Place the ground beef-vegetable mixture at the bottom of a baking pan and top with mashed sweet potatoes.
10. Sprinkle with fresh parsley and bake in the oven for 25 minutes.

Husband Approved

Hubby says: "Even better than what I remember having as a kid."

Kid Approved

Daughter says: "I like this best with the cauliflower mashed on top instead of sweet potatoes but it's good either way."

Inspired by Grandma Margaret

Sloppy Joe's

Husband Approved

Hubby says: "Just as good as my mom used to make. And you don't even really miss the bun."

Another traditional American favorite from my childhood is Sloppy Joes. Although conventional serving would call for a hamburger bun, this recipe is still satisfying and delicious when served in a lettuce wrap or cabbage wrap. Also another great recipe that tastes almost better as leftovers, so feel free to make extra for later.

1. Heat in a skillet:
   - 2 T butter
2. Add:
   - ½ cup minced onions
   - ½ cup chopped celery
   - ½ cup chopped green bell pepper
   - ¼ cup chopped jalapeno pepper (optional)
3. Cook on medium heat until softened than add:
   - 1 ½ lbs grass-fed organic ground beef or bison
4. Cook and stir until meat is lightly browned. Add:
   - ½ cup chopped mushrooms
   - 4 T chili sauce (no sugar variety)
   - ½ cup water
   - Celtic Sea salt and pepper to taste
5. Simmer uncovered over low heat around 15 minutes or until thickened.

Note: You can make this recipe ahead of time and freeze or refrigerate for fast and easy on-the-go meals.

Kid Approved

Daughter says: "I like this recipe served as a salad topping with lots of shredded lettuce and cheese instead of in a lettuce wrap...but that's good too."

Inspired by Grandma Margaret and Joy of Cooking

Stuffed Cabbage Rolls

Husband Approved

Hubby says: "This dish is best with sausage filling and extra cayenne pepper so it's nice and spicy."

Kid Approved

Daughter says: "I like this recipe, but I wouldn't want to eat it every day. It is good, and is fun to eat...like an egg roll!"

When I was a kid, my dad would take me every year to "Folk Fest" in Milwaukee, Wisconsin. It was special quality time, making great memories. Folk Fest was a huge event with food, costumes, dancing, marketplace, and education about cultures from around the world. I remember enjoying the cabbage rolls as one of our favorite ethnic dishes we would try. This recipe is fairly simple and worth the extra time to make and then bake. It makes great leftovers too!

1. Preheat oven to 375°.
2. In a large pot of boiling water, blanch cabbage leaves for 2 minutes to soften, then plunge into cold water to stop the cooking process. Drain and dry them on a towel. You'll need:
   - 8 large cabbage leaves
3. Combine in a large skillet and cook until done:
   - 1 lb ground beef or mixture of beef and pork sausage
   - ½ cup finely chopped onions
   - 2 T finely chopped fresh parsley
   - 2/4 tsp Celtic Sea Salt
   - ½ tsp Thyme
   - 1 clove garlic, pressed
   - ¼ tsp paprika
   - A few grains of cayenne
4. Divide the meat mixture into 8 parts. Put one part on each cabbage leaf. Fold outer leaves in, then roll into log shape. Secure if necessary with toothpicks.
5. Place Cabbage Rolls seam side down into buttered baking dish.
6. Dot each roll with
   - ½ tsp butter
7. Pour into dish:
   - ½ cup beef broth
8. Bake covered 50 minutes

Inspired by Joy of Cooking

Taco Salad

Husband Approved

Hubby says: "I love this recipe and the leftovers are great too."

Kid Approved

Daughter says: "The more toppings the better. I like mine with lots of tomato and cheese."

Just because we are not having shells or tortillas doesn't mean we can't enjoy a good taco now and again. We make it into a salad! Fast and easy, especially in the power pressure cooker or slow cooker for those extra busy days. Pre-shred the cheese and prep your veggies ahead of time for extra time saving.

1. Brown 1-2 lbs ground beef and chopped onions until brown and fully cooked. Drain off the grease.
2. Add ¼ cup **Homemade Taco Seasoning** (see condiments section) and ¼ cup water. Add more water if needed.
3. Continue cooking until flavors are fully blended.
4. Serve on shredded lettuce and top with choice/s of:
   - Shredded cheese
   - Diced fresh tomato
   - Chopped onion
   - Sour cream
   - Sliced black olives
   - Guacamole
   - Salsa (no sugar version, or make your own)
   - Pico de Gallo
   - Fresh cilantro

Variations:
- Use shredded chicken instead of the ground beef.
- Use ground turkey.

PORK RECIPES

DITCHCANDIDA.COM

Note: Pork is not considered a "clean" meat according to guidelines in Leviticus. Therefore, if you are following the Theologenic Lifestyle, substitute other cuts of clean meat for the recipes in this chapter, or simply omit them.

Bacon & Asiago Pork Chops

If you're in the mood for pork chops, you have to try this recipe. It's a little messy on the grill so use a grill pan or screen for best results. You can also bake them, but grilled is so delicious! Use a meat thermometer if needed to make sure the pork is completely cooked before serving.

Ingredients: (serves 4)

4 thick boneless pork chops

½ cup shredded asiago cheese
½ cup chopped sweet onions
½ cup chopped pre-cooked bacon

Celtic Sea salt and Pepper to taste

1. Cut a pocket into all 4 of the pork chops.
2. If you haven't already, cook the bacon until it's done but not too crispy.
3. Chop up the bacon, and in a bowl, combine it with equal parts of chopped onion and shredded asiago cheese. Now stuff this mixture into each pork chop and set aside.
4. Prepare a cool grill and place the stuffed pork chops slightly upright, (to avoid spilling the stuffing), onto a grill screen which is placed on the grill grate.
5. Once the cheese is melted and holds the stuffing together better, place the chops on their side and cook until the chops are just cooked through. You only need to flip them once to cook the other side. This shouldn't take long, but will depend on how thick your chops are.

*Note: Alternatively, you can bake the stuffed chops in a 400° oven for 25-30 minutes or until done.

Husband Approved

Hubby says: "Bacon, cheese, and pork chops? Definitely a winning combination."

Kid Approved

Daughter says: "I loved the flavor but they were a little messy to eat."

Inspired by Smoked and Grilled.com

Homemade Breakfast Sausage

Sometimes, it's hard to find breakfast sausage without nitrates, nitrites, or sugar….but we still like enjoying sausage now and again especially with recipes like our Sausage and Kale Soup. If you can't find good sausage, here is a great alternative recipe where you can make your own!

Ingredients:
- 2 lbs ground organic pastured pork
- 1 T Celtic Sea Salt
- 2 tsp black pepper
- 2 tsp finely chopped fresh sage or 1 tsp dried ground sage
- 1 tsp fennel powder
- 1 tsp garlic powder
- ½ tsp rosemary leaves
- ½ tsp dried thyme
- 1/8 tsp clove
- Dash of cayenne pepper (optional)

1. Combine ground pork with other ingredients and mix well.
2. Form into one inch patties. (Recipe makes about 15)
3. Store in the freezer until ready to use. I like to vacuum seal them in 2-3 serving packages.

To Cook: Heat in a heavy skillet over medium heat for 5-7 minutes until cooked through.

Husband Approved

Hubby says: "This is a winner. Great sausage either by itself or in other recipes."

Kid Approved

Daughter says: "I love sausage and this is really good. My favorite is the Sausage and Kale Soup, but it's really good with eggs too."

Inspired by Wellness Mama

Crockpot Chile Verde

Husband Approved

Hubby says: "Great flavor with a great southern flair. A winner any time."

Kid Approved

Daughter says: "I like this recipe, especially with lots of yummy toppings."

Here is another super fast and easy crockpot recipe for those days you're wanting a one-pot, throw-it-together-in-the-morning-and-have-dinner-ready-when-you-get-home, kind of recipe. Since most of the ingredients are staple pantry items anyway, it's also a great dish for those days you just don't know what to fix. Plus, it's delicious!

Ingredients: (serves 4)

- 2 pounds pork roast, boneless and cubed
- 3 cloves garlic, minced
- 2 Anaheim chilies, chopped
- 1-2 jalapeño peppers, diced
- 1 poblano pepper, chopped
- 1 onion, chopped
- 3 (4 oz.) cans diced green chiles
- 4-5 tomatillos, chopped
- 2 cups chicken broth (homemade)
- 1 (8 oz.) can diced tomatoes
- 2 tsp fresh oregano
- 1 tsp salt
- 1 tsp freshly ground pepper
- ½ tsp cumin
- ½ tsp paprika

Optional toppings for serving:

Cilantro, shredded cabbage, shredded lettuce, fresh tomato, avocado, sour cream, shredded cheese.

1. Combine all ingredients in a crockpot slow cooker and stir gently to incorporate spices.
2. Cook on LOW setting for 6-8 hours.
3. Shred meat and serve with desired toppings listed above.

Inspired by The Warrior Wife

Crockpot Pork Loin Casserole

When I was getting my Master's degree, my Crockpot was one of my best "kitchen" friends. When time is tight, it's so handy to throw ingredients in…set the temperature…and have dinner ready when I needed it. Easy, delicious, and very little mess to clean up during preparations and dinner. This recipe is one of those favorites that makes a really good meal with almost no effort. Serve on its own or over Spaghetti Squash.

Husband Approved

Hubby says: "Simple and delicious. I love the textures and flavors of this dish."

Ingredients: (serves 4)

1 ½ lbs pork loin
1 (15 oz) can tomato sauce
2 medium zucchini, sliced
1 onion, rough chopped
1 clove garlic, minced
1 head cauliflower, separated into medium florets
2 T basil, dried
¼ tsp black pepper, freshly ground
½ tsp Celtic Sea salt, (optional)

1. Add all ingredients to a large crockpot.
2. Cook on high for 3-4 hours or on low for 7-8 hours.

Note, you may need to add a little water to the bottom of the crockpot, especially if you'll be cooking on high setting and you have a large crockpot.

Kid Approved

Daughter says: "Yummy. I especially like the veggies in this dish."

Inspired by paleoplan.com

Grilled Pork Tenderloin with Sauerkraut

I love sauerkraut. It's so delicious and so very good for our gut…and so often when I ask others if they like sauerkraut I get a disgusted face and a vehement "no." Often, however, those same people find that they really do like sauerkraut when they try my lacto-fermented version. If you think you don't like sauerkraut, you may too be thinking of a time when you tried that nasty canned version. Canned sauerkraut is like canned peas or canned asparagus. There is simply NO comparison to fresh or properly prepared lacto-fermented. I encourage you to give it another shot if you don't think you like it. And, your gut will thank you too!

This dish is fast and simple to prepare and tastes amazing. If you don't want to fire up the grill outside, use a grill pan or electric grill pan like the George Foreman Grill.

Ingredients per serving:
- 4 oz pork tenderloin, thick sliced
- 1 oz green onion, chopped
- 3 oz fresh lacto-fermented sauerkraut
- ½ tsp caraway seed
- Cumin, Celtic Sea Salt, Pepper, and Sage (to taste)

1. Season pork with cumin, sage, salt, and pepper.
2. Grill until cooked inside but not dry.
3. In a small skillet, lightly saute green onions in butter or coconut oil until translucent.
4. Add caraway and heat through.
5. Serve pork, topped with onions and fresh sauerkraut. Note: never cook/heat the sauerkraut as it will kill the beneficial probiotics in the dish.

Husband Approved

Hubby says: "Pork tenderloin is so good, almost like a cross between ham and bacon. This dish is good and makes great leftovers."

Kid Approved

Daughter says: "I didn't used to like sauerkraut but now I love it. I like this recipe with extra onion."

Inspired by In the Kitchen with MRC.

Mustard & Onion Pork Chops

Husband Approved

Hubby says: "Any pork chop is a good pork chop."

Kid Approved

Daughter says: "I wouldn't want to eat this every day, but once in awhile it's good."

Growing up, whenever we had pork chops, my mom would fix them with onions and mustard. For the longest time, this was just how I thought all pork chops tasted. It's still a favorite way to fix them, even though my horizons have expanded in my adult years. You can find the recipes for both the mustard and the onion mix in the Condiments section.

Ingredients: (serves 4)

4 boneless pork chops
4 T Homemade Dijon Mustard
4T Homemade Onion Soup Mix
Celtic Sea salt and Pepper to taste

1. Heat a grill pan on medium-high heat and lightly grease with coconut oil or butter.
2. Add pork chops and cook one side until nice and brown, about 7 minutes.
3. Flip pork chops and baste with mustard, spreading about 1 T per chop. Sprinkle each chop with some onion soup mix.
4. Cover and cook until done (meat thermometer reads 170).

Inspired by Mom

Pork Chops with Roasted Garlic

Garlic is so good for our health, especially when battling candida. This recipe originally called for red wine, but I found that the dark balsamic did a wonderful job as a substitute, making a sauce with rich flavor. This recipe also works with chicken breasts if you prefer chicken over pork.

Ingredients:
- 20 cloves garlic
- 4 T Butter
- 4 boneless pork chops, medium to thin cut
- ¼ cup dark balsamic vinegar
- 1 bay leaf
- ½ cup beef broth
- Celtic Sea salt and pepper
- Chopped chives, for garnish

1. Preheat oven to 350°.
2. Place garlic cloves on a large sheet of parchment paper. Sprinkle with salt and pepper, and drizzle with 2 T of melted butter.
3. Fold the edges and top of parchment paper to seal. Place on a baking sheet and roast garlic for 1 hour, or until golden and slightly soft but not falling apart. Set aside. (This step can be done on prep day or in advance.)
4. Meanwhile, sprinkle pork chops on both sides with salt and pepper. Heat 2 T butter in a large skillet over medium high heat. Add the pork chops and cook them for a couple of minutes on each side (no need to cook all the way through yet.)
5. Remove chops and set aside. Add to the pan the roasted garlic then add balsamic vinegar and bay leaf.
6. Stir, scraping pan, to cook mixture about 5-7 minutes or until reduced by about two-thirds.
7. Add beef broth and bring to low boil. Remove bay leaf.
8. Add pork chops back to pan, stir to coat, then cook an additional 4-5 minutes until finished cooking through.
9. Place pork chops on serving plates, drizzle with lots of garlic cloves and sauce, then top with chopped chives.

Husband Approved

Hubby says: "This recipe is like a fancy restaurant-type dinner. Lots of flavors and very good."

Kid Approved

Daughter says: "I didn't think I would like this recipe as much as I did and now I can't wait to have it again."

Inspired by Renee Drummond

Roast Pork Loin

Generally if I serve pork, it is either chops or loin. These cuts tend to be less "cured" so tend to be better cuts to prepare. This recipe uses lots of flavorful herbs for a delicious finished dish. Since this roast does take about an hour and a half to cook, you'll want to fix it on a day you are home to watch the stove. Or, you can fix it in the pressure cooker at high pressure for 35 minutes.

Ingredients: (serves 6)
- 1 pork loin, ideally free-range or heritage
- ¾ tsp Celtic Sea salt
- ¾ tsp black pepper
- ½ cup melted coconut oil or butter
- 5 cloves garlic, minced
- 1 tablespoon fresh thyme, minced
- ¼ cup fresh parsley, minced
- 1 tablespoon fresh rosemary, minced
- 1 tablespoon fresh sage, minced
- 1 cup balsamic vinegar

Husband Approved

Hubby says: "The herbs lend lost of great flavor to this pork loin. Delicious."

Kid Approved

Daughter says: "I liked this even better the next day reheated."

1. Preheat oven to 350°.
2. In a small saucepan, heat balsamic vinegar on low heat until reduced and syrupy. Once nice and thick, remove from heat and set aside.
3. In a medium bowl, combine remaining ingredients other than the pork and mix well.
4. Place pork loin on a greased or lined baking dish. Brush with herb baste, using all the herbs.
5. Bake for 45 minutes to 1 hour or until a thermometer inserted into the center reaches 160 degrees.
6. Brush with balsamic vinegar glaze and bake an additional 10 minutes.
7. Remove from the oven and let rest 10-15 minutes before serving.

Inspired by Dr. Steven Gundry

Rosemary Roasted Pork Tenderloin

Rosemary is one of those aromatic herbs that is delightful in the garden and even more enjoyable in culinary dishes. The combination of flavors with rosemary and mustard make this a very enjoyable and easy dish; and a fun choice when entertaining. Serve with sweet potato fries, baked sweet potatoes, or any other vegetable side of your choice.

Ingredients:
- 16 oz pork tenderloin
- ¼ cup **Homemade Mustard** (Dijon-style)
- ¼ cup rosemary sprigs, chopped
- 4 tsp garlic powder
- ¾ cup course ground black pepper

Husband Approved

Hubby says: "I liked this recipe. The flavor with the mustard and pepper made it very tasty."

1. Preheat oven and baking dish to 350°.
2. In a medium bowl, combine all ingredients except pork, mix well.
3. Set aside about 1/3 cup of sauce and refrigerate.
4. Place remaining sauce in large re-useable bag with pork. Seal bag and turn to coat.
5. Allow mixture to marinate for about 30 minutes or while oven is preheating. (Or you can do these steps the night before.)
6. Drain marinade from meat and discard.
7. Place meat in a lightly greased roasting pan. Pour reserved marinade over the top.
8. Bake uncovered for 40-45 minutes or until meat thermometer reads 160°.
9. Slice and serve.

Makes about 3-4 servings.

Kid Approved

Daughter says: "I don't like much pepper, but I love rosemary and mustard so this was a one thumb kind of dish."

Inspired by In the Kitchen with MRC

SEAFOOD RECIPES

DITCHCANDIDA.COM

Note: Shrimp, Crab, and Lobster are not considered "clean" meats according to guidelines in Leviticus. Therefore, if you are following the Theologenic Lifestyle, substitute other cuts of clean meat for the recipes in this chapter, or simply omit them.

Blackened Herb Fillets

This is a somewhat spicy recipe that coats the fish. It's great with red snapper, trout, salmon, or any of your favorite fillets. I especially like to use trout, but feel free to experiment with what varieties you like best.

Ingredients:
- ½ cup melted coconut oil
- 3 T paprika
- 2 ½ tsp dried onion flakes
- ¼ tsp cayenne pepper
- 1 ½ tsp dried thyme
- 1 ½ tsp dried oregano
- 1 ½ tsp dried basil
- ¾ tsp cumin
- 1 tsp Celtic Sea salt
- ¼ cup fresh mint leaves
- 4-6 fresh fish fillets

Husband Approved

Hubby says: "Excellent flavor in this recipe with just enough heat."

1. Combine all herbs except mint in a small shallow bowl and mix well.
2. Put melted oil in another shallow bowl and place side by side with herb mixture.
3. Heat large skillet on high heat.
4. Dip fish fillets in oil and coat well, then dip in herb mixture and coat both sides.
5. Cook in hot skillet on one side (1-3 minutes) until herbs turn dark but not burned, then flip over carefully and cook on the other side.
6. Reduce heat to low and cook until fish is fully cooked.
7. Sprinkle fresh chopped mint onto fish before serving.

Kid Approved

Daughter says: "I like fish and this was good, but just a little spicy."

Inspired by pH Miracle Diet

Cashew Dusted Cod

This recipe is a great choice if you're wanting something yummy that feels a little "fancier" yet without the fuss or mess. Super fast to make and crazy easy…plus it tastes so good. The combination of cod with cashews makes a delightful dish any time of day.

Ingredients:

4		cod fillets, 6 ounces each
2	T	Greek yogurt
4	T	chives, chopped
1		tsp horseradish
1		zest from lemon
½		cup cashews, very finely chopped

1. Preheat oven to 425 degrees.
2. Place cod in a lightly-greased, shallow baking dish.
3. In a small bowl, mix the Greek yogurt, chives, horseradish, and lemon zest. Season mixture with sea salt and pepper.
4. Cover cod evenly with mixture and top with cashews.
5. Bake for 18-20 minutes or until the fish is done, and the crust is golden and crunchy.

Husband Approved

Hubby says: "This is a delicious choice if you're in the mood for seafood."

Kid Approved

Daughter says: "I loved the flavor but the texture of the fish with the crunchy nuts wasn't my favorite. Tasted good."

Inspired by The Whole Journey

Chili Rubbed Tilapia with Asparagus

Not everyone likes fish, but tilapia is a light fish with simple flavors that blend well with herbs and spices. Tilapia, Cod, and Pollock are some of my favorite fish, especially since we live in the heartland…about as far from the ocean as we can get so fish is rarely fresh.

Substitute broccoli or other vegetable if Asparagus is not in season…but if you can get fresh asparagus, be sure to use it! So delicious.

Ingredients per serving:
- 8 oz fresh asparagus, tough ends trimmed, cut into 1 inch pieces
- 1 T chili powder
- ½ tsp garlic powder
- ¼ tsp Celtic Sea Salt
- 8 oz tilapia or other white fish
- 3 tsp coconut oil
- Lemon zest

1. Bring 1-2 inches of water to a boil in a medium saucepan.
2. Put asparagus in a steamer basket over the boiling water, cover, and steam until tender-crisp (about 4 minutes).
3. Meanwhile, combine spices and dredge filets in mixture to coat.
4. Heat coconut oil in large skillet over medium high heat. Add fish and cook 5-7 minutes, turning once, or until thoroughly cooked but not dry.
5. Add lemon zest, a pinch of salt, and asparagus to the pan and cook an additional 2 minutes until warmed.

Husband Approved

Hubby says: "I like spicy so enjoy this recipe with extra chili powder added to my fish filet."

Kid Approved

Daughter says: "I don't like spicy, but this isn't too bad, especially when mom makes it with less chili powder and extra asparagus! The asparagus is the best part."

Inspired by In the Kitchen with MRC.

Cilantro Lime Grilled Shrimp

Husband Approved

Hubby says: "Shrimp is good just about any way it's prepared, but grilled? Oh yeah, that's the best."

Kid Approved

Daughter says: "I love shrimp and especially like this recipe when mom serves it with fresh cucumber salad."

If you like shrimp, you'll love this recipe. It's simple to make and so good. You can prep the shrimp and let it marinate the night before, then whip these up as a fancy breakfast with the veggie side of your choice. Tastes great cold, too as an addition to your favorite salad.

1. Gently toss together:
   - 2 lbs peeled and de-veined shrimp
   - ¼ cup coconut oil
   - Zest from 2 limes
   - 1/8 tsp red chili flakes
2. Let sit at room temperature for about 20 minutes to marinate. (If you're in a hurry, you can make this mixture ahead of time)
3. Preheat grill or grill pan to medium heat.
4. Drain shrimp if necessary and either skewer or place in a grill basket.
5. Grill shrimp 2-3 minutes per side until bright pink and cooked through (careful not to overcook or shrimp will become rubbery).
6. Sprinkle with:
   - ½ cup chopped fresh cilantro
   - Celtic Sea salt to taste

Creole Shrimp Lettuce Wrap

Husband Approved

Hubby says: "I enjoy good Creole flavors and you can't go wrong with grilled shrimp. What a delicious combination."

Before my daughter was born, I wasn't a huge fan of spicy or southern foods. For some reason, while I was pregnant I craved them and now I love them. This Creole recipe isn't too terribly spicy (unless you want it to be) and has the perfect blend of garlic, onion, and peppers to make a delicious dish. Since the filling needs time to marinate, make it the night before.

Ingredients:
(1 serving)

- 4 oz shrimp, cooked
- Chopped fresh parsley
- 1 oz chopped green onion
- 1 oz chopped bell pepper
- 1 oz chopped celery
- 1 tsp garlic
- ½ tsp onion powder
- 2-3 T Homemade Mayo
- 2 oz cucumber, chopped
- Creole seasoning to taste
- Hot Sauce to taste (no sugar)
- Large leaf lettuce for wraps

1. Combine shrimp, parsley, vegetables, mayo, garlic, onion powder, Creole seasoning and hot sauce in large bowl. Stir to combine.
2. Cover and marinate for 2 hours or overnight in the refrigerator.
3. Cut cucumber into long thin strips and set aside.
4. Wash lettuce leaves and dry.
5. To assemble wraps, place some of the shrimp mixture onto a lettuce leaf and top with cucumber. Carefully roll up wrap and use toothpicks to hold in place if necessary.
6. Repeat until all ingredients are used.

Kid Approved

Daughter says: "Spicy isn't my thing, but I do love shrimp."

Inspired by In the Kitchen with MRC

Ginger Salmon & Kale Salad

Ginger is another superfood in fighting Candida. You're sure to love this recipe if you like Salmon…and it tastes good even as a breakfast. You'll need to allow time to marinate both the salmon and the kale, so allow for a couple hours before dinner…or make ahead.

Husband Approved

Hubby says: "I didn't think I liked greens like kale until my taste buds started to change after getting off sugar. This salad is quite good."

Ingredients: (serves 4)

For the Salmon:
1 pound wild-caught salmon
½ cup coconut aminos
2 tsp grated ginger
1 T Xylitol
salt and pepper to taste

For the Kale Salad:
3 cups chopped kale
1 cup shredded carrots
½ cup diced cucumber
½ cup chopped green onion
1 cup shredded red cabbage
1/4 cup olive oil
1/4 cup balsamic vinegar
2 T Xylitol or stevia equivalent
2 T Homemade Mustard (Dijon or regular)
salt and pepper to taste

- Warm sauté pan on low and add coconut aminos, ginger, Xylitol, and seasoning. Heat marinade until everything is combined and liquid.
- Let cool for 2 minutes and then pour over salmon. Allow the salmon to marinate for 20 minutes. Grill to desired texture.
- Meanwhile, combine kale, carrots, cucumber, green onions, and cabbage.
- In a separate bowl, whisk the olive oil, vinegar, Xylitol, mustard, salt and pepper to make dressing. Pour over the salad for at least an hour before serving to allow the kale leaves to soften.
- Top with Salmon or serve on the side.

Kid Approved

Daughter says: "Kale, cucumbers, and salmon go so well together. And it makes for a colorful salad, too!"

Inspired by The Whole Journey

Goat Cheese Shrimp

If you don't like goat cheese, you can substitute feta cheese or crumbled bleu cheese in this recipe. To make the noodles, a spiralizer slicer is handy, but you can just slice them small or use a julienne peeler.

Ingredients:
- 1 tsp coconut oil
- 1/3 small onion, thinly sliced
- 1 clove minced garlic
- 5 oz uncooked shrimp, thawed, peeled, de-veined
- freshly ground salt & pepper
- 1 Roma tomato, diced
- pinch of crushed red pepper
- 1/3 tsp chopped fresh basil
- 1 zucchini
- 1 oz goat cheese

1. Heat the coconut oil over medium heat in a large skillet.
2. Add the onions and sauté for about 5 minutes, until softened.
3. Add the shrimp and garlic. Cook the shrimp for about 1 minute on each side, until just opaque. Remove the shrimp from the pan.
4. Add the tomato, 1 tablespoon of water, crushed red pepper, and basil.
5. Bring to a boil then reduce to a simmer and cook for about 5 minutes, adding more water, a little at a time if needed to keep it from burning, but not too much.
6. Add the zucchini and sauté over medium heat until slightly softened, about 3 minutes, then add the shrimp and heat through, about 1-2 minutes more. Serve with crumbled goat cheese.

Husband Approved

Hubby says: "This recipe is a nice light meal for those times you just want something simple but good."

Kid Approved

Daughter says: "Fresh basil AND shrimp? Oh yeah, that's a delicious combination! I like this recipe best with feta cheese."

Inspired by Shepherd's Diet

Grilled Salmon & Herbs

Salmon has a unique flavor and I've found that most people either love it or hate it. If you are one who loves it, try grilling the salmon filets with herbs.

Ingredients: (1 serving)
1 salmon filet per person
1 tsp dried dill
1 tsp garlic powder
1 tsp onion powder
1 tsp parsley
1/8 tsp fennel

1. Mix herbs together in a small bowl.
2. Brush grill pan or grill basket with coconut oil to avoid sticking.
3. Sprinkle herbs onto salmon filets and grill on medium low heat until cooked.

Husband Approved

Hubby says: "I'm a take it or leave it kind of guy when it comes to fish. This salmon has good flavor though, so if you like salmon, you'll love this one."

Kid Approved

Daughter says: "I don't like salmon, but I still tried it. This was good with lots of garlic."

Inspired by Grandma Margaret

Grilled Shrimp & Vietnamese Coleslaw

Husband Approved

Hubby says: "I like this recipe with Creole seasoned grilled chicken and served on a plate without the lettuce."

Kid Approved

Daughter says: "The fresh mint is so good in this recipe and I especially like it with lots of shrimp."

This recipe is super easy to make and very tasty. It's a great make-ahead recipe where you can make the "coleslaw" portion and store until ready to eat. Also great served salad-style without the lettuce if you prefer. Add some microgreens for extra flavor and nutrients or mix in some sauerkraut for an additional probiotic and digestive enzyme boost. Try replacing the shrimp with grilled chicken breast or pork loin for some variety.

Ingredients:
(1 serving)

- 4 oz shrimp, peeled & de-veined
- 4 oz thinly sliced cabbage
- 2 oz thinly sliced cucumber
- 1 oz sweet bell pepper, sliced
- 1 oz green onion, chopped
- 1 T fresh mint
- 1 packet stevia
- Zest from one lime
- Pinch of crushed red pepper
- Celtic Sea Salt to taste
- Large leaf lettuce for wraps

1. Grill or broil shrimp until pink.
2. Combine remaining ingredients except lettuce in a large bowl and mix to make "slaw".
3. Serve shrimp and slaw in a lettuce leaf wrap.

Inspired by In the Kitchen with MRC

Pesto Shrimp

My good friend Emily shared this recipe and it is absolutely delicious. The flavors of shrimp and pesto go so very well together. Make up a bunch of pesto, freeze in ice cube trays, then store for future use when you want to make this recipe on the fly. Great as a salad topping too!

Ingredients:
  1 tsp coconut oil
  1/3 small onion, thinly sliced
  1 clove minced garlic
  5 oz uncooked shrimp, thawed, peeled, de-veined
  freshly ground salt & pepper
  Basil Pesto (see recipe in Condiments Section)
  Finely shredded fresh parmesan cheese

Husband Approved

Hubby says: "Any recipe with shrimp is a winner in my book."

1. Heat the coconut oil over medium heat in a large skillet.
2. Add the onions and sauté for about 5 minutes, until softened.
3. Add the shrimp and garlic. Cook the shrimp for about 1 minute on each side, until just opaque. Remove the shrimp from the pan.
4. Make **Basil Pesto** and serve over Shrimp, garnished with fresh grated parmesan cheese.

Kid Approved

Daughter says: "This is so good, especially with extra parmesan."

Inspired by Emily Waterman

Roasted Fish with Dill

Dill is one of my favorite herbs. It smells so very amazing and is so very good for our bodies. Dill can help with bad breath, constipation, digestive issues, bloat, and gas. And best of all it tastes amazing. Fresh is always best if you can find it locally. Dill flavors blend well with fish. Try this recipe with salmon, halibut, trout, or any other favorite.

Ingredients:
- 1 T butter
- 2 tsp minced fresh Dill
- 5 ounces of fish (salmon, trout, etc.)
- Celtic Sea salt and freshly ground black pepper to taste

1. Preheat the oven to 475 degrees.
2. Place the butter and half the Dill in a roasting pan just large enough to fit the salmon and place it in the oven. Heat about 5 minutes, until the butter melts and the herb begins to sizzle.
3. Add the fish to the pan, skin side up. Roast 4 minutes. Remove from the oven, then peel the skin off. (If the skin does not lift right off, cook 2 minutes longer.)
4. Sprinkle with salt and pepper and turn the fillet over. Sprinkle with salt and pepper again.
5. Roast 3 to 5 minutes more, depending on the thickness of the fillet and the degree of doneness you prefer.
6. Spoon a little of the butter over each and garnish with the remaining Dill.

Husband Approved

Hubby says: "I'm a big fan of dill and enjoy this recipe, especially with some oven roasted vegetables."

Kid Approved

Daughter says: "I like most fish, and especially like this recipe with trout or cod."

Inspired by Shepherd's Diet

Sardine Salad

Sardines are one of those ingredients that people either seem to love them or hate them…with very little in between. Personally, I love them and sardines are a great choice on the Ditch Candida program. Sardines are a cold water, fatty fish that are low in mercury and rich in vitamin D and Omega 3's. Serve this as a main dish or as a side dish. It's great either way!

Husband Approved

Hubby says: "Personally, I'm not a big fan of sardines so it's not a big winner in my book, but I can see where it would be good if you like sardines."

Ingredients: (serves 2)

1 (4 oz) can sardines, drained
½ cup thinly sliced fennel bulb
½ cup cucumber, peeled and small diced
¼ cup red onion, small diced
½ avocado, diced
3 tsp extra virgin olive oil
1 tsp balsamic vinegar
1 tsp fresh dill, finely minced
Celtic Sea Salt and pepper to taste
Chopped fresh dill for garnish

1. To make dressing, in a small bowl whisk together the olive oil, balsamic vinegar, and fresh dill. Set aside.
2. Meanwhile, in a medium bowl, add the sardines and break them up with a fork into small crumbles.
3. Add the remaining ingredients and toss.
4. Pour on the dressing, gently mix, and add salt and pepper to taste.

Note: This salad is excellent served with fresh cucumber slices, cheese crackers, or sliced sweet bell peppers.

Kid Approved

Daughter says: "Yum-o-rific!"

Inspired by The Whole Journey

Tuna Salad

Tuna salad makes a great light meal or even snack. Easy to make, economical, loaded with energy, and delicious. Our version uses either homemade mayonnaise, yogurt, or crème fraiche since most commercial mayo has sugar and canola oil. For a lighter version, try omitting the mayo altogether.

Husband Approved

Hubby says: "I'm not usually a tuna lover, but this is pretty good.

Ingredients:
- 1 can tuna in water
- ¼ tsp dry mustard or ½ tsp **Homemade Mustard**
- 1 tsp diced lacto-fermented pickles
- Dash paprika
- Celtic Sea Salt to taste
- 2 tsp - 2 T **Homemade Mayonnaise**, yogurt, or crème fraiche

Optional Additional Ingredients:
- Cubed Cheddar Cheese
- Fresh Peas
- Diced Celery
- Shredded carrots
- Finely chopped shallots, green onions, red onion, or sweet onion
- Diced sweet bell pepper
- Diced fresh tomato
- Fresh herbs like parsley or cilantro
- Sauerkraut or other lacto-fermented vegetables
- Microgreens
- Hard boiled egg

Kid Approved

Daughter says: "I could eat this every day. I especially like it with lots of pickles and fresh cilantro."

Combine ingredients in a small bowl. Amount of mayonnaise depends on personal preference and how moist you like your tuna salad.

Serve in a lettuce wrap, or as a topping to your favorite greens salad.

Snacks

Snacking is a fundamental part of our culture and is helpful when on any healthy diet plan. Choosing the RIGHT snacks is important. We show you how.

Snacks are an important addition to consider in our menu plans and in the Ditch Candida program. When we are hungry, or find ourselves with those "munchies", it becomes more tempting to grab something processed. Until we can start creating new neurological patterns in how we approach food, we need to make sure we have plenty of healthy snacks on hand that are easy to grab when the desire to eat hits us. Included in this section are several great snacks that we especially enjoy. Not all snacks take extra preparation, however. Here are a few you can have on hand that take little or no preparation:

- **Fresh vegetables.** Not just the proverbial carrot sticks...although they are great too!....fresh vegetables are a top snack choice. The trick is to take a moment on your prep day to wash, peel, cut, dice, or otherwise prepare the vegetables so they are ready to eat. By preparing them ahead of time, you have plenty of options ready to grab-and-go when the snack attack hits. Some of our favorites for snacking include carrots, broccoli, cauliflower, celery, cherry tomatoes, sweet bell pepper, radish, snap peas, and my personal favorite...jicama.
- **Cheese.** Cheese can make a great quick snack and it has proteins that are filling. Some great snacking cheeses are string cheese, cottage cheese, and sliced hard cheeses.
- **Yogurt.** Yogurt is a fantastic snack, especially because you get the double duty of added probiotics. Yogurt is super easy to make yourself, too. If you buy your yogurt, just be sure to get the unflavored versions since most commercial yogurt, especially flavored, contains added sugar. Stick with organic versions made with high quality milk. If you like your yogurt a little sweeter or flavored, add stevia, our Pumpkin Syrup, cacao powder, or a few drops of food grade essential oil.
- **Nuts.** Nuts make great snacks too. We have a few good additonal recipes for you to spice up (literally) your nuts, but nuts are good plain too. Nuts can be difficult to digest, however, because they naturally contain enzyme inhibitors that protect the nut while dormant (waiting to be planted and become a tree). To make nuts more digestible, purchase raw organic nuts and soak them first before eating. Soaking for 12-24 hours in warm water will "trick"

the nuts into releasing those enzyme inhibitors, thinking it is time to start growing. After soaking, you can dehydrate them again to make them nice and crispy.
- **Seaweed Snacks**. Sea vegetables are nutritious and very good. Commercially you can find dried seaweed "chips" that make great snacks. You can also buy Nori sheets (what they use to make sushi) to snack on too. Just watch the labels to make sure there are no added ingredients that may derail your progress.

Be sure to also check out our Vegetable Sides section. Just about any recipe included there can also be used as a snack, as can many of our dessert recipes.

And don't forget to drink lots of water. Sometimes when we think we are hungry, it's actually our bodies trying to tell us we are thirsty and to drink more. So keep that water bottle or thermos handy and drink, drink, drink. The more water you drink the better your body will be able to flush out those toxins and function well.

Cheese Chips

Cheese chips make a tasty snack or side dish. They took me a couple tries to get them right when I first made the recipe, since cheese can just melt away to almost nothing…so learn from my mistakes and follow the instructions, especially watching the cheese carefully while broiling! Now that I have the hang of making them, I make them regularly since they are so crazy good. I hope you think so too!

Ingredients:

Any hard cheese of your choice (firmer varieties like cheddar, asiago, or parmesan tend to work best)

Husband Approved

Hubby says: "I don't tend to gravitate to raw cheese as a snack, but I love the flavor of cooked cheese. These chips are a winner!"

1. Line a baking sheet or cookie sheet with parchment paper.
2. Put small piles (about an 1/8 cup or so) of shredded cheese or folded pieces of sliced cheese onto the parchment paper, spacing evenly. Keep in mind that the cheese will spread while it melts, so allow some space between piles.
3. Turn the oven or toaster oven to broil and put cheese in the oven.
4. Watch carefully!!! Don't just walk away. This is definitely not a multitask kind of recipe.
5. Remove cheese after the cheese starts to bubble and brown around the edges.
6. Allow to cool completely.
7. Remove carefully with a spatula. Blot off excess oil with a paper towel if necessary.
8. Store in an airtight container. Use as you would chips for snacking or dipping.

Kid Approved

Daughter says: "Any cheese is a good cheese, especially a toasted, crunchy cheese chip!"

Inspired by Wellness Mama

Cinnamon Spiced Nuts

All I can say is YUM! This recipe just tastes too good to be HEALTHY. But yep, it sure is and makes an amazing snack, chopped up as a topping, or finely crushed as a crust. In our house, it's a staple item to have in the pantry.

Husband Approved

Hubby says: "Having good snacks to grab when you're craving something is a must and these are the perfect choice to have on hand. They also make great snacks at work and are loaded with energy."

Ingredients:

4 Cups Nut of Choice (Pecans, Almonds, Cashews, or combinations)
1 Egg White
Pinch of Salt
¼ Cup Stevia (Cup-for-Cup) or about ¼ tsp liquid
2 teaspoons Cinnamon
2 teaspoons Vanilla

Variation:
Add ½ tsp pumpkin pie spice

1. In a medium bowl, combine egg white and salt. Whisk until frothy.
2. Add stevia, cinnamon, and vanilla. Whisk to combine all ingredients.
3. Add the nuts and stir to coat thoroughly.
4. Line a baking pan with parchment paper and spread nuts evenly.
5. Roast in the oven at 150 degrees or in your dehydrator at the highest setting for about 2 hours or until crunchy.

Kid Approved

Daughter says: "So good, especially the pecans! Crunchy with just enough sweet."

Inspired by Nourishing Traditions

Curried Cashews

If you like a snack with crunch, sweet, and spicy…then you have to try these curried cashews. The recipe is also amazing with pecans and hazelnuts too. Adjust the Xylitol or stevia to your personal preference. There are also different styles of curry powder on the market, too…so experiment to find the combination that you like.

Ingredients:

- 3 cups cashews, whole or pieces
- 2 T curry powder
- 1 T Celtic Sea salt
- 1 T Xylitol or Cup-for-Cup Stevia
- 2 T water
- 1 tsp coconut oil, melted

1. Preheat oven to 200° or use a dehydrator at the highest setting.
2. Line a baking sheet with parchment paper or if using a dehydrator, use the liner inserts for your trays to avoid sticking.
3. Mix together all the ingredients other than the cashews until well blended.
4. Toss in the cashews and coat.
5. Spread nuts as an even layer on the baking sheet or dryer sheets.
6. Roast for 45-50 minutes in the oven or 6-8 hours in the dehydrator or until crispy.
7. Transfer to an airtight container.

Husband Approved

Hubby says: "These are so good. I love having crunchy snacks with a little kick."

Kid Approved

Daughter says: "I like these nuts. The cinnamon nuts are my favorite, but these are really good too."

Inspired by Get Inspired Everyday

Eggplant Jerky

Eggplant is such an amazing vegetable because there are so many things we can do with them. If you'd like a fun and new way to prepare eggplant, try making jerky. You do need a good dehydrator for this recipe, but the results come out almost like a cross between bacon and beef jerky. It's sweet, salty, and deep-flavored with chewy goodness.

Ingredients:

1 large eggplant (about 1 lb) Organic is best so you can leave the skins on
½ cup oil
4 T balsamic vinegar
8-10 drops English Toffee flavored Stevia (Sweetleaf)
½ tsp paprika
Sprinkle of Celtic Sea salt

1. Wash eggplant and slice into thin strips. For ease in snacking you can cut long strips in half crosswise.
2. In a large bowl, whisk together oil, vinegar, stevia, and paprika. Place strips in the mixture a few at a time, turning to make sure each is completely coated.
3. Marinate 2 hours.
4. Place on dehydrator sheets, spacing close but not overlapping.
5. Place a solid tray at the bottom of your dehydrator or line bottom of unit with parchment paper to catch drips.
6. Dehydrate at 115° for 12-18 hours or until dry and fairly crisp.
7. Store strips in an airtight container.

Inspired by Everyone Eats Right

Husband Approved

Hubby says: "This recipe surprised me when I found out it was a vegetable. I didn't know what it was until AFTER I tried it and I really liked it."

Kid Approved

Daughter says: "I could eat these all the time. So yummy."

Fried Cheese Sticks

Husband Approved

Hubby says: "This is one of my favorite treats and I can never get enough of them when served. I could make a whole meal just out of cheese sticks."

Kid Approved

Daughter says: "These are sooo good!. I like them with mom's pizza sauce drizzled on top."

Who doesn't love a good cheese stick dipped in pizza sauce? This recipe is quick and easy, and super good. The trick is to have the cheese really cold before cooking them. Check out our recipe for "Pizza" for a great pizza sauce dipping recipe to go with these as a snack, an appetizer, or side dish. If your family is anything like mine, you may want to double this recipe so you have enough!

Ingredients:

½ pound of Mozzarella cheese, cut into sticks (or use string cheese)
2 eggs
½ cup almond flour
1 tsp Italian Seasoning (see Condiments section for recipe)
½ tsp Celtic Sea salt
1 cup coconut oil

1. About 2-3 hours before making, put cheese sticks in the freezer to get nice and cold…and firm.
2. Combine almond flour, Italian seasoning, and salt on a plate or shallow tray; mix well.
3. Crack eggs into another shallow tray or low bowl and beat well until creamy.
4. Melt coconut oil on medium-high heat in a shallow pan that is at least 1 inch deep. Oil needs to be hot before adding cheese.
5. Remove cheese from the freezer. Dip cheese sticks, one at a time, into the egg mixture then into the flour mixture, then back into the egg mixture, and then the flour mixture until well coated (they need to be fully coated or the cheese will escape and spread out in the pan).
6. Carefully drop cheese into hot oil, cooking 3-4 at a time, and cook for a couple of minutes, turning until all sides are golden brown.
7. Remove with a slotted spoon or pasta scoop and cool slightly on a paper towel lined plate.
8. Repeat until all the cheese is cooked.

Inspired by Wellness Mama

Guacamole

Husband Approved

Hubby says: "The spicier the better. I like this one with extra taco seasoning and cayenne pepper."

Kid Approved

Daughter says: "I could eat the whole bowl of this just by itself."

Personally, I don't love avocado. I know it's healthy and many love them, but for me the best and only way to enjoy avocado is with guacamole. Fresh made with some fresh veggies or veggie chips, it is the perfect snack…or even lunch.

1. Peel and mash with a fork:
   - 1 or 2 ripe avocados
2. Add:
   - Diced fresh tomato
   - Finely chopped scallion or sweet onion (about ¼ cup)
   - Lime zest (or a couple drops of food-grade Lime Essential Oil)
   - 1 T fresh chopped cilantro
   - 1 tsp Homemade Taco Seasoning (optional but highly recommended)

Optional additional ingredients:
- Dash of paprika
- Seeded and finely chopped jalapeno pepper
- Seeded and finely chopped sweet bell pepper
- ½ tsp coriander
- Cayenne pepper

Garnish with optional ingredients like:
- Fresh cilantro
- Fresh parsley
- Pimiento
- Black Olives

Homemade Beef Jerky

Jerky is such a great snack and making your own is so much better than anything you can find at the store. For one thing, jerky is expensive to buy…and another thing is most commercial jerky contains sugar. You will need a dehydrator for this recipe. Although it IS possible to make jerky in the oven, the dry times are long and you never want to leave an oven unattended…so for safety reasons…and much better results…use a dehydrator. This recipe is simple and delicious. Be sure to use the best quality, lean meat you can find.

Ingredients:
1 pound London broil steak, Sirloin, or flank steak (very lean and grass fed is best)
¼ cup coconut aminos
¾ teaspoon all natural liquid smoke
¾ teaspoon chili powder
½ teaspoon Celtic Sea salt
¼ teaspoon fresh cracked pepper
¼ teaspoon garlic salt
¼ teaspoon onion powder
¼ teaspoon smoked paprika
dash of cayenne pepper

1. Place the steak in the freezer for 2 hours to firm it up and make it easier to slice thinly.
2. Remove it from the freezer and trim any visible white fat. Any fat left on the meat will spoil after drying.
3. Slice the steak into 1/8 inch pieces. For London broil slice it with the grain, for flank steak slice it against the grain.
4. Whisk together the ingredients for the marinade and combine the marinade with the beef slices in a shallow dish or a Ziploc bag. Cover and marinate in the refrigerator overnight or up to 24 hours turning occasionally to evenly coat.
5. Remove the meat from the marinade and pat it dry with paper towels.
6. Evenly place the strips on dehydrator sheets lined with parchment paper, careful not to let them overlap.
7. Dehydrate the beef for 3-4 hours at 145 degrees F, flipping once half way through.

Recipe from Danielle Walker: (http://againstallgrain.com/2013/01/07/smoky-beef-jerky/)

Husband Approved

Hubby says: "Jerky is one of my all time favorite snacks. Love this recipe."

Kid Approved

Daughter says: "All jerky is hard to chew, but worth the work. So yummy!"

Kale Chips

Getting away from processed foods and junk food, we no longer eat things like potato chips. But sometimes you just crave a salty snack or side. Kale chips make a wonderful alternative and are super easy to make, store well, and offer that salty satisfaction. Vary the flavor with different herbs or spices to find the flavors you like best. In making kale chips, it is important to preheat the baking sheet so it's nice and hot.

1. Preheat oven to 325° and place your baking sheet in the oven to preheat too. You want the baking sheet nice and hot.
2. Wash, de-stem, and leaf:
   - 2-3 bunches kale
3. Melt 1/2 T Coconut Oil and pour over kale.
4. Add additional seasoning depending on preference:
   - Celtic Sea Salt
   - Garlic Powder
   - Fresh or Dried Dill
   - Italian Seasoning
   - Taco Seasoning
   - Chili Seasoning
   - Paprika
   - Fresh or Dry Parsley
5. Massage kale gently with hands to evenly coat leaves with oil and seasoning. Wash hands.
6. Carefully remove preheated baking sheet from the oven and drop kale leaves on baking sheet. You will hear them sizzle.
7. Bake at 325 for 10 minutes, stir, rotate baking sheet, and bake another 10-15 minutes until kale is crispy and not burned.
8. Remove from oven and let sit on hot baking sheet an additional 3 minutes to crisp up even more as they cool.
9. Store in an airtight jar.

Husband Approved

Hubby says: "These are good. For taste, I give these two thumbs up, but for texture I give them one."

Kid Approved

Daughter says: "I could eat a whole batch of these in one sitting. I especially like them flavored with dill."

Mediterranean Hummus

Husband Approved

Hubby says: "This makes a great snack with some fresh veggies."

Kid Approved

Daughter says: "I like this hummus with fresh cucumbers!"

Hummus is so good and makes a great snack, but since hummus usually has tahini and chickpeas…it's usually off the list. However, you can make your own version substituting almond butter for the tahini and sweet potato for the chickpeas.

Ingredients:
  2 cloves garlic, minced
  ¼ cup yogurt
  ¼ tsp cumin
  1 tsp Celtic Sea salt
  1 avocado
  1 T almond butter
  2 T roasted red peppers
  1 Baked Sweet Potato, skins removed
  A couple pitted black olives
  3-4 T Olive Oil
  Dash nutmeg

Optional additional ingredients:
  Roasted Beets
  Shredded carrots
  Peas

Add all ingredients except oil to a food processor and blend until well mixed. Slowly add oil until hummus reaches desired consistency. Serve immediately or chill.

Nut Butter

Commercial nut butters tend to be loaded with sugars…and we don't know for sure the quality of the nuts or how they were handled. Nuts are more easily digested when soaked first which releases enzyme inhibitors. For a full explanation on nuts, soaking for increased digestibility, and making nut butters and nut milks, check out our full online course in the Living Foods Academy at www.HealthyHomesteadLiving.com. Making your own is easy and so delicious. Cashew butter is like a dessert…almost like cake batter. Give it a try and see for yourself.

1. Place in a large bowl and stir:
   - 4 cups warm filtered water
   - 4 cups raw organic nuts of choice (pecans, walnuts, almonds, cashews, macadamia…or a mixture)
   - 1 T Celtic Sea Salt
2. Cover the bowl with a plate and leave in a warm place for 7-12 hours.
3. Drain the nuts in a strainer. Shake well to remove excess water.
4. Blot dry with paper towel or clean kitchen cloth and transfer to a food processor.
5. Grind with the S blade for about 5 minutes or until a smooth butter forms.
6. Add:
   - ¾ cup coconut oil
   - ¼ cup Cup-for-Cup Stevia or equivalent
7. Process for another minute or so until butter is well mixed and smooth.
8. Store in an airtight container in the fridge for up to 3 weeks.

Variations:
Add additional course chopped nuts at the end for a "Chunky" version.
Add cacao nibs or stevia sweetened chocolate chips, form into balls for a no-bake dessert.
Add ¼ cup cacao powder and 2 tsp vanilla for a "Chocolate" version.

Inspired by Nourishing Traditions.

Husband Approved

Hubby says: "Cashew butter is my favorite and almond butter is a close second."

Kid Approved

Daughter says: "This is so good in my lunches, especially cashew with chocolate."

Onion Rings

Onion rings are a favorite in our household and onions are a powerhouse food in fighting candida. We like these onion rings as snacks, as the perfect side to a bun-free hamburger, or as a hamburger topping. For extra flavor, try using our Homemade Seasoning Salt.

Ingredients:
1 large sweet onion, peeled and thinly sliced into whole rings
½ cup or so almond flour
½ cup garlic powder
1 tsp Celtic Sea salt or Homemade Seasoned Salt
½ tsp pepper
2 eggs
Coconut oil

1. Heat oil over medium/high heat in large, deep skillet or deep fryer.
2. Mix flour and spices on a large plate.
3. Beat eggs in a large, flat bowl.
4. Dip separated onion rings into egg mixture then flour mixture.
5. Carefully drop into hot oil and cook about 3 minutes per side until golden brown and crispy.
6. Remove to towel-lined plate. Allow to cool.

Husband Approved

Hubby says: "More please!"

Kid Approved

Daughter says: "I especially like the little crispy ones."

Rosemary Almonds

Nuts are one of my favorite snacks since they are so delicious, filling, and healthy. This recipe is simple to make and smells so good when cooking. If you can't find fresh rosemary, use dried (if you must) but there is a significant difference in flavor between the two. I usually make this as a double or triple batch since it doesn't usually last very long in our house. For variety, try substituting other nuts like cashews and Macadamia nuts.

Husband Approved

Hubby says: "Delicious and satisfying. I love having these on hand when I'm at work. They give me a great boost of energy and curb hunger and sweet cravings."

Ingredients:

2 cups raw almonds, blanched*
2 T fresh rosemary, minced
2 tsp Celtic Sea salt
Ghee or Coconut Oil

1. *To blanch almonds, place almonds in boiling water for 1 minute (no longer). Drain off water and run the almonds under cold water to cool. Shake the water off in a colander, then pop off the skins.
2. Heat a large pan over medium heat. Add enough ghee or coconut oil to coat the bottom of your pan.
3. Add the almonds. Stir frequently to avoid burning, and saute until golden brown, about 5-7 minutes.
4. Turn down the heat to low and add the rosemary and salt. Continue stirring and cook another 2 minutes or so until the rosemary becomes fragrant.
5. Remove from heat and allow to cool on paper towels to absorb any excess oil.
6. Enjoy warm or cool.

Inspired by the Primalist.com

Kid Approved

Daughter says: "I like these nuts. The cinnamon nuts are my favorite, but these are really good too."

Sweet Potato Chips

Sometimes you just want the salty crunch of those good ol' chips….and with this recipe you can have it by making your own…and out of sweet potatoes. Super delicious and easy. You'll need a dehydrator to get the best results and get that desired "crunch".

Ingredients:

3-4 organic sweet potatoes, scrubbed clean
2-3 T coconut oil
Celtic Sea Salt

1. Preheat oven to 425°.
2. Using a mandolin slicer (for best results) or sharp knife, carefully slice sweet potatoes into uniform ¼ inch slices. The more uniform the better for even drying.
3. Place slices in large bowl with melted coconut oil and mix by hand to evenly coat sweet potatoes.
4. Spread evenly on baking sheet/s, being careful to not overlap chips.
5. Sprinkle with desired amount of Celtic Sea salt.
6. Bake 15-20 minutes until cooked and just starting to crisp on the edges.
7. Remove from oven and allow to cool slightly.
8. Arrange chips on dehydrator trays then dry at 135° for 6-8 hours or until crispy and fully dry.
9. Store in an airtight container.

Husband Approved

Hubby says: "Sweet potato chips are one of my favorite snacks and we like to smuggle them in to movie theaters and enjoy them instead of popcorn while watching the film."

Kid Approved

Daughter says: "These are so good either as a snack or as a side dish to things like hamburgers or sloppy joes."

Almond Torte

Husband Approved

Hubby says: "This makes a pretty good cake substitute although the texture is a bit different so takes some getting used to. Great flavor, though."

Kid Approved

Daughter says: "I don't normally like regular cake very much, and this one is even better."

You'll need a spring-form pan for this recipe. I also recommend lining the bottom with a sheet of parchment paper to make the torte easier to remove since it does tend to be a bit fragile. Torten and tortes are basically traditional cakes made with nut flours, making them the perfect choice on the Ditch Candida program. For best results, make sure all ingredients are at room temperature before starting the recipe.

1. Preheat oven to 350°
2. Beat :
   - 6 egg yolks
3. Add gradually and beat until creamy:
   - 1 cup Cup for Cup Stevia or equivalent in liquid
4. Add:
   - Zest of one lemon and 1 orange
   - 1 tsp cinnamon
   - 1 ½ cup almond flour
5. In a separate bowl or stand mixer, whip until stiff but not dry:
   - 7 egg whites
6. Carefully fold egg white mix into batter without over mixing.
7. Fold into spring-form pan, lined with parchment paper.
8. Bake 40 minutes or until done.
9. Let cool in the pan, remove side, then top with Stevia Frosting, Pumpkin Spice Syrup, or Hot Fudge Topping.

Variations:
- Use Pecan Flour for a richer, moister cake
- Add 1 tsp vanilla and 3 T cacao powder to the batter for a chocolate version
- Mix ½ hazelnut flour and ½ pecan or walnut flour

Inspired by Joy of Cooking

Carrot Cake

Cake in general is challenging without the gluten in regular wheat flour, so when converting recipes we got a little creative. The texture of this recipe is not going to be as light and fluffy as traditional cake, but we think it's a pretty tasty rendition. We hope you think so too.

Husband Approved

Hubby says: "Not normally my choice of cakes anyway, this one has great flavor and a nice alternative once in awhile."

1. Preheat oven to 350° and line an 8x8 baking pan with parchment paper.
2. In a large bowl or Stand Mixer, whisk together:
   - 1 cup finely shredded zucchini (it should look like puree)
   - 6 T melted butter
   - 2 T melted coconut oil
   - ¾ cup Xylitol or Cup-for-Cup stevia (or equivalent)
   - 1 large egg
   - 1 T vanilla
   - ½ cup chopped pecans
   - 1 ½ cups grated carrots
3. In a separate bowl, combine:
   - ¾ cup almond flour
   - 1 tsp baking powder
   - 1 tsp baking soda
   - 1 tsp cinnamon
   - ½ tsp Celtic Sea salt
4. Slowly add flour mixture to batter, folding just until combined. Don't over-mix.
5. Pour into prepared pan and bake for 30 minutes or until cake springs back gently when touched.
6. Allow to cool and top with **Cream Cheese Frosting**.

Kid Approved

Daughter says: "I love this cake with lots of frosting!"

Inspired by Grandma Margaret and Joy of Cooking

Cheesecake

My all time favorite dessert is cheesecake. I love the creamy, smooth goodness. Even as a child, when my mom would ask me what kind of birthday cake I wanted, my response was always, "cheesecake." So for those of you out there who love cheesecake like I do, here is a great alternative you can enjoy!

Husband Approved

Hubby says: "Another delicious dessert alternative. You'd never guess it's sugar-free and gluten-free."

Kid Approved

Daughter says: "Yummy for my tummy. I love this cheesecake!"

Ingredients: (serves 6)

For the crust:
- 1 cup of pecan meal (or pecans ground in the food processor)
- 2 T coconut oil
- 1 egg
- ¼ tsp cinnamon
- ½ tsp stevia (or to taste)
- 2 drops each of lemon essential oil and orange essential oil

For the filling:
- 4 (8 oz) packages cream cheese, softened
- 3 eggs
- 1 tsp vanilla
- Zest of one lemon
- 4 drops lemon essential oil (food grade only)
- 2-3 tsp stevia or ¾ cup xylitol (or to taste)

1. Preheat oven to 325°.
2. Line a spring-form pan with parchment paper. In large bowl, combine crust ingredients and press into bottom of pan.
3. In a separate bowl, combine filling ingredients and mix until smooth. Pour over crumbled crust.
4. Place a pan of water in the oven. This creates a "steam" effect and a moist cooking environment.
5. Bake cheesecake for 1 ½ hours. Turn oven off, and let it sit in the oven for another ½ hour.
6. Remove from oven and allow to cool completely. Refrigerate for at least 2 hours before removing sides of pan.
7. Slice and enjoy.

Inspired by Grandma Margaret

Chocolate Chip Cookies

Just because you're on the Candida Program doesn't mean you have to give up goodies. This Chocolate Chip Cookie Recipe is a handy one to have on hand to whip up quickly when you are in the mood, or have on hand to help when those sweet cravings hit.

Made with almond flour, the texture will be a bit different than traditional cookies, yet still delicious and you'd never guess they are sugar free! Be sure to use a quality brand of Stevia Sweetened Chocolate Chips.

Husband Approved

Hubby says: "Any cookie is a great treat and these are good. A bit "cakey" for my personal taste so one thumbs up on this one."

Ingredients:
- 2 cups Almond Flour
- ½ cup softened (not melted) Butter or coconut oil
- ¼ to 1/3 cup "Cup-for-Cup" Stevia
- 1 large egg
- ½ teaspoons Baking Soda
- pinch of Celtic Salt
- 1 tablespoon pure Vanilla
- 1 cup (or less) Lily's Stevia Sweetened Chocolate Chips

1. Preheat oven to 350 degrees.
2. Mix the almond flour, baking soda, stevia, and salt in a bowl. Add the softened butter or coconut oil (or a mix of both) and stir well by hand until mixed. It should form a thick dough that is hard to stir.
3. Add the egg and mix well. This should make the dough more formable and easier to mix. If needed, add a tsp or two of milk to thin. Finished dough should be easy to form.
4. Add chocolate chips and stir by hand until incorporated.
5. Form dough into tablespoon size balls and bake for 10 minutes or until tops are starting to be golden brown.
6. Let cool at least 5 minutes and serve.

Note: If you place a sheet of Parchment Paper on the baking sheet prior to adding dough, cleanup will be much easier, and you can easily slide the whole sheet of baked cookies onto a cooling rack without disturbing the shape of the cookie while hot.

Kid Approved

Daughter says: "I love these cookies and they are so yummy as a treat, a snack, or added to my lunch at school. Best with lots of chocolate chips!"

Recipe Adapted from Wellness Mama.com

Chocolate Mocha Gelatin Pie

Gelatin pies, also known as chiffon pies, are light since they're primarily egg white based. This chocolate and coffee version is a delicious treat and a great one to serve when you have friends over for dinner or attending a family function and need to bring a dessert. Since we don't bake these pies, rather use light heat to set them, be sure to use quality organic eggs.

Husband Approved

Hubby says: "A dessert with chocolate AND coffee just has to be good! And this one is really enjoyable."

1. Prepare by baking and cooling:
   - **Grandma's No Roll Pie Crust**
2. Combine and stir until smooth in small bowl:
   - 1 T gelatin
   - ¼ cup cold strong black coffee
3. In a separate medium bowl, combine and stir until smooth:
   - 6 T cacao powder
   - ½ cup Cup for Cup Stevia or equivalent
   - ½ cup boiling strong black coffee
4. Stir in the soaked gelatin until it is dissolved.
5. Cool slightly and pour mixture gently onto:
   - 4 lightly beaten egg yolks
6. Move mixture to a double boiler over (not in) boiling water and heat until mixture thickens.
7. Chill until almost set then beat with a wire whisk. Add:
   - 1 tsp vanilla
8. In a separate bowl, whip until stiff but not dry:
   - 4 egg whites
   - ½ cup Cup for Cup Stevia or equivalent
9. Carefully fold egg whites into chocolate mixture. Fill the pie shell. Chill until filling is set and firm.
10. Serve topped with **Homemade Whipped Cream**

Kid Approved

Daughter says: "I don't really love the taste of coffee, so this one isn't my favorite.

Inspired by Joy of Cooking

Chocolate Pudding

Husband Approved

Hubby says: "This is really good with lots of whipped cream on top."

Kid Approved

Daughter says: "So good. I especially like it frozen as a pudding pop."

Pudding is a wonderful dessert, but the way we make it, you can also use it as a great snack. The secret is in the avocados. Avocado creates the base for the texture of the pudding and contains healthy fats. You won't taste the avocado, though since we doctor it up with magnesium-rich cacao powder and other tasty ingredients. Use a blender or food processor to get your pudding nice and creamy!

1. Combine in a food processor or blender:
   - 3 medium avocados
   - ¼ tsp liquid stevia
   - ¼ cup cacao powder
   - 3 T almond butter
   - 1 tsp ground cinnamon
   - 1 tsp ground nutmeg
   - ½ tsp almond extract (optional)
   - 1 T grass-fed beef gelatin
2. Blend until well mixed and the consistency you like.
3. Chill before serving.

Variation:
- Top with slivered toasted almonds
- Top with Homemade Whipped Topping
- Freeze in Freezer Pop Containers to make your own Frozen Pudding Pop treats.

Inspired by Cultured Food Life

Chocolate Truffles

Husband Approved

Hubby says: "Warning. Once you start eating these, you just can't stop."

Kid Approved

Daughter says: "I love these. They pretty much just melt in your mouth and are like chocolate cheesecake bites."

These truffles are so rich and creamy and oh so delicious. They are easy to make, but have a couple steps with time in between to chill so plan accordingly. Set this recipe aside as a great option for holidays, parties, or special occasions…and also great for everyday sweet cravings.

1. In a large bowl or Stand Mixer, whip:
   - 2 blocks of softened cream cheese
   - 3 T cacao powder
   - 2 T Cup-for-Cup Stevia or Xylitol
2. Form into bite-sized balls and place on parchment or wax paper lined baking sheet.
3. Refrigerate until well chilled and firm.
4. Once firm, heat double boiler and melt, stirring constantly and watching carefully so you don't scorch:
   - 1 bag of Stevia Sweetened Chocolate Chips
5. Using thongs or slotted spoon, lightly coat truffle balls with chocolate then carefully transfer to wax paper lined platter or baking sheet.
6. Return the the refrigerator to chill completely.

Variations:
- Add a couple drops of preferred Food Grade Essential Oil to the melted chocolate before coating. Try Peppermint, Spearmint, Wintergreen, or Orange.
- Top with Chopped Cinnamon Spiced Nuts or Toasted Sliced Almonds after coating with melted chocolate and before final chill.

Inspired by Taste of Home

Coffee Chocolate Custard

Personally, I don't care for coffee or anything flavored with coffee, but my hubby sure does and I know there are many of you out there like him. So, we wanted to include this simple dessert for your enjoyment. You do need a good powerful blender to make this recipe.

1. Preheat oven to 300°.
2. In a blender, add:
   - 1 oz. Stevia sweetened chocolate chips
   - 1 cup strong, hot coffee
   - 1 cup whole organic milk
   - 3-4 T xylitol (or stevia equivalent)
   - 1/8 tsp Celtic Sea salt
   - 2 eggs
3. Pour mixture into individual custard cups or ramekins.
4. Add about 1 inch of hot water to a heavy stone or ceramic baking dish then place custard cups into the dish with water.
5. Bake for 30-50 minutes. To test for doneness, insert a knife near the edge of a cup. If the blade comes out clean, the custard will be solid all the way through when cooled.
6. Remove from heat and allow to cool.
7. Chill at least 2 hours before serving.

Husband Approved

Hubby says: "Coffee and chocolate together make a truly delicious dessert."

Kid Approved

Daughter says: "I don't really like coffee, but I can see where this would be really good for anyone who does."

Inspired by Grandma Margaret and Joy of Cooking

Cream Cheese Cookies

Husband Approved

Hubby says: "The more recipes like these, the less you feel like you are missing out on the sugar sweets. These are really good and very sweet."

Kid Approved

Daughter says: "I love it when Mom puts cookies in my lunchbox, and these are a fun treat. I especially liked dipping them in the Fudge Sauce she makes."

Converted from a traditional recipe, these cookies taste like a cross between Sugar Cookies and Shortbread. Make the dough ahead of time and store in the freezer. Then, any time you want some great treats, pull out the dough and bake. I usually make several batches at once so there are plenty in the freezer when needed. Use parchment paper as a liner for the baking sheet to make it easier to transfer cookies to the cooking rack after baking. They will be VERY soft until cooled, but will firm up once completely cool.

1. Blend until creamy:
   - ½ cup butter
   - 1 cup Cup-for-Cup Stevia, 1 ½ T. Powder, or 1 tsp liquid
   - 1 well-beaten egg
   - 4 oz. softened cream cheese
   - 2 T. Yogurt
   - 1 tsp vanilla
2. Beat in:
   - 1 ¾ cup Almond Flour
   - 1/8 tsp baking soda
   - ½ tsp baking powder (aluminum free)
   - ½ tsp salt
3. Place dough on sheet of parchment paper or wax paper and carefully form into a log. Wrap in paper and place in the freezer at least 2 hours or until firm.
4. Preheat oven to 350°. Slice dough into ¼ inch rounds and place on parchment lined baking sheets.
5. Bake for 12-15 minutes.
6. Transfer to cooling racks and cool completely.

Inspired by Joy of Cooking

Cream Cheese Frosting

Traditional frosting is pretty much just pure sugar. In our version, we substitute stevia. You wouldn't want to eat this recipe every day, but for those special occasions and birthdays it gives you a better option. Use with Almond Torte or Carrot Cake for a holiday treat.

1. Cream together with hand mixer or stand mixer:
   - 4 oz. (½ package) softened cream cheese
   - 1 ½ T milk
2. Add slowly:
   - ¾ cup Cup for Cup Stevia
3. Flavor with:
   - 1 tsp vanilla
   - ½ tsp cinnamon

   OR:
   - Zest from one lemon, lime, or orange

   OR:
   - 1 tsp vanilla
   - 1 T cacao powder

4. Chill briefly to firm, then use to top your favorite dessert.

Husband Approved

Hubby says: "Rich and creamy, this frosting tastes like regular frosting."

Kid Approved

Daughter says: "The chocolate version is my favorite!"

Inspired by Joy of Cooking

French Silk Pie

Decadently rich, this pie is truly one of those special occasion or chocolate craving kind of treats. Make this recipe for potluck or family gatherings, holidays, birthdays, or just a day you want some extra special pampering. It's so good, you'll never guess it's actually good for you and completely Ditch Candida friendly.

1. Prepare **Grandma's No Roll Pie Crust** and bake crust at 350 oven for 10 minutes. Cool completely.
2. In a large bowl or Stand Mixer, whip:
   - 2 blocks of softened cream cheese
   - 3 T cacao powder
   - 2 T Cup-for-Cup Stevia or Xylitol
3. Pour into prepared pie crust.
4. Refrigerate until well chilled and firm.
5. Top with **Homemade Whipped Cream**
6. Serve chilled.

Husband Approved

Hubby says: "Best chocolate pie ever!"

Kid Approved

Daughter says: "I love this pie, but can only eat a small piece before getting full."

Inspired by Grandma Margaret

Grandma's No Roll Pie Crust

Husband Approved

Hubby says: "You'd never guess this was made with almond flour instead of regular flour. Light, flaky, and delicious."

Kid Approved

Daughter says: "This crust is my favorite part of the pies...except maybe the whipped cream."

Just because we are temporarily off fruits and sugar doesn't mean we can't enjoy a good pie now and again. Use this recipe for our Pumpkin Pie, French Silk Pie, or even as a base for quiche or pot pies. My Grandma Margaret gave me this recipe when I was around 10 years old and just learning to bake. I converted it more recently to ingredients that would work for the Ditch Candida program. A favorite then and still a favorite now, I hope you enjoy it too.

1. Put directly into glass or stoneware pie pan:
   - 1 ½ cups almond flour
   - 1 packet stevia powder
   - 1 tsp Celtic Sea Salt
2. Melt:
   - ½ cup coconut oil
3. Add to oil:
   - 2 T milk
4. Whisk oil and milk until well blended then pour into pie pan with almond flour mixture.
5. Mix with your hands until a soft dough forms, then press gently into the bottom and sides of pie pan to form the crust.

For baked pies: Fill with desired filling and bake as directed for pie.
For no-bake pies: Place pie crust in 350 oven for 10-12 minutes until golden brown.

Recipe from Grandma Margaret

Homemade Ice Cream

Husband Approved

Hubby says: "I love ice cream and this one is best just plain."

Kid Approved

Daughter says: "Yummy for my tummy!"

Ice Cream is such a special treat when you are going through the Ditch Candida program. You do need an Ice Cream Maker of some kind, and we recommend the Cuisinart version because you don't need any salt or other accessories. Since Ice Cream is a frozen dish, limit how much or how often you have it if you are having digestive issues, since cold foods add extra stress to the digestive system. Look for high quality cream from grass-fed organic antibiotic-free cows. Grandma Margaret always said the quality of a recipe is only as good as the quality of the ingredients and this especially holds true with Ice Cream!

1. Pre-freeze the ice cream bowl if using a Cuisinart Ice Cream Maker.
2. Remove ice cream bowl from freezer, assemble machine, and add:
   - 2 cups Heavy Cream
   - 1 cup Whole Milk
   - 1 T vanilla
   - ½ tsp liquid stevia (vanilla flavored is especially good)
3. Turn on machine. Ice cream will be ready in about 15-20 minutes.

Variations:
- Add ½ tsp cacao powder, mixed with 1 tsp melted coconut oil for chocolate ice cream.
- Add 4-5 drops of Food Grade Peppermint Essential Oil for peppermint ice cream.
- Add 3-4 drops of Food Grade Lemon Essential Oil and grated Lemon Zest for lemon ice cream.

Toppings:
- Serve with Zucchini Brownies
- Top with Homemade Hot Fudge Syrup (see Condiments)
- Top with Pumpkin Syrup (see Condiments)

Homemade Marshmallows

Marshmallows are a classic snack and treat for me as a kid growing up. Whether it was part of making s'mores or just enjoying the fluffy, sweet goodness, we often enjoyed the sticky and delicious marshmallow. Believe it or not, marshmallows are easy to make yourself. Say "hello" to true indulgence, without the guilt.

Ingredients:

4 T grass fed gelatin powder
1 ½ cups water
1 T Marshmallow Root
1 tsp liquid stevia
1 tsp vanilla

Husband Approved

Hubby says: "Slightly different flavor than commercial marshmallows but even better."

1. In a small saucepan, bring 1 1/2 cups of water to boil. Reduce heat and add marshmallow root. Simmer on low for 5 minutes. Let cool and strain, reserving 1 cup of the "tea."
2. Pour ½ cup of marshmallow tea into a small bowl or mixer bowl and add the gelatin. Whisk well then set aside.
3. Pour the other ½ cup of marshmallow tea back into the saucepan and heat to boiling. Keep at a rolling boil for 8 minutes.
4. Slowly pour hot mixture into gelatin mixture (which will be hardened by now). Add stevia.
5. Turn on the mixer or hand mixer and turn to high speed. Blend with the mixer for another 10-15 minutes or until it forms a stiff cream (it should form gentle 'peaks').
6. Pour whipped marshmallow mixture into a parchment paper lined baking dish or lasagne pan.
7. Let sit at least 4 hours or overnight. Marshmallows should now be firm but spongy.
8. Flip onto a cutting board and cut with a well oiled pizza cutter.
9. Store in an airtight container at room temperature. (Do not refrigerate or they will get soggy).

Variations:
- Add flavored stevia instead of plain.
- Add food grade essential oils such as mint, orange, lemon…
- Add cacao powder during mixing stage for chocolate flavored

Inspired by Grandma Margaret

Kid Approved

Daughter says: "Ooey Gooey goodness!"

Lemon or Lime Sorbet

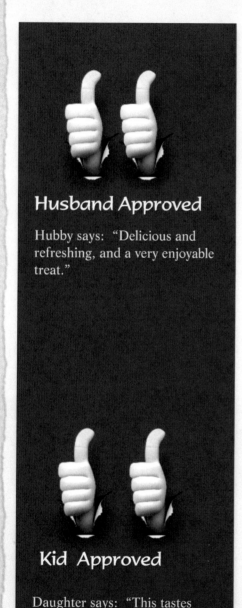

Husband Approved

Hubby says: "Delicious and refreshing, and a very enjoyable treat."

Kid Approved

Daughter says: "This tastes like frozen lemonade! I love it."

You'll need an ice cream maker for this recipe. We love the Cuisinart version because you don't need salt so it's a fast and easy way to make homemade versions without the sugar. Light and tangy, this sorbet is a delightful treat. Be sure to only use high quality food-grade essential oil for this recipe.

Ingredients:
- 3 cups water
- 1 cup Cup-for-Cup Stevia or 2 tsp liquid stevia
- 2 T lemon or lime zest
- 5-6 drops lemon or lime essential oil
- Pinch of Celtic Sea salt

1. Combine ingredients in a medium bowl. Cover and refrigerate 2-3 hours or overnight.
2. Prepare ice cream maker.
3. Pour mixture into ice cream maker and follow directions according the the machine you have. Process until thick…about 15-20 minutes. Sorbet should have a soft, creamy texture.

Variation:
Add 1 cup fresh basil to the mixture before cooling. Strain out basil leaves before adding to the ice cream maker. The basil infuses the sorbet with delicious undertones. Other fresh herbs may also be used.

Macadamia Nut "Cake"

This "cake" is great for those special occasions, entertaining, or for a simple dessert. We always recommend purchasing nuts raw, soaking them for 24 hours, then drying them in the dehydrator to make them crispy again before consuming. This extra step will make the nuts more digestible and the nutrients more bio-available.

Ingredients: (serves 8)

1 ½ cups macadamia nuts
1 cup crème fraiche
½ cup Xylitol or Cup-for-Cup stevia (or equivalent)
1 tsp vanilla
6 egg whites
Pinch of Celtic Sea salt

Husband Approved

Hubby says: "A dessert with simple flavors and nutty texture. I enjoyed it."

Kid Approved

Daughter says: "Another great dessert, especially with lots of frosting."

1. Preheat oven to 325°.
2. Prepare two 8-inch cake pans by cutting two rounds of parchment paper to fit the bottom of the pans. Place the parchment paper into buttered pans and then butter the parchment paper so they are well greased. Sprinkle a little almond flour into the bottom of the pans.
3. In a food processor, process macadamia nuts to a powder.
4. Add the cultured cream, sweetener, and vanilla and process well.
5. Place egg whites in a glass or stainless steel bowl with a pinch of salt and beat until stiff peaks form.
6. Fold the macadamia nut mixture into the egg whites, careful not to over-mix.
7. Divide the mixture between the two pans and spread gently so that it touches the sides.
8. Bake for 40 minutes or until the layers pull away from the sides of the pan.
9. To serve, let cool and place the two layers, one on top of the other, on a plate. If desired, you can add some **Cream Cheese Frosting** between the layers and on the top, flavored with chocolate or vanilla.
10. Garnish with chopped macadamia nuts if desired.

Inspired by Nourishing Traditions

Meringue Cookies

Husband Approved

Hubby says: "An interesting texture yet very good."

Kid Approved

Daughter says: "Yummy. I especially like the chocolate ones."

Light and crunchy, these meringue cookies are a fun treat and great for birthday parties, family gatherings, or just plain old snacking. You'll need a good mixer to make these to get the egg whites nice and fluffy. After baking, it will be tempting to peek and open the oven…but refrain or your cookies may not turn out the way you want them. Try dipping meringue cookies in our Pumpkin Syrup or Hot Fudge Syrup for extra flavor.

1. Preheat oven to 375°.
2. Whip until frothy and stiff peaks start to form:
   - 3 egg whites
3. Add gently and gradually, whipping constantly:
   - 1 cup Cup-for-Cup Stevia or equivalent
   - 1 tsp vanilla powder
   - 2 T cacao powder (optional for chocolate flavored)
4. Drop from a teaspoon onto greased or parchment paper lined baking sheets and put into preheated oven.
5. Immediately turn heat off on oven and do not open oven door for at least 2 hours, preferably overnight.

Variations:
- Add a few drops of peppermint essential oil (food grade only)
- Add a few drops of lemon essential oil (food grade only)
- Sprinkle with finely chopped nuts or Spiced Nuts before baking
- Sprinkle with cinnamon before baking

Recipe from Grandma Margaret

Pecan Tart

Not everyone has a tart pan in their kitchen, but if you do this is a great recipe in which to use it…or a great excuse to get one! Almost like a pecan pie, but without all that nasty corn syrup normally found in tarts and nut pies.

You can also substitute Walnuts with the same recipe for a whole new dessert experience, equally good.

Ingredients:
1 recipe **Grandma's No Roll Pie Crust**
1 1/3 cup Pecan halves or pieces (or pecan meal)
4 T butter, melted
¾ cup xylitol or cup-for-cup stevia
2 eggs
1 tsp coffee extract
1 tsp vanilla
½ tsp Celtic Sea salt

1. Preheat oven to 350°.
2. Line a 10 inch French-style tart pan with pie crust dough.
3. Process pecans in a food processor to a fine powder.
4. Add remaining ingredients and blend until smooth.
5. Pour into tart shell and bake for about 40 minutes.

Husband Approved

Hubby says: "I love pecans and this is a delicious recipe. Just enough sweet and a great nutty flavor."

Kid Approved

Daughter says: "This is good, especially with some home-made Ice Cream or Whipped Topping."

Inspired by Nourishing Traditions

Pumpkin Cheesecake

I love cheesecake. It's my favorite dessert, and adding the rich goodness of pumpkin just makes it even better! We use this recipe as a substitute for birthday cakes, take it to family gatherings as a healthy dessert, and make it just for everyday enjoyment. Easy to make and oh so good!

Ingredients for the Crust:
1 cup of nuts such as almonds, pecans, or hazelnuts (ground in the food processor to a fine powder)…or use 1 cup nut flour
2 T coconut oil or butter
1 egg
½ tsp cinnamon
1 packet stevia or xylitol

Ingredients for the Filling:
12 oz pumpkin puree (1 can or 1 ½ cups homemade)
2 T coconut oil
2 (8 oz) packages cream cheese
3 eggs
1 tsp pumpkin pie spice
1 tsp vanilla
Stevia or Xylitol to taste (I use about 2 tsp powdered stevia)

1. Preheat oven to 375°.
2. Mix crust ingredients and press into the bottom of a 9 inch pie pan and place in preheating oven for about 10 minutes until crust is slightly toasted (careful not to burn).
3. In the meantime, mix filling ingredients with mixer until well blended.
4. Pour into toasted crust then return to preheated oven. Cook for 35-45 minutes or until top doesn't wiggle in the center.
5. Remove and let cool.
6. Chill at least 2 hours or overnight before serving.
7. Top with **Homemade Whipped Cream.**

Husband Approved
Hubby says: "A winner for any occasion!"

Kid Approved
Daughter says: "I love pumpkin pie. And I love cheesecake. This recipe combines two of my close favorites. So good."

Inspired by Wellness Mama

Pumpkin Pie

A classic on Thanksgiving, pumpkin pie is good just about anytime. Since our version doesn't use sugar or wheat flours, it's actually healthy and loaded with nutrients, so enjoy a slice without any guilt. Not just a dessert, pumpkin pie also makes a great breakfast or snack too! Be sure to use organic pumpkin and good quality, organic cream.

1. Prepare **Grandma's No Roll Pie Crust**.
2. Preheat oven to 425°.
3. Mix until well blended:
   - 2 slightly beaten farm-fresh eggs
   - 2 cups cooked or canned pumpkin (or squash)
   - 1 ½ cups evaporated milk or cream
   - ¾ cup Cup-for-Cup Stevia (or equivalent)
   - ½ tsp salt
   - 1 tsp cinnamon
   - ½ tsp ginger
   - ¼ tsp nutmeg
   - 1/8 tsp cloves
4. Pour the mixture into the pie shell and bake 15 minutes at 425. Reduce temperature to 350° an additional 45 minutes or until an inserted knife comes out clean.
5. Allow to cool, then serve with **Homemade Whipped Cream**.

Note: Be sure to use a glass or stoneware pie pan and NOT aluminum. Aluminum cookware and bakeware are toxic and will tend to leach toxins into the food in which it is cooked.

Husband Approved

Hubby says: "Pumpkin Pie is one of my favorite desserts, especially with lots of whipped cream."

Kid Approved

Daughter says: "I like having pumpkin pie or brownies as an alternative to birthday cake. Such a treat and so yummy."

Inspired by Grandma Margaret and Joy of Cooking

Pumpkin Squares

Husband Approved

Hubby says: "I love these. One of my absolute favorites. For a sweet tooth like me, this is one treat that really satisfies my cravings."

Kid Approved

Daughter says: "This is good both as a full bite or, the fun way to eat it...which is by eating each layer at a time, starting with the whipped topping."

I converted this recipe from one that my sister-in-law would bring to family events and it was one of my husband's favorites. Loaded with sugar and processed ingredients, however, I made it a mission to come up with a viable and healthier alternative that was still delicious. The recipe below is my version which is so delicious and a real treat. It does take a little more time and work to prepare, so I save this recipe for those special occasions.

1. Start with the crust. Combine in a large bowl:
   - 1 ¾ cups pecan meal or finely ground pecans
   - 1/4 cup xylitol
   - 1 stick of melted butter
2. Spread in a 9 x 13 pan.
3. In a separate large bowl or stand mixer, mix together until smooth:
   - 2 eggs
   - ¾ cup xylitol or stevia equivalent
   - 2 (8 oz.) packages cream cheese
4. Spread over crust and bake at 350° for 20 minutes. Set aside and let cool.
5. In a 2 quart saucepan over medium heat, stir together:
   - 3 egg yolks (set aside the egg whites, you'll use them later)
   - 1 (16 oz.) can pumpkin
   - ½ cup xylitol or stevia equivalent
   - ½ cup whole organic milk
   - ½ tsp Celtic Sea salt
   - 1 tsp cinnamon
6. Cook over medium heat until thick (about 5-10 minutes)
7. In a small bowl, soften 1 package Knox unflavored gelatin in ¼ cup of water. Stir into pumpkin mixture and let cool completely.
8. Beat until stiff and then carefully fold into COOLED pumpkin mixture:
   - 3 egg whites
   - ¼ cup xylitol or stevia equivalent
   - 1 tsp vanilla
9. Spread on top of cooled cream cheese mixture.
10. Top with Homemade Whipped Cream. Chill for 8 hours or put in the freezer until completely set up (1-2 hours).

Inspired by Angela Breedlove

Spiced Butternut Chips

Butternut squash makes delicious chips for snacking or as a side dish. We like making these to take on hiking trips, horseback riding trail rides, bike rides, or camping trips because they are so yummy yet so filling. If you don't have a dehydrator, you can make them in the oven. Just turn the heat down to 250 after step 6.

Ingredients:

- 1 medium butternut squash
- 2 T melted coconut oil
- ½ tsp cinnamon
- Pinch of nutmeg, ginger, cloves, and allspice
- Pinch of Celtic Sea Salt
- 3-6 drops of liquid stevia

1. Preheat oven to 450°.
2. Peel butternut squash and slice thinly (1/8 inch). (Tip: Use a mandolin slicer to make this easier.) Place in a large bowl.
3. In a small bowl, mix melted oil, stevia, and spices. Stir to combine well.
4. Pour the spice/oil mixture over the squash and stir to coat.
5. Arrange slices close to each other on a baking tray lined with parchment paper or an oven chip tray.
6. Bake 20 minutes or until squash is softened. Watch them closely so they don't burn or overcook.
7. Transfer chips to dehydrator trays and dry at 125° for 8-12 hours or until crisp and dry.
8. Store in an airtight container.

Husband Approved

Hubby says: "Delicious and satisfying, these are a nice snack that satisfy that craving for sweet as well and crunchy."

Kid Approved

Daughter says: "These don't taste at all like squash. I love the cinnamon flavor!"

Inspired by Martina Slajerova, KetoDiet

Stevia Frosting

Traditional frosting is pretty much just pure sugar. In our version, we substitute stevia. You wouldn't want to eat this recipe every day, but for those special occasions and birthdays it gives you a better option. Use with Almond Torte or Carrot Cake for a holiday treat.

1. Cream together with hand mixer or stand mixer:
   - 4 oz. (½ package) softened cream cheese
   - 1 ½ T milk
2. Add slowly:
   - ¾ cup Cup for Cup Stevia
3. Flavor with:
   - 1 tsp vanilla
   - ½ tsp cinnamon

   OR:
   - Zest from one lemon, lime, or orange

   OR:
   - 1 tsp vanilla
   - 1 T cacao powder

4. Chill briefly to firm, then use to top your favorite dessert.

Husband Approved

Hubby says: "Rich and creamy, this frosting tastes like regular frosting."

Kid Approved

Daughter says: "The chocolate version is my favorite!"

Inspired by Joy of Cooking

"Sugar" Cookies

You won't be able to roll these out and cut them into pretty shapes with cookie cutters like traditional sugar cookies, but for a tasty treat, these rank right up there as a delicious dessert and work great for a take-along for family gatherings or kid parties.

Husband Approved

Hubby says: "Not a bad cookie considering sugar cookies are normally loaded with stuff that is unhealthy (but tastes so good). These are a great alternative."

Ingredients: (Makes 12-15 cookies)

½ cup (1 stick) melted butter
2 tsp powdered stevia
1 tsp almond extract
1 tsp vanilla extract
1 pastured egg
4-5 drops orange essential oil (food grade)
2 cups blanched almond meal or almond flour
¼ teaspoon Celtic Sea salt

1. Preheat oven to 325°. Line a cookie sheet with parchment paper.
2. In a large mixing bowl, combine the melted butter, egg, vanilla and almond extracts, stevia and orange essential oil.
3. Add almond meal and sea salt and mix to combine well.
4. Scoop into tablespoon sized balls (the size of half a golf ball), about 12 per cookie sheet.
5. Freeze for at least 15 minutes, then bake at 325 for 6 minutes. Flatten with spatula or fork and bake an additional 5 – 7 minutes. Let cool, then serve.

Kid Approved

Daughter says: "These cookies are good and make a great dessert in my school lunches."

Inspired by Dr. Steven Gundry

Thin Mint Cookies

Husband Approved

Hubby says: "Who doesn't love chocolate with a trace of mint? Bring on the cookies!?

Kid Approved

Daughter says: "These are too good to really be good for you. I love them."

I love mint, and these cookies taste a lot like the Girl Scout variety. I never get tired of these cookies so love to have them on hand for those hormone or stress induced cravings for "comfort food". The cacao is loaded with magnesium which is especially good for helping with PMS symptoms, and the Peppermint Essential Oil gives great flavor while helping with balancing the digestive system. Win-win all around with great flavor!

1. Preheat oven to 225°.
2. In a large bowl, combine:
   - 1 ¾ cup almond flour
   - 1/3 cup cacao powder
   - 3 T. Stevia/Xylitol, 18-20 drops liquid stevia, or 1 ½ tsp powder
   - 1 tsp baking powder (aluminum free)
   - ¼ tsp Celtic Sea Salt
3. Beat in:
   - 1 large pastured egg, beaten
   - 2 T. melted coconut oil
   - ½ tsp vanilla
   - 10 drops Liquid Stevia
   - 4-5 drops food grade peppermint essential oil
4. Place dough between two sheets of parchment paper and roll out to 1/8 inch thick. Remove top piece of parchment paper.
5. Using a 2 inch cookie cutter, cut out circles and place on parchment paper lined baking sheet. Repeat with remaining dough.
6. Bake cookies until firm, about 40-50 minutes. Turn off oven and leave cookies in the oven to continue to crisp. Let cool completely.
7. Once cool, heat double boiler and melt, stirring constantly and watching carefully so you don't scorch:
   - 1 bag of Stevia Sweetened Chocolate Chips
   - 1 T. melted coconut oil
   - 4-5 drops food grade peppermint essential oil
8. Dip cookies into melted chocolate mix, using two forks or tongs to fully coat cookie. Place dipped cookie on waxed paper to cool and set.

Inspired by Healing Gourmet

Zucchini Brownies

Husband Approved

Hubby says: "One of my favorite desserts is brownies and ice cream and I never would guess while eating these that they are made with vegetables!"

Kid Approved

Daughter says: "Pass me another, please?"

Brownies are our go-to choice for birthdays since they are cake-like and delicious. This recipe is so incredibly moist and fudgy…you'd never guess it was actually good for you! Top with Homemade Ice Cream for a truly decadent treat.

1. Preheat oven to 350° and line an 8x8 baking pan with parchment paper. Set aside.
2. In a large bowl or Stand Mixer, whisk together:
   - 1 cup finely shredded zucchini (it should look like puree)
   - 6 T melted butter
   - 2 T melted coconut oil
   - 1 large egg
   - ½ cup Xylitol or Cup-for-Cup Stevia (or equivalent stevia)
   - 1 T vanilla
3. Add slowly, folding through slowly until just combined:
   - ¾ cup almond flour
   - 1/3 cup cacao powder
   - 1 tsp baking powder
   - ¼ tsp Celtic Sea Salt
4. Fold in ¼ cup Stevia-Sweetened Chocolate Chips
5. Pour into prepared pan.
6. Bake for 30 minutes or until the brownies spring back when gently touched.
7. Allow to cool; cut into squares.

Inspired by Cafe Delites

Avocado Olive Dip

This recipe is for a dip, but it's so good and so filling that you could just about make it into a snack all by itself. Try serving with Cheese Chips, Sweet Potato Chips, fresh vegetables, or shred some leftover grilled chicken and smear this dip on it and serve cold.

Ingredients (about 6 servings)

3 ripe avocados, peeled, seeded, mashed
1 (6 ounce) can black olives, drained, sliced
1 (4 ounce) can chili or jalapeno peppers, drained
7 or 8 small green onions, chopped
3 large tomatoes, chopped
3 or 4 garlic cloves, minced
6-8 drops of lemon essential oil (food grade)
5 or 6 fresh basil leaves, finely chopped

Husband Approved

Hubby says: "I love how this dip is so filling and gives me lots of energy so I can get my work done. Tastes great too."

1. Combine the avocados, olives, chili peppers, green onions, tomatoes, garlic, olive oil, lemon essential oil, and basil in a large bowl and mix well.
2. Chill, covered, for at least two hours.

Kid Approved

Daughter says: "Super good with cheese chips, especially with extra basil."

Inspired by What Would Jesus Eat?

Avocado Tomato Dressing

Avocados contain healthy fats that give your body lots of needed energy when repairing. Combined with tomato and herbs, this dressing is delicious and filling. Avocado can turn brown quickly from oxidization so only make what you need (you may want to half this recipe) and serve it right away.

Ingredients (about 6 servings)

1 avocado, pitted
1 cup chopped tomatoes, unpeeled, unseeded
2 tablespoons extra-virgin olive oil
1 clove garlic, minced
2 tablespoons chopped fresh parsley or 1 ½ teaspoons dried parsley
1 tablespoon chopped fresh basil or 1 teaspoon dried basil
¼ teaspoon Celtic sea salt

Cut avocado in half and remove the seed. Use a large spoon to scoop out the flesh. Mix in a blender with all remaining ingredients. Blend until smooth. Add water if you desire a thinner dressing. Makes about one cup.

Use as a dressing for any lettuce salad. Serve with fresh vegetables.

Husband Approved

Hubby says: "I don't really like raw tomato. This dressing is smooth and creamy and has a very mild flavor."

Kid Approved

Daughter says: "I could eat this dressing all by itself!"

Inspired by The Daniel Fast Cookbook

Balsamic Vinaigrette Dressing

This dressing makes a wonderful addition to salads, roasted vegetables, and various other recipes. It is about as simple as it gets for a dressing or sauce and you can adjust according to personal preference and usage. Be sure to use high quality balsamic vinegar for best results.

Commercial dressings are loaded with preservatives and often contain sugar. Even if the ingredients list doesn't say "Sugar", it may be disguised as other names or forms of sweeteners. You'd hate for something as simple as a commercial salad dressing, often even marketed as "healthy", to slow your progress.

You can make this recipe as individual servings or make larger batches to store in an airtight bottle for future use. No need to refrigerate, just give it a shake before pouring. Note that we don't give exact measurements because the amount you make at one time may vary.

1. Mix together in a bowl:
   - 1 part high quality aged balsamic vinegar
   - ½ part oil such as olive, avocado, or hazelnut
   - Dash of garlic powder
   - Dash of Celtic Sea salt
2. Serve or store in airtight glass bottle.

Husband Approved

Hubby says: "I don't care for any vinegars, so my opinion is a bit jaded. If you like balsamic, you'll love this dressing."

Kid Approved

Daughter says: "I love balsamic and especially love this when mom makes a microgreen salad with feta cheese and fresh herbs."

Basil Pesto

Traditional pesto generally contains pinenuts, which we want to avoid on the Ditch Candida program…yet replace them with blanched or soaked almonds (or leave out altogether) and you have a delicious sauce for a wide variety of recipes. Use as a salad dressing, top it on vegetables, or add to grilled chicken or shrimp. The possibilities are endless and so very delicious. Grow your own basil or buy organic for best results.

Note: Basil comes in a wide range of varieties, made obvious when looking at a seed catalog to grow your own. Pretty much any and all basil makes delicious pesto. Some varieties will be more sweet, others spicy. Choose a variety according to personal preference.

Using a food processor with the S blade makes this recipe super fast and easy.

Make a bunch at once, then freeze for later use. Freeze in an ice cube tray for individual servings easily accessed and thawed when you need it.

Husband Approved

Hubby says: "Pesto makes a great topping on roasted vegetables."

1. Combine in a food processor:
   - 1 ½ cups fresh basil
   - ½ cup fresh parsley (optional)
   - 2 cloves garlic
   - ¼ cup soaked raw almonds (optional)
   - ¾ cup grated fresh parmesan cheese
2. Pulse until mixture forms a thick puree.
3. Very slowly drizzle in while pulsing:
   - About ¾ cup olive oil

Kid Approved

Daughter says: "I could eat this straight. My favorite is pesto as a topping on sliced garden cucumbers in the summer."

Inspired by Joy of Cooking

Blue Cheese Dressing

Salad dressings are so versatile and easy to make, and so much better than the commercial alternatives that are filled with undesirable ingredients. This blue cheese dressing is flavorful and great on a Cobb Salad, Buffalo Chicken Salad, or just about any salad, and also makes a great veggie dipping sauce or topping for chicken, pork, or beef.

Ingredients:

1 cup Homemade Mayonnaise
½ cup sour cream
½ cup buttermilk
4 oz (½ cup) blue cheese crumbles
2 T fresh chopped chives
3 dashes coconut aminos
Pinch of Celtic Sea salt
½ tsp black pepper

1. In a medium bowl, whip with a wire whisk the mayo, sour cream, and buttermilk.
2. Add remaining ingredients and stir to combine.
3. Store in an airtight glass container in the refrigerator for up to 3 weeks.

Variation:
- Add crumbled bacon bits

Husband Approved

Hubby says: "I don't normally go for blue cheese. This dressing surprised me and is really good on the Buffalo Chicken Salad."

Kid Approved

Daughter says: "I like this dressing as a dipping sauce for carrots and red bell pepper slices."

Inspired by Renee Drummond

Caesar Dressing

Caesar Salads are one of my favorites but commercial dressings so often contain sugars and unhealthy fats. After I found this recipe and adjusted a couple of the ingredients, I was so excited to not only get to enjoy Caesar Salad again, but I found the flavors to be even better as homemade! Whip up a batch on your prep day and have it in the refrigerator when you need it. Fresh dressings usually will keep well refrigerated for about 1-2 weeks.

Ingredients: (serves 8)

- 4 anchovy fillets
- 2 garlic cloves, peeled
- 3 T Dijon Mustard (homemade)
- 1 T balsamic vinegar
- Zest from one lemon
- 3-4 dashes coconut aminos
- ½ tsp Celtic Sea salt
- ¼ cup freshly grated Parmesan cheese
- ½ cup extra virgin olive oil

1. Combine all of the ingredients except the olive oil in a blender or food processor (using the S blade).
2. Pulse until well blended.
3. With the machine on low, slowly drizzle in the olive oil in a small stream until it's all incorporated.
4. Scrape down the sides, blend again for a few seconds, then give the dressing a taste.
5. Adjust flavor according to personal preference by adding more of whatever ingredient you think it may need…such as more cheese or more salt.
6. Store in an airtight glass container in the refrigerator for up to 2 weeks. Dressing may separate. If so, just give it a shake to reincorporate before serving.

Husband Approved

Hubby says: "A delicious dressing if you like Caesar."

Kid Approved

Daughter says: "This is even better than the dressing you get at restaurants!"

Inspired by Pioneer Woman

Cinnamint Dressing

I love cinnamon! And, I love mint! When I came across this recipe, I knew I HAD to try it…and I was not at all disappointed. Delicious on a greens salad, or pour over roasted vegetables. This is especially good in the summer when the fresh mint in the garden is overflowing the pots and you're looking for recipes to use it in! If you aren't growing mint…you might consider it. Easy to grow and so very delicious!

Ingredients (about 4 servings)

5 tablespoons carrot juice
½ cup olive oil
Zest from 2 lemons
½ teaspoon lemon pepper
½ teaspoon cinnamon
1/8 teaspoon paprika
1 tablespoon fresh mint, finely chopped

Put all ingredients together except mint in a food processor or blender. Blend until smooth. Stir in mint.

Husband Approved

Hubby says: "I didn't expect to like this from the ingredients but it is surprisingly tasty."

Kid Approved

Daughter says: "This dressing is really good. It makes my mouth happy."

Cucumber Dressing

Husband Approved

Hubby says: "I don't really like cucumber much, but I can see where this would be a hit for anyone who does."

Cucumbers are a light and refreshing vegetable and cooling to the body. This dressing is delightful in the heat of summer when you are craving something cool and smooth with delicious flavors. Serve over a tossed salad or use a little less almond milk and make it into a thicker dip for fresh vegetables.

Ingredients (about 4 servings)

- 2-3 teaspoons carrot juice
- 1 large cucumber, peeled and seeded
- ½ red bell pepper
- ½ small onion
- 1 cup almond milk
- 1 teaspoon dried basil
- 1 tablespoon coconut aminos

Put all ingredients together in a food processor or blender. Blend until smooth.

Kid Approved

Daughter says: "Light and creamy dressing that is especially good with baby carrots!"

Inspired by pH Miracle Diet

Cucumber Sour Cream Dressing

The use of fresh herbs in dressings makes a world of difference. In this recipe we use fresh dill, which ranks up there in my top favorites for fresh herbs. Combine dill with cucumber and you have a refreshing and delicious treat. Try this dressing on salads, over cold grilled chicken breast leftovers, or added to lettuce wraps.

Ingredients (about 6 servings)

½ cucumber, peeled, seeded, grated
¼ teaspoon Celtic Sea salt
2 teaspoons Dijon mustard
1 tablespoon white balsamic vinegar
Celtic salt and freshly ground pepper to taste
½ cup sour cream
¼ cup plain yogurt
1 tablespoon snipped fresh dill

1. Place the cucumber and the ¼ teaspoon of salt in a small sieve set over a bowl; toss to combine.
2. Drain for 10 minutes.
3. Combine the mustard, vinegar, and salt and pepper to taste in a blender or food processor for a few seconds.
4. Add the sour cream, yogurt, and dill.
5. Blend until smooth, scraping down the sides occasionally.
6. Add the drained cucumber and blend just until combined.

Husband Approved

Hubby says: "I love dill and the fresh dill in this recipe makes it delicious and smell amazing."

Kid Approved

Daughter says: "I especially love this recipe with shredded chicken and cheese in a lettuce wrap with microgreens and tomato. So yummy!

Inspired by What Would Jesus Eat?

Curried Carrot Almond Dressing

Husband Approved

Hubby says: "This is a great dressing for salads, but I especially like it with the homemade onion rings!"

Kid Approved

Daughter says: "I don't really like curry, but this was pretty good!"

Fresh carrot juice is so very nutritious and combined with a few other ingredients can make an amazing dressing or dip. This one combines the savory of curry with the nutty of almonds to make a really delicious dressing. Although we mention the garlic as "optional", in our opinion…don't leave out the garlic. If anything, add a little extra!

Ingredients (about 4 servings)

½ cup almonds, soaked and blanched with skins removed (a rubber garlic roller takes the skins off fast)
1 cup fresh carrot juice
1/3 to ½ teaspoon curry powder
½ teaspoon dried onion
Coconut aminos, to taste
Dash or lemon or lime zest, to taste
Optional: 1 clove fresh or 2 cloves roasted garlic

Put all ingredients in a blender and blend at high speed until smooth. If you want this more for a dip, then use more almonds and less carrot juice and process to desired thickness.

Inspired by pH Miracle Diet

Ginger Almond Dressing

Husband Approved

Hubby says: "This is a delicious dressing with lots of "zing.""

Ginger is a powerful ally in this war against candida! Combine ginger with garlic and scallions and you have a powerhouse dressing that tastes amazing while it reinforces the system in this battle. Try this dressing on a salad, over spaghetti squash or zucchini noodles, or as a dip with fresh veggies.

Ingredients (about 4 servings)

3 scallions (white part only)
Peeled fresh ginger (3 inch piece)
2 garlic cloves
4 tablespoons almond butter
1 teaspoon olive oil
Coconut aminos, to taste
1 cup water
Optional: 1-2 sun dried tomatoes packed in olive oil

In a food processor, process the scallions, ginger, and garlic until smooth. Add almond butter, oil, and coconut aminos and process until the mixture is blended. Slowly add the water to the desire consistency, can be more than one cup. Continue processing until well blended. Serve on non-starchy vegetables, salads, or get creative and let us know your favorite uses.

Kid Approved

Daughter says: "This one was a little spicy for me but I liked the flavors, especially with extra almond butter."

Inspired by pH Miracle Diet

Dilly Herb Cheese Dip

This creamy dip is light and full of flavor. Fresh dill is so aromatic and blends well with the garlic and cheese. My favorite is to serve this dip with fresh cucumber spears or baby carrots. Kids especially seem to like this dip. Add a little extra yogurt to make a wonderful salad dressing.

Ingredients (about 4 servings)

8 ounces cream cheese, softened
¼ cup plain yogurt
2 tablespoons fresh dill, chopped
2 tablespoons fresh parsley, chopped
2 small green onions, chopped
½ teaspoon minced garlic
½ teaspoon Celtic salt

1. Combine the cream cheese and yogurt in a food processor or blender and process for 1 to 2 minutes.
2. Add the dill, parsley, green onions, garlic, and salt; process for 30 seconds or just until blended.
3. Serve with raw vegetables.

Husband Approved

Hubby says: "Dill is my favorite herb and this dip is super good."

Kid Approved

Daughter says: "Finger licking good! I love this dip and will pretty much lick the bowl clean too when mom serves it."

Inspired by What Would Jesus Eat?

Herb Dressing

We tend to find a few favorite dressings and then just stick to those few. If you're looking to shake things up a bit and try something new, give this dressing a shot. The herbs blend well to give it a zesty and aromatic flavor that works great on any salad, vegetable, or even as a marinade on top of chicken. We hope you like it as much as we did.

Ingredients (about 2 servings)

1 teaspoon dry mustard
1 teaspoon fresh parsley
1 teaspoon dill weed
½ teaspoon Celtic sea salt
¼ teaspoon tarragon
¼ teaspoon ground black pepper
1/8 teaspoon thyme
1/3 cup oil (extra virgin olive oil is best)
Pinch of oregano

Combine all ingredients and mix well.

Husband Approved

Hubby says: "I love dill and the dill combined with the other herbs makes this a really good dressing."

Kid Approved

Daughter says: "I liked this dressings, especially served on spaghetti squash with some parmesan cheese."

Inspired by pH Miracle Diet

Italian Dressing

You can't go wrong with a good classic Italian Dressing and when you make your own, not only do you get the freshest ingredients for the best flavor, but you don't have to worry about all those additives found in commercial varieties. This dressing is easy to make, economical, and stores well.

Husband Approved

Hubby says: "This is one of my favorite dressings, especially served over grilled chicken breast or grilled vegetables."

Ingredients (about 8 servings)

½ cup extra-virgin olive oil
2 tablespoons fresh lemon zest
1 clove garlic, minced
1 teaspoon dried basil
½ teaspoon dried oregano flakes
¼ teaspoon Celtic Sea salt

Place all ingredients in a blender and mix to combine. Refrigerate until chilled.

Use with any lettuce salad. Drizzle over tomato slices with avocado and basil. Serve with cheese slices. Or serve over grilled chicken breast.

Kid Approved

Daughter says: "I love this dressing on a salad, but it's also really good on mom's roasted butternut squash!"

Inspired by The Daniel Fast Cookbook

Jalapeno Popper Dip

Husband Approved

Hubby says: "Oh yeah, this is a winner. Good as a dip or in eggs, this is one of my all time favorites."

Kid Approved

Daughter says: "So cheesy and creamy. I like it with lots of extra bacon."

This recipe is a family favorite and a common request for holidays and get-togethers. Serve with sweet potato chips, fresh vegetables slices, or homemade crackers. I sometimes make this just for the leftovers as my husband's favorite Sweet Potato Quiche is when I add this Jalapeno Popper Dip to the egg mixture before baking…or add it to scrambled eggs for a special treat. It's also wonderful added to your lettuce wraps. Best served warm, but can also be served cold. If you don't like "heat", be sure to remove all the seeds and membranes from the jalapenos.

Ingredients:
- 6-8 slices of bacon, cooked crispy and diced (or add extra if you love bacon)
- 2 (8 oz.) Packages of cream cheese, softened
- 1 cup homemade mayonnaise or crème fraiche
- 4-6 jalapeño peppers, deseeded and chopped fine
- 1 cup cheddar cheese, shredded
- ½ cup mozzarella cheese, shredded
- ¼ cup diced green onion
- ½ cup shredded fresh parmesan cheese

1. Preheat oven to 350°.
2. Combine all ingredients except parmesan cheese in a medium bowl.
3. Stir well to fully combine.
4. Transfer to an oven safe shallow dish. I use a glass lasagne pan.
5. Top with shredded parmesan cheese.
6. Bake for 20-25 minutes or until cheese is bubbly and well melted.
7. Allow to cool slightly and serve warm.

Inspired by Christina Cooper

Queso Dip

We love queso. Just because we don't have the chips during our Ditch Candida time-frame, doesn't mean we can't still enjoy some good queso. Serve this dip as a dressing, on cauliflower rice with pico de gallo and grilled chicken, or use your imagination and enjoy!

Ingredients (about 8 servings)

16 ounces cottage cheese
8 ounces pepper jack cheese, grated
4 ounces jalapeno, de-seeded and diced fine
Cilantro, to taste (and then add a little more if you like cilantro as much as I do)
Chili powder or **Homemade Taco Seasoning**, to taste

1. Blend cottage cheese in blender until smooth.
2. Heat cottage cheese in saucepan over medium heat, stirring occasionally. Slowly add pepper jack cheese until melted completely.
3. Add jalapeño, cilantro, chili powder and stir.

Husband Approved

Hubby says: "I love this queso dip served on just about anything."

Kid Approved

Daughter says: "More please!"

Inspired by In the Kitchen with MRC

Homemade Ranch Dressing

Ranch is so versatile and pretty much becoming an American classic. Commercial varieties have sugar…and sometimes even the dreaded corn syrup! Try making your own for a much better and healthier version that will keep you on track with ditching your candida.

Ingredients:

- ¼ cup dried parsley
- 1 T dill
- 1 T garlic powder
- 1 T onion powder
- ½ tsp basil
- ½ tsp black pepper

Mix all ingredients and store in an airtight jar.

To make dressing, add 1 T dressing mix to 1/3 cup **Homemade Mayonnaise** or Greek Yogurt. Add milk to desired consistency if needed.

Husband Approved

Hubby says: "Well, it's not Hidden Valley but it does work well as a good alternative."

Kid Approved

Daughter says: "Ranch is one of my favorite salad dressings…but I really love Balsamic too!"

Inspired by Wellness Mama

Red Pepper Dip

We especially like this dip in the summer when fresh sweet bell peppers are in the garden. Try mixing and matching your pepper choices for a variety of flavor. Orange, yellow, purple…they all taste amazing. Did you know….look at the bottom of the pepper…does it have 3 lumps or 4? The peppers with 4 lumps are better for fresh eating and recipes like this one, and the peppers with 3 lumps are especially good for cooking.

Ingredients:

½ cup red bell peppers, fresh or roasted
1 tsp dried basil
1 garlic clove
1 cup cottage cheese

1. Place all ingredients except cottage cheese in a blender or food processor and mix until well chopped and combined.
2. Add the cottage cheese and mix until well blended.
3. Chill, covered, for at least 1 hour.

Uses:
- Serve with fresh vegetables
- Spread onto lettuce wraps
- Use as a salad dressing
- Serve over eggs
- Spread on **Pancakes** then top with shredded cheese and favorite toppings for mini "Pizza" alternative. Broil until cheese is bubbly.

Husband Approved

Hubby says: "I'm not usually much of a dip fan, but this was especially good as a dressing or spread."

Kid Approved

Daughter says: "I like this recipe as a salad dressing. It's creamy and tastes really good."

Red Pepper Walnut Pesto

This recipe takes a couple extra steps and pre-planning but is so worth the extra effort. Make it on your prep day when you're multitasking in the kitchen anyway and enjoy it as snacking during the week with fresh vegetables or try serving it over roasted or grilled eggplant!

Ingredients (about 8 servings)

- 6 ounces red bell pepper
- 2 medium garlic cloves, peeled
- ¾ cup walnuts, toasted
- ½ cup sun-dried tomatoes
- 2/3 cup fresh basil leaves
- ½ cup grated parmesan cheese
- ½ teaspoon Celtic sea salt
- ¼ teaspoon black pepper
- ½ cup olive oil

1. Preheat oven to 400°.
2. Halve and de seed/de vein red peppers, place skin side down on oven rack.
3. Roast 15 to 20 minutes or until skin is well shriveled but not blackened. Place in bag for 15 minutes to steam.
4. Place garlic cloves in a medium sized saucepan, add cold water to cover and bring to a boil. Reduce heat and simmer for 5 minutes or until soft enough to pierce with fork.
5. Remove using a slotted spoon and set aside to drain.
6. Place all ingredients in a blender. Blend for 30 seconds or until desired consistency is reached.

Husband Approved

Hubby says: "Great flavor and filling. Makes a delicious snack or appetizer."

Kid Approved

Daughter says: "This is so good, especially with extra parmesan and served over roasted or grilled vegetables."

Inspired by Vitamix Cookbook

Sun-Dried Tomato Dip

To me, tomatoes exemplify the image of sunshine in summer. Sun-dried tomatoes carry that nostalgic flavor and this recipe makes a delicious dip that is perfect with veggies, on leftover turkey slices, or on a cucumber salad. Make your own sun-dried tomatoes with the surplus garden tomatoes by slicing them and dehydrating them. So yummy!

Husband Approved

Hubby says: "Even though tomatoes aren't my favorite, the sour cream and cream cheese make this recipe almost taste like a dessert than a dip."

Ingredients (about 4 servings)

10 oil-packed sun-dried tomatoes, drained, chopped
8 ounces cream cheese, softened
1 cup sour cream
1 teaspoon Celtic Sea salt
½ teaspoon freshly ground black pepper
2 scallions, sliced

1. Combine the sun-dried tomatoes, cream cheese, salt, pepper, and scallions in a food processor.
2. Process until desired consistency.

Kid Approved

Daughter says: "Smooth and creamy with a pretty pink color. This dip is FUN to eat."

Inspired by What Would Jesus Eat?

Wowie Zowie Almond Dressing

Husband Approved

Hubby says: "A really great dressing with so much for the palate. Sweet, zesty, sour, savory, and nutty…all in one delicious treat."

Kid Approved

Daughter says: "I love this dressing on cauliflower rice with grilled chicken. Reminds me of some fancy Chinese food from a restaurant."

This dressing is a favorite in our house, especially with the kids! It is rich and sweet with a creamy nut butter taste that works great on salads, over cauliflower rice, or on top of any steamed vegetables! You have got to try this one and experience it for yourself.

Ingredients (about 6 servings)

1 cup raw almond butter
½ cup water
zest of one lemon plus a couple drops of lemon essential oil
2 tablespoons of coconut aminos or 1 teaspoon Celtic salt
2 teaspoons xylitol or stevia equivalent
1 tablespoon dried onion (powder or flakes, but we use flakes)
2 cloves garlic
1 tablespoon grated fresh ginger root
1 tablespoon sesame oil

In a blender or food processor, combine almond butter, water, lemon, and coconut aminos or salt. After this is well blended leave the blender on and add onion, garlic, ginger, and oil. Blend well and add additional water if required for thinner consistency. Can be served warmed or cool.

Inspired by pH Miracle Diet

Yogurt Cucumber Dip

We put this recipe in the dressings and dips section, but it really is a good Snack option too, especially in early summer when radishes and cucumbers are fresh from the garden or farmers market. This recipe has such amazing flavor and is so refreshing and light. If you can't find fresh mint, you can substitute dry…but it won't quite be the same. Be sure to use yogurt that doesn't have any added sugar. Yummy!

Ingredients (about 4 servings)

2 cups plain yogurt
2 tablespoons minced fresh mint
2 cloves garlic, crushed
2 large cucumbers, peeled, sliced
Watercress and radish slices (or other vegetables of choice)

1. Combine the yogurt, mint, garlic, and cucumbers in a bowl; mix well.
2. Serve on a bed of watercress and radish slices.

Husband Approved

Hubby says: "The mint and the cucumbers give this recipe a cooling and refreshing flavor, and makes a great snack with a big glass of iced tea after a day having fun in the sun."

Kid Approved

Daughter says: "Radishes are so delicious, but a bit spicy, so they're super yummy with this dip. I love mint and I love cucumbers, too!"

Inspired by What Would Jesus Eat?

Homemade Cajun Seasoning

We used to buy the commercial version until I found out how easy this was to make…and how many additives where added to store-bought. Use this with our Chicken Salad recipe or add it to chicken, casseroles, or eggs. Adjust the cayenne pepper to your desired level of spicy!

Ingredients:

½ cup paprika
1/3 cup Celtic Sea Salt
¼ cup garlic powder
2 T black pepper
2 T onion powder
2 T oregano
1 T thyme
1 T cayenne pepper (or to taste)

Mix all ingredients and store in an airtight jar. We usually double this recipe and make a bunch all at once as it doesn't usually last very long otherwise.

Husband Approved

Hubby says: "The spicier the better, I say. This is great for just about anything. I like it on my roasted vegetables."

Kid Approved

Daughter says: "I love mom's chicken salad, but normally don't like things too spicy, so just one thumb up."

Inspired by Wellness Mama

Homemade Chili Seasoning

Making your own Chili Seasoning is so worth it! For one, you know there is no added sugar or preservatives, but the flavor is so good, you'll never look back and buy those silly packets again. Great for more than just making chili too. Add to scrambled eggs, put a pinch in chicken or egg salad for extra kick, or add it to shredded chicken for a spicier version. The sky is the limit on the fun experiments you can try.

Ingredients:
- ½ cup Chili Powder
- ¼ cup Garlic Powder
- 3 T. Onion Powder
- ¼ cup Oregano
- 2 T. Paprika (we use Smoked Hungarian)
- ¼ cup Cumin
- 1 T. Thyme

*For extra "heat" add Cayenne Pepper to taste

Note: We don't add salt to our chili powder as you will want to salt to taste on each individual recipe.

Mix all ingredients and store in an airtight jar. We usually double this recipe and make a bunch all at once as it doesn't usually last very long otherwise.

¼ cup of the Seasoning Mix is equivalent to 1 packet of commercial seasoning.

Husband Approved

Hubby says: "I love chili and the flavors of this seasoning are great on just about anything…well, except maybe ice cream."

Kid Approved

Daughter says: "I love Mom's chili and it's good when she adds the seasoning to my eggs, too!"

Homemade Italian Seasoning

If you like Italian, you'll love this seasoning. Use it to make your own pizza sauce, salad dressings, and so much more. Be creative. It's great on chicken with some melted cheese....or try it on fresh tomatoes as a great snack.

Ingredients:
- ½ cup Basil
- ½ cup marjoram
- ½ cup oregano
- ¼ cup rosemary
- ¼ cup thyme
- 2 T garlic powder

Note: We don't add salt to our Italian seasoning as you will want to salt to taste on each individual recipe.

Mix all ingredients and store in an airtight jar. We usually double this recipe and make a bunch all at once as it doesn't usually last very long otherwise.

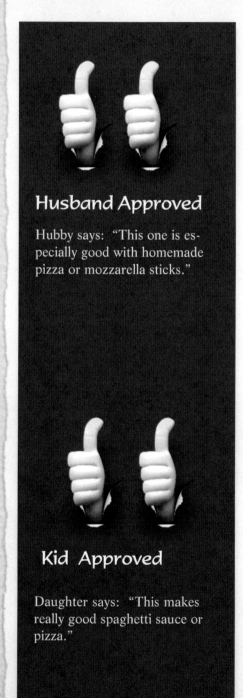

Husband Approved

Hubby says: "This one is especially good with homemade pizza or mozzarella sticks."

Kid Approved

Daughter says: "This makes really good spaghetti sauce or pizza."

Inspired by Wellness Mama

Homemade Onion Soup Mix

Husband Approved

Hubby says: "Hard to judge just the dry mix but I know I love everything made with it so it must be 2 thumbs up."

Kid Approved

Daughter says: "I especially like this one as a dip or on steak."

This is a staple item in my pantry since it's so good and makes recipes just sing. If you garden, make your own dried onion flakes in your dehydrator…or buy the ingredients in bulk and save. Great for dips, sauces, and dressings but also incredible on steaks, pork chops, or in soups. Have fun with this one, especially since it's LOADED with healthy ingredients that help with your cleanse.

Ingredients:

- 1 cup dried or dehydrated onion flakes
- 2 tsp onion powder
- 2 tsp garlic powder
- 1 tsp celery powder
- 1 tsp black pepper
- 2 tsp Celtic Sea Salt
- 1 tsp turmeric

Mix all ingredients and store in an airtight glass jar. I usually make this in big batches at once so I always have plenty on hand.

About ¼ cup of the above mix is equivalent to 1 packet of the commercial onion soup mix.

** Add ¼ cup to 2 cups beef broth for a quick and easy French Onion Soup
**Add ¼ cup to yogurt or sour cream for a super veggie dip
**Excellent on roasts, steaks, chops, lamb, or other meats as a rub.

Inspired by Wellness Mama

Homemade Seasoned Salt

Sometimes you just want a little more kick to your salt in a recipe, but commercial seasoned salt is usually made with unhealthy salts, and usually anti-caking agents, MSG, and sometimes even sugar. The alternative? Easy. Make your own! This version works great in a wide variety of recipes.

Ingredients:

½ cup Celtic Sea Salt (finely ground)
¼ cup onion powder
¼ cup garlic powder
¼ cup black pepper
2 T chili powder
3 T paprika
2 T dried parsley
1 T red pepper flakes (optional)

Mix all ingredients and store in an airtight spice jar. Use instead of regular salt in any recipe you want a little extra flavor.

Husband Approved

Hubby says: "This is especially good on eggs, casseroles, and roasted veggies."

Kid Approved

Daughter says: "I like this seasoned salt on the roasted turnips or radishes. So yummy."

Inspired by Wellness Mama

Homemade Taco Seasoning

Taco Seasoning is so easy to make and handy to have on hand, plus it is so much better than those packets that are expensive and often contain sugars, MSG, and GMO's, too! Use for seasoning meats, adding to soups, and making amazing sauces and dips. I make big batches so I always have plenty on hand. Store in an airtight jar to keep the flavors fresh.

Ingredients:
½ cup chili powder
¼ cup cumin
1 T garlic powder
2 T onion powder
1 tsp oregano
1 tsp paprika
¼ tsp turmeric

Note: We don't add salt to our taco seasoning as you will want to salt to taste on each individual recipe.

Mix all ingredients and store in an airtight jar. We usually double this recipe and make a bunch all at once as it doesn't usually last very long otherwise.

¼ cup of the Seasoning Mix is equivalent to 1 packet of commercial seasoning.

Husband Approved

Hubby says: "I love Southwest cuisine and anything made with this seasoning has been a winner."

Kid Approved

Daughter says: "I love tacos and the flavor of the spices. I especially like this seasoning on my scrambled eggs."

Inspired by Wellness Mama

RECIPES

CONDIMENTS & SAUCES RECIPES

DITCHCANDIDA.COM

Barbecue Sauce

My hubby is a huge BBQ fan and was so bummed when I said he couldn't have his favorite commercial BBQ sauce…until he tried this one. The base recipe is just a starting point if you choose to experiment a little and create your own original recipe. Most commercial versions contain a great deal of sugar, but by making it yourself you can substitute stevia instead.

1. Saute until brown:
   - ¼ cup onion
   - 1 T coconut oil
2. Add and simmer 20 minutes:
   - ½ cup water
   - 1 T coconut aminos
   - 1 T balsamic vinegar
   - Zest from one lemon
   - ½ tsp liquid stevia
   - 1 cup organic tomato sauce (1 large or 2 small cans)
   - ½ tsp Celtic Sea Salt
   - ¼ tsp paprika
   - ¼ tsp black pepper
   - 1 tsp dry mustard
   - ½ tsp chili powder (or to taste)
3. Use immediately or store in an airtight glass jar in the fridge for up to 1 week.

Optional additional ingredients:
- Diced green chilies
- ½ tsp cumin
- ¼ tsp ginger
- 1 tsp coriander
- Pinch of cayenne pepper

Husband Approved

Hubby says: "Oh yeah! Got me some BBQ again. Perfect for those warm summer days when you put some chicken on the grill."

Kid Approved

Daughter says: "My dad makes the best BBQ chicken, especially when mom makes the sauce!"

Inspired by Joy of Cooking

Bolognese Sauce

Another traditional favorite, Bolognese Sauce makes a great topping on Eggplant Parmesan, Spaghetti Squash, Zucchini noodles, with Meatballs, or as a topping on Meatloaf. Such a versatile recipe and super easy. Make extra and freeze or can (pressure can) for future use. A family favorite and a common "go-to" when guests join us for dinner.

Husband Approved

Hubby says: "Who doesn't love a good red sauce, and this version has such good flavor but without the traditional sugars. I love this on meatloaf or with meatballs."

Ingredients: (about 4 servings)	
6 dried mushrooms	¼ cup finely chopped onion
1/3 cup butter	1 cup chopped lean beef
¼ cup minced lean ham or Canadian bacon	2 tablespoons tomato paste
¼ cup finely chopped carrot	1 strip lemon peel
	Nutmeg
	1 cup beef stock
	½ dry white wine
	¼ cup whipping cream

1. Reconstitute the mushrooms, reserving them and the liquid.
2. Melt butter in a large saucepan; add in the lean ham, carrot, and onion.
3. Stir and cook for 1 to 2 minutes. Then add in the lean beef and brown over a medium heat, stirring occasionally.
4. Add the mushrooms, their liquid, the tomato paste, lemon peel, a pinch of nutmeg, the beef stock, and the white balsamic.
5. Partially cover and simmer slowly for one hour.
6. Remove from heat, take out lemon peel and stir in the whipping cream.
7. Serve immediately or store for future use.

Kid Approved

Daughter says: "I love this sauce over vegetable noodles and topped with lots of fresh parmesan cheese!"

Inspired by Joy of Cooking

Grandma's Special Spaghetti Sauce

This recipe is adapted from Grandma Margaret's Special Meatball Bomber & Spaghetti recipe. Every Christmas, Grandma would make her famous meatballs with this special homemade sauce. I recommend trying it with the meatballs, but it's amazing on its own too.

If you like canning, you can make big batches of this sauce and preserve it to have it handy and ready. Use a pressure canner (not the same as the electric pressure cookers we use for other recipes in this program) and process at 10 lbs of pressure for 20 minutes.

Ingredients:
- 1 large (24 oz) can of tomato sauce rinsed with a little water
- 2 cans tomato paste plus 2 cans water
- 1 T Parsley flakes
- ½ tsp oregano
- 1 T garlic powder
- 1 T onion powder
- 1 T parmesan cheese, grated
- 1 T Romano cheese, grated
- Celtic Sea salt and pepper to taste

Mix all ingredients in a large saucepan and heat on low until flavors are well combined. Careful not to boil.

Note: We recommend serving this with Grandma's **Meatball Bombers.** (See recipe in Beef section) If you are making the meatballs, prepare as directed then simmer meatballs in sauce for 1 hour on low.

Husband Approved

Hubby says: "Best spaghetti ever, especially with the meatballs!"

Kid Approved

Daughter says: "You don't even miss the pasta noodles when you have this recipe, especially with zucchini noodles instead."

Inspired by Grandma Margaret

Homemade Ketchup

Husband Approved

Hubby says: "You don't even miss the traditional version with the full flavors of this recipe."

Kid Approved

Daughter says: "So good. I even like to lick it off my fingers."

Ketchup is one of those condiments that is so hard to find commercially without sugar. The good news is that it is easy to make at home. Granted, no homemade ketchup will taste just like commercial since we don't use sugar or high fructose corn syrup...but I think the homemade version is even better! Adjust the spices to your personal flavor preference and use organic tomato paste if possible.

Combine in a bowl and whisk until well combined:
- 1 (6 oz) can organic tomato paste
- 2 T white balsamic vinegar
- ¼ tsp dry mustard
- ¼ tsp garlic powder
- ¼ tsp onion powder
- ¼ tsp cinnamon
- ¼ tsp Celtic Sea salt
- Pinch of ground cloves
- Pinch of ground allspice
- 1/8 tsp cayenne pepper (optional)
- Stevia or xylitol to taste
- ¼ cup to 1/3 cup water depending on thickness preference

Optional additional ingredients:
- ¼ tsp fennel powder
- Pinch of dried basil
- Pinch of dried oregano
- 1/8 tsp ground black pepper

Place in an airtight glass jar and store in the refrigerator for up to 2 months....if it lasts that long.

Delicious with our No-Bun Hamburgers and/or Sweet Potato Fries.

Inspired by Grandma Margaret

Homemade Mayonnaise

Sauces and condiments were a hard thing to give up when I first started the candida program…but with a little creativity I found out I didn't have to give them up completely! I just had to make my own instead of relying on commercial versions that inevitably were using unhealthy ingredients. This mayo is a great alternative. Just be sure that all ingredients are at room temperature before starting or they won't emulsify correctly.

Ingredients:

4 egg yolks (must be organic and farm fresh is best)
1 T Apple Cider Vinegar or Balsamic Vinegar
½ tsp dried mustard
2/3 cup liquid oil (olive or avocado)
2/3 cup coconut oil

1. Put egg yolks into a blender or food processor and blend until smooth.
2. Add vinegar and mustard and blend until mixed.
3. SLOWLY add oil while blending at low speed, starting with liquid oil…adding a couple drops at a time until it starts to emulsify.
4. Continue to slowly add the rest of the oils until completely incorporated and creamy.
5. Store in the fridge. Use within a week or so.

Husband Approved

Hubby says: "I'm not usually a mayo fan, but added to other recipes, this is really good."

Kid Approved

Daughter says: "I like this in tuna salad, chicken salad, or on top of my hamburgers."

Inspired by Wellness Mama

Homemade Mustard

Husband Approved

Hubby says: "Even better than store-bought."

Kid Approved

Daughter says: "Yummy and fun to make. I love helping mom make mustard, and it smells so good too."

Mustard is one of the easiest things in the world to make and the flavor is so much better than anything you can find at the store. If you like a more traditional yellow mustard, use white or yellow mustard seeds. If you like a spicier "Dijon" style mustard, use brown or black mustard seeds or a combination.

1. Grind in a coffee grinder (or use a mortar and pestle) until they are coarse ground for spicier mustard and smoother for traditional mustard:
   - 6 T mustard seeds
2. Pour the semi-ground seeds into a bowl and add:
   - ½ cup dry mustard powder
   - 2 tsp salt
   - 1 tsp turmeric
   - ¼ cup minced fresh herbs like dill, parsley, or sage (optional)
3. Slowly pour in:
   - ½ cup cold water
4. Stir well until fully mixed and let stand for about 10 minutes. The longer you let it sit, the mellower the mustard will be.
5. Add:
   - 3 T white balsamic vinegar (or whey for fermented mustard)
6. Mix thoroughly and taste. Add stevia or xylitol if needed or a sweeter mustard is preferred.
7. Pour into a glass jar and store in the fridge. Mustard may be runny at first but will thicken overnight. Best if you wait at least 12 hours before using.

Inspired by Grandma Margaret

Hot Fudge Sauce

Husband Approved

Hubby says: "Be still my heart. This hot fudge topping is good on ice cream, in coffee, on pancakes, and just right out of the jar!"

Sometimes you just need CHOCOLATE, especially if you're looking for a better alternative to top your pancakes, waffles, ice cream, or other desserts like cheesecake. This Hot Fudge Sauce recipe is super delicious and completely guilt free. Plus, by using cacao powder, you have the added benefit of a magnesium-rich super-food.

1. Combine in a medium saucepan and whisk until well combined:
   - 1 cup cacao powder
   - ½ cup xylitol
   - 1 cup heavy cream
2. Turn on the heat to medium low and continue whisking briskly as it warms. Careful not to overheat.
3. As the mixture heats to warm, add:
   - 1 stick (½ cup) organic salted butter, cut into pieces
4. Heat until hot but not boiling. Once hot and well mixed, add:
   - 3 tsp vanilla
5. Let the sauce cool in the pan for 5 minutes, then transfer it to a mason jar or other glass container. Serve when warm or store in the fridge for future use. (Note: it will become more solid as it cools.)

Kid Approved

Daughter says: "Mom has me spoiled with homemade ice cream with this hot fudge topping. Ice cream other places just isn't the same anymore."

Inspired by Grandma Margaret and Renee Drummond

Pumpkin Spice Syrup

Husband Approved

Hubby says: "Man o man! This makes the best coffee ever! More like a dessert than a beverage."

This is a very versatile recipe that is so delicious. It has so many wonderful uses that really spice up a dish so I like to keep some on hand in the fridge all the time. My favorite is as an ice cream topping, but it also makes a truly amazing latte that would rival any fancy coffee shop.

Ingredients:
- 1 ¼ cups water
- ½ cup pumpkin puree, fresh or canned
- ½ cup Cup-for-Cup Stevia
- ½ tsp vanilla
- 1 tsp cinnamon
- ½ tsp allspice
- ½ tsp ginger

1. Place all ingredients in the order listed into a Vitamix or other blender.
2. Blend on low speed a couple seconds then slowly increase speed to high.
3. Blend for 3 minutes or until mixture is thick and syrupy.
4. Syrup will be hot. Use immediately if you want a hot version or allow to cool and store in an airtight glass container in the fridge until ready to use.

Uses:
- Ice cream topping…also good with added chopped pecans
- Pumpkin Pie Latte: combine ½ cup syrup with ½ cup hot milk and 1 ½ cups hot coffee and blend on high for 10 seconds.
- Pumpkin Chai Latte: combine ½ cup syrup with 1 cup milk and ½ cup chai spice tea…blend on high for 10 seconds.
- Swirl in yogurt as a delicious flavoring.

Kid Approved

Daughter says: "Um, yes please! This is so good, especially on ice cream."

Inspired by Vitamix cookbook

Soy Sauce Alternative

Every so often we come across a recipe that calls for "Soy Sauce", but since we need to avoid all soy, and especially all high gluten products, here is a great homemade alternative that tastes pretty darn close, if I do say so myself. You can also use Coconut Aminos if you don't notice any setbacks (since coconut IS a fruit and we want to try to limit our coconut intake (other than coconut oil).

Ingredients:
- 2 cups beef bone broth
- 2 tsp balsamic vinegar
- ¼ tsp liquid stevia
- ¼ tsp garlic powder
- ½ tsp onion powder
- Celtic Sea salt, pepper, and ginger powder to taste
- 1 tsp fish sauce

1. Mix all ingredients except fish sauce in a saucepan and bring to a low simmer.
2. Simmer until reduced by half (10 minutes or so).
3. Taste test and add more salt/pepper/ginger if needed.
4. Remove from heat and add fish sauce.
5. Stir well and let cool.
6. Store in airtight glass bottle in the fridge.

Husband Approved

Hubby says: "A pretty tasty alternative and great on No Rice Sushi."

Kid Approved

Daughter says: "I like Oriental dishes, and could barely tell a difference in this recipe from store bought."

Inspired by Wellness Mama

Homemade Vanilla

Vanilla is so easy to make and tastes better than any vanilla extract you can find at the store. I was visiting a friend once who had just returned from Mexico where she had purchased some fancy vanilla. We did a blind taste test between my vanilla, the Mexican vanilla, and some commercial vanilla she had in her cupboard. Hands down, my vanilla was picked as the best by everyone who tried the taste-test. Choose good quality Grade A vanilla beans for best results.

Husband Approved

Hubby says: "I was one of the 'guinea pigs on the taste test and definitely enjoyed the flavor of this one best."

Kid Approved

Daughter says: "Vanilla makes many of my favorite recipes taste great. Especially Homemade Ice Cream!"

Ingredients:

  1 bottle of desired size with tightly sealing lid
  2-3 vanilla beans per pint, depending on bottle size
  Vodka or Spiced Rum

1. Place vanilla beans, whole or sliced, into a tight sealing bottle. We use the flip-top style bottles.
2. Add vodka or spiced rum to fill the bottle.
3. Seal the bottle and give the bottle a gentle shake.
4. Place in a cabinet or other dark place and let sit for 8 weeks or longer. The longer it sits, the better vanilla flavor. Give the bottle a gentle shake about once a week for the first eight weeks.
5. Add to your favorite recipes.

Note: I usually make my vanilla in liter-size bottles to make larger quantities. Then, you can transfer to smaller bottles if desired after the initial 2 months of steeping time. Homemade vanilla makes great gifts, too.

Homemade Whipped Cream

Husband Approved

Hubby says: "Pumpkin pie just isn't complete without whipped cream."

Kid Approved

Daughter says: "I could eat this by itself as a dessert. I love eating it off my pie first, then enjoying the pie."

Sometimes, a little whipped cream on top of a piece of pumpkin pie or brownie just adds that extra "oh yeah!" The commercial convenience whipped topping (can't call it cream because it doesn't even contain any milk) is loaded with toxic ingredients. Once you get used to the original version, sweetened with a little stevia, you'll never want to use that store-bought version again.

Chill mixing bowl at least 2 hours before making this recipe for best results. You can use a hand mixer, but a stand mixer works best.

Add to the chilled mixing bowl:
- 1 cup heavy cream
- ½ tsp vanilla
- ½ tsp liquid stevia
- 1 tsp gelatin (optional, but helps cream hold its form longer)

Mix with wire whisk attachment on medium-high speed until stiff. Watch carefully, as over-whipping will cause the separation of fat molecules and you will find yourself with sweet butter instead.

Serve on top of your favorite dessert.

Note: I've seen a really nifty tool out on the market that uses no electricity and whips up the whipped cream in about 30 seconds. My favorite version is made by Pampered Chef. I recommend it if you make whipped cream very often…or want to make it more often but find it tedious to make.

RECIPES

BEVERAGES & TONIC RECIPES

DITCHCANDIDA.COM

Almond Milk

It's so easy making your own nut milks and the flavor is so much better than anything you can find at the store. In fact, the first time I made Almond Milk, we did a blind side-by-side taste test with my daughter and some of her friends…and the homemade won out hands down. Plus, you know there are no preservatives or filler ingredients. You do need some equipment for making nut milks including:
- Quality Blender such as Vitamix or Blendtec
- Cheesecloth or nut bag for straining

For a full tutorial on nuts, including making your own nut milks and nut butters with videos and printable instructions, check out our full Nuts course at HealthyHomesteadLiving.com.

1. Add to your Vitamix or other high powered blender the following:
   - 1 cup nut of choice (almond, cashew, etc.)
   - 4 cups pure water
   - 1 tsp vanilla
   - ½ tsp stevia or xylitol (or to taste)
   - Pinch of Celtic Sea salt
2. Blend until frothy.
3. Meanwhile, place a fine mesh strainer lined with cheesecloth or nut bag over a bowl.
4. Carefully pour nut milk into lined strainer and strain completely to separate the pulp. Pulp may be dehydrated and ground into almond flour.
5. Transfer nut milk to glass jar and refrigerate or enjoy immediately. Will store for about 1 week.

Note: Some settling or separation may occur while storing. This is normal and your milk is still good. Just shake gently to re-mix. Never consume milk that smells "off". Nut milks are an excellent choice as a beverage or as a dairy substitute in many recipes as it is lower in calories and contains healthy fats.

Husband Approved

Hubby says: "I am now the designated daily Almond Milk maker and I take my job seriously. Fresh almond milk is so good and my favorite for my daily energy smoothies."

Kid Approved

Daughter says: "I love drinking this by itself, but it's good in other recipes, too!"

Chai Latte

I used to enjoy ordering a chai latte once in awhile when at business meetings or out with friends. Cinnamon, is one of those spices that I just love! Here is a simple homemade version without the sugar.

You'll need a disposable tea bag or tea ball that allows you to add your ingredients and steep to make the tea. Or, you can substitute a coffee filter and tie it up with kitchen twine.

1. Combine in a tea bag or tea ball:
   - 1 T roobois tea
   - ½ tsp garam masala
   - 1/8 tsp cinnamon
   - ¼ tsp nutmeg
2. Place into teapot filled with water and bring to boil.
3. Once boiling, remove from heat and steep for 10 minutes.
4. Remove tea bag/tea ball.
5. Add:
   - 8 oz almond milk
   - Stevia or Xylitol to taste
6. Serve hot or cold.

Husband Approved

Hubby says: "I usually like coffee more than tea, but this is good."

Kid Approved

Daughter says: "This tea is such a treat, and it smells so good."

Inspired by Executive Chef Ken Blue

Citrus Cream Smoothie

Smoothies make a fantastic "fast food", and there are so many great variations and additives. You can "sneak" in some really healthy ingredients that you can't even taste, making them the perfect choice for picky eaters. This smoothie uses a citrus food grade essential oil of your choice. Try it with Orange for a creamsicle flavor or a few drops of both lemon and lime for a refreshing treat.

Husband Approved

Hubby says: "This smoothie reminds me of sherbet-style ice cream. It's almost too good to be so healthy."

Ingredients:
- 1 cup almond milk
- 1 cup cream cheese
- 1 cup ice
- 1 T coconut oil
- 1 tsp vanilla
- 3-4 drops of citrus food grade essential oil
    - (orange, lemon, tangerine, lime, etc)
- Stevia or Xylitol to taste (about 2 T)

Optional additional ingredients:
- Kale leaves
- Kelp powder

Combine ingredients in a powerful blender and process until smooth.

Variation:
- After blending, pour into your ice cream maker for a delicious ice cream.
- Pour into popsicle molds and freeze until firm to make smoothie pops.

Kid Approved

Daughter says: "I love smoothies for breakfast and this one is so good. I especially love it when mom makes it into frozen smoothie pops!"

Crème de Mint Smoothie

I love this smoothie as a quick breakfast, snack, or dessert. It only takes a couple minutes to make and has healthy fats and proteins for lots of energy. Plus, it tastes amazing. The cool and refreshing flavor of mint is especially good on hot days.

I especially love this smoothie when it's made with fresh, homemade almond milk.

Ingredients:
- 1 cup almond milk
- 1 cup cream cheese
- 1 cup ice
- 1 T coconut oil
- 1 T vanilla
- Sprig of fresh mint leaves
- 2 tsp cacao powder (optional)
- Stevia or Xylitol to taste (about 2 T)

Combine ingredients in a powerful blender and process until smooth.

Variation:
- After blending, pour into your ice cream maker for a delicious mint ice cream.
- Pour into popsicle molds and freeze until firm to make smoothie pops.

Husband Approved

Hubby says: "I don't normally gravitate towards mint so didn't expect to like this as much as I did the first time I tried it. Now, it's a welcome special treat."

Kid Approved

Daughter says: "I love smoothies for breakfast and this one is one of my favorites. I especially love it when mom makes it into frozen smoothie pops!"

Hot Cocoa

Husband Approved

Hubby says: "This hot cocoa is so good it could be a dessert."

Kid Approved

Daughter says: "Mom makes the best hot cocoa and I would never guess it didn't have any sugar!"

My daughter really loves hot cocoa, especially after being outside on cold winter days. Just because we aren't feeding the candida with sugar, doesn't mean we can't enjoy a nice mug of hot cocoa once in awhile. We just tweak a couple ingredients to make it Ditch Candida approved. Personally, I like this version better than the original!

The following recipe is for one serving. Feel free to adjust depending on how much you want/need to make:

1. Add to a small saucepan:
   - 1 cup almond milk (or regular whole milk)
   - 1 ½ T cacao powder
   - ¼ tsp vanilla
   - Dash of pumpkin pie spice
   - Stevia or Xylitol to taste (about 1 T if using cup-for-cup)
2. Heat on low, whisking gently to fully combine all ingredients until mixed and to desired temperature.
3. Pour into mug or coffee cup.
4. Top with **Homemade Whipped Cream** or add **Homemade Marshmallows**

Lemonade

Lemon is one of those incredibly refreshing flavors that is especially good on hot days in the summer. Traditional lemonade contains loads of sugar and lemon juice (if you're lucky and have the real version instead of the chemical substitutes). Both sugar and lemon juice are not part of the Ditch Candida program, but we can still make delicious and refreshing lemonade using a few simple substitutes. Make up a big batch and have a pitcher in your refrigerator for those times you're especially craving sweets. You'll be amazed at how a glass of our lemonade satisfies that craving without jeopardizing your progress.

1. Fill a pitcher with pure, filtered water.
2. Add a few drops of Food Grade Lemon Essential Oil to taste (Note: for a ½ gallon pitcher, I usually add about 8-10 drops of oil)
3. Add Stevia or Xylitol to taste.
4. Chill well in refrigerator.

Variations:
- Add Fresh Basil, Fresh Cilantro, Fresh Mint, or Fresh Goji Leaves for added flavor
- Pour over crushed ice for a extra special treat
- Freeze into ice cubes and add to your water for a hint of lemon infusion
- Add a couple drops of Food Grade Lavender Essential Oil
- Add a couple drops of Food Grade Lime, Grapefruit, or Orange Essential Oil

Husband Approved

Hubby says: "Who doesn't love the refreshing goodness of Lemonade?"

Kid Approved

Daughter says: "I love mom's lemonade, especially with some herbs added in!"

Old Fashioned Root Beer

Believe it or not, root beer is pretty easy to make…and a fun project with the kids. It doesn't taste exactly like store-bought…and I think it's BETTER because they use chemical compounds to create the flavors rather than real ingredients.

For an extra special treat, mix with **Homemade Ice Cream** (recipe in Dessert section) for the best Root Beer Floats you'll ever experience!

Husband Approved

Hubby says: "This is especially good as a root beer float!"

Ingredients:
- ½ cup sassafras root bark
- ½ tsp wintergreen leaf
- 1 cinnamon stick
- 2 tsp vanilla
- Dash of coriander
- Dash of allspice
- 3-4 drops Lime Essential Oil
- 3 quarts filtered water
- 1 bottle seltzer water
- Stevia or Xylitol to taste

1. In a large pot, add sassafras root bark, wintergreen, cinnamon, coriander, and allspice, and add 3 quarts of water.
2. Bring to a boil then reduce heat to simmer for about 15-20 minutes.
3. Strain through a fine-mesh strainer or cheesecloth to remove all the herbs.
4. Let cool completely, and add lime essential oil and sweetener to taste.
5. Mix with seltzer water for carbonation according to personal preference. I find about 50:50 is pretty good but you may prefer a little less root beer and more seltzer.

Kid Approved

Daughter says: "Even better than cans! I love this with ice cream added, too."

Inspired by Wellness Mama

Pumpkin Spice Latte

Husband Approved

Hubby says: "Anything coffee is a winner and this recipe is more like a dessert than a beverage."

Kid Approved

Daughter says: "I don't like coffee but I can see where it would be good if you did....Now the Chai Latte is REALLY good!"

Sometimes you just want a fancy latte like what you get at those over-priced coffee shops. Oh how we love our comfort beverages as much as our comfort foods! Here is a great option that's fun, easy, delicious and good for you!

Make it for your friends or family as a special treat that will wow them with you culinary expertise! Or, just make a cup for yourself on those days you need a little extra love.

1. Add to your Vitamix or other high powered blender the following:
   - ½ cup **Pumpkin Spice Syrup** (see recipe in Condiments section)
   - ½ cup whole organic milk
   - 1 ½ cups hot coffee
2. Blend about 10 seconds or until frothy.
3. Top with Optional **Homemade Whipped Cream**

Variation: Pumpkin Spice Chai Latte

4. Add to your Vitamix or other high powered blender the following:
   - ½ cup **Pumpkin Spice Syrup**
   - 1 cup milk
   - ½ cup strong brewed **Chai Tea**
5. Blend about 10 seconds or until frothy.

Sweet Tea

If you live in the south, sweet tea is a considered almost a staple food on the table. Culturally, sweet drinks are for some, a necessity. If you've been used to drinking lots of carbonated beverages and sweet drinks, switching to water cold turkey may be a challenge. Here is a version, using Stevia or Xylitol that works well, tastes delicious, and is easy to make. We love having a pitcher of this in the fridge all summer for that cool and refreshing drink.

Note: We recommend using quality, organic tea leaves. The best tea for this beverage is Black, Green, Peko, or Oolong. You can buy tea bags, but loose leaves tend to be better quality. If you use loose tea, steep in a tea ball or tie them up in a coffee filter.

1. Fill a pitcher with almost boiling water and add 4 small tea bags or 1 large tea bag, or 3 T loose tea leaves.
2. Let steep until cooled. Remove tea bags.
3. Add Stevia or Xylitol to taste.
4. Chill well in refrigerator.

Variation: Make Sun Tea!

1. Fill a pitcher with water and add tea bags.
2. Place pitcher in a sunny location for 2-3 hours.
3. Remove tea bags.
4. Add Stevia or Xylitol to taste.
5. Chill well in refrigerator.

Note: Carry some stevia or Xylitol with you when you away from home so you can order unsweetened tea at a restaurant and sweeten it yourself.

Husband Approved

Hubby says: "I love sweet tea and it's so refreshing to have other options besides water with meals."

Kid Approved

Daughter says: "Sweet tea is a great treat, especially after I've been helping mom in the garden."

MENU PLANS & SHOPPING GUIDES

DITCHCANDIDA.COM

Menu Plan for Week 1

Monday:

Breakfast: Sweet Potato Quiche *pre-made on prep day, Herbal Tea or Coffee, Water
Lunch: Sausage & Kale Soup *possible Pressure Cooker Recipe, Side Salad, Water
Dinner: Grilled Chicken Breast, Roasted Carrot Sticks with Pecans (see recipe on Roasted Root Vegetables), Water
Snacks: Cottage Cheese with Tomatoes & Sauerkraut
Treats: Chocolate Chip Cookies

Tuesday:

Breakfast: Scrambled Eggs with toppings of choice, Sautéed Onions & Mushrooms, Herbal Tea, Water
Lunch: Leftover Sausage & Kale Soup, Caprese Salad, Water
Dinner: Chicken Fried "Rice", Water
Snacks: Spiced Nuts
Treats: Leftover Chocolate Chip Cookies

Wednesday:

Breakfast: Sweet Potato Quiche *pre-made on prep day, Herbal Tea, Water
Lunch: No Bean Chili with favorite toppings (cheese, sour cream, fresh cilantro) *CrockPot or Pressure Cooker Recipe, Water
Dinner: Salad-in-a-Jar with Balsamic Dressing *pre-made on prep day, Water
Snacks: String Cheese
Treats: Cream Cheese Cookies

Thursday:

Breakfast: Fried Eggs (with butter or ghee), Herbal Tea, Water
Lunch: Leftover No Bean Chili, Water
Dinner: Tuscan Style Eggplant (or Tuscan Style Chicken depending on preference), Water
Snacks: Kale Chips
Treats: Small Serving of Lily's Stevia Sweetened Chocolate

©2017 Healthy Homestead Living, a division of Strive 4 Savvy, LLC
All rights reserved. Do not duplicate, distribute, train from, or create derivative works from without permission.

Friday:

Breakfast: Huevos Rancheros, Yogurt, Herbal Tea, Water
Lunch: Southern Chicken Salad in Lettuce Wrap, Microgreen Salad, Water
Dinner: Baked or Grilled Cod Filets, Steamed Broccoli with Cheese, Water
Snacks: Hard Cooked Eggs, Kale Chips
Treats: Chocolate Pudding

Saturday:

Breakfast: Pumpkin Muffins, Yogurt, Herbal Tea, Water
Lunch: Vegetable Lasagna, Side Salad, Water
Dinner: Hungarian Mushroom Soup, Water
Snacks: Vegetables with Almond Butter, String Cheese
Treats: Homemade Ice Cream with Zucchini Brownies

Sunday:

Breakfast: Omelets with Favorite Toppings, Herbal Tea, Water
Lunch: Leftover Hungarian Mushroom Soup
Dinner: Pot Roast *CrockPot or Pressure Cooker Recipe, Oven Roasted Butternut Squash, Water
Snacks: Yogurt
Treats: Leftover Zucchini Brownies

©2017 Healthy Homestead Living, a division of Strive 4 Savvy, LLC
All rights reserved. Do not duplicate, distribute, train from, or create derivative works from without permission.

Grocery List for Week 1

Since this is the first week, we've included staple pantry items needed for the week in addition to the ingredients for the recipes listed. Keeping in mind our tips on saving money, you may want to buy in bulk on certain items if possible, as it will save you in the long run.

Produce:

3 large bunches of Kale
4-5 medium-large Sweet Potatoes
1 large Zucchini
Lettuce
Preferred Salad Toppings (Cucumber, Cauliflower, Broccoli, etc.)
2-3 Tomatoes
1 Bag Onions
2-3 Sweet Bell Peppers
1 package Microgreens (or grow your own)
4 packages sliced Mushrooms or 3-4 lbs Fresh Mushrooms (Cremini, Shitake, or Button)
2 large Eggplant
1 large bag Organic Carrots
1 large Cauliflower
1 Butternut Squash
Fresh or Frozen Broccoli
Frozen Peas

Refrigerator Items:

2 dozen Eggs
1 package unsweetened yogurt
1 package Cheddar Cheese (and/or preferred cheese like Pepper Jack, Swiss, Colby)
1 package Mozzarella Cheese
Milk
Cream (if making Ice Cream)
Butter
2 packages Cream Cheese
1 package Crème Fresh
1 package Cottage Cheese
Almond Milk
1 package String Cheese

Meats:

2 lb frozen or fresh Chicken Breasts (pasture raised/organic)
2 lbs Ground Beef
Chuck Roast
1 package Cod Filets
1 package organic sausage (no nitrites, nitrates, or sugar)

Canned/Jar Items:

5 cans Diced Tomato (no sugar added)
2 cans Pumpkin
1 can chicken
Dijon Mustard (no sugar)
Bubbies Sauerkraut (or other lacto-fermented brand)
Coconut Oil
Olive Oil or Avocado Oil
Chicken Broth (or make your own)
Beef Broth (or make your own)
Balsamic Vinegar

©2017 Healthy Homestead Living, a division of Strive 4 Savvy, LLC
All rights reserved. Do not duplicate, distribute, train from, or create derivative works from without permission.

Spices/Herbs/Nuts:

Celtic Sea Salt*
Almond Flour
Almonds
Pecans
Cacao Powder
Cinnamon*
Smoked Paprika*
Oregano*
Garlic Powder*
Onion Powder*
Dill*
Basil*
Cilantro*
Cumin*
Thyme*
Red Pepper Flakes*
Vanilla (or make your own with Vanilla Beans and Vodka)*

*Hopefully you have most of these already in your pantry.

Other:

Lily's Stevia Sweetened Chocolate Chips
Tea of Choice (we love Chai)
Liquid Stevia
Cup-for-Cup Stevia Powder
Baking Soda*
Baking Powder*

Prep Day Recommendations for Week 1

To save time as the week progresses, take a couple hours on a prep day to set things up for the week. Here are a few recommendations that go along with the menu plan for Week 1:

- Hard Boil 1 Dozen Eggs (10-15 minutes)
- While eggs are boiling, grill Chicken Breasts, making enough for Monday dinner plus extras for "Salad-in-a-Jar" and Chicken Fried "Rice". (10-15 minutes)
- Clean and wash all vegetables, then chop up items for salads. Prepare "Salad-in-a-Jar" for the number of people you need them for, taking account the menu plan is for twice in the week per person. (20 minutes or so after eggs and chicken have cooled enough to add to the jars)
- Shred Cheeses. I buy in blocks rather than pre-shredded as it's more economical and has fewer preservatives. If you have a food processor with a shredding blade, shredding cheese is fast and easy. Place the cheese in the freezer for a couple minutes before shredding to facilitate easier work. (10 minutes)
- Make Chocolate Chip Cookies (15-20 minutes)
- While cookies are baking, make dough for Cream Cheese Cookies and freeze. (15 minutes)
- Make 2 (or more) Sweet Potato Quiches. These reheat very well. Vary the ingredients between quiches for a different palate/flavor for each meal. (40 minutes total oven time, but you can multitask while it cooks)
- Make Kale Chips. (5 minutes)
- (Optional) At the same time, Pre-Roast Butternut Squash as it takes the same temperature in your oven. (20 minutes) When cool, store in sealed container in the fridge until needed.
- Make Spiced Nuts. (10-15 minutes)

Note: Since it's the first week, and sweet temptations are most challenging, if you have extra time…go ahead and also make a batch of *Thin Mint Cookies* and/or *Chocolate Truffles*. The more "goodies" you have on hand, the easier it will be to make good choices and avoid those things that are going to slow down your progress.

Total Prep Time: Less than 2 hours

©2017 Healthy Homestead Living, a division of Strive 4 Savvy, LLC
All rights reserved. Do not duplicate, distribute, train from, or create derivative works from without permission.

Menu Plan for Week 2

Monday:
Breakfast: Omelets with preferred toppings (go for some veggies like broccoli, asparagus, mushrooms), Herbal Tea
Lunch: Garden Vegetable Soup
Dinner: Taco Salad
Snacks: Guacamole with Veggies
Treats: Pumpkin Pie with Homemade Whipped Topping

Tuesday:
Breakfast: Leftover Garden Vegetable Soup, Herbal Tea
Lunch: Italian Zucchini
Dinner: Smoked Trout, Oven Roasted Radishes (or turnips), Side Salad with Microgreens
Snacks: Hard Cooked Eggs and/or Cottage Cheese
Treats: Leftover Pumpkin Pie

Wednesday:
Breakfast: Leftover Smoked Trout, Fried Egg, Herbal Tea
Lunch: No Rice Sushi
Dinner: Ratatouille
Snacks: Spiced Nuts
Treats: Meringue Cookies

Thursday:
Breakfast: Tomato Basil Parmesan Soup, Herbal Tea
Lunch: Leftover Ratatouille, Fresh Tomato Slices with Microgreens and Cilantro
Dinner: Greek Style Stuffed Peppers
Snacks: Cashew or Almond Butter with Veggies
Treats: Thin Mint Cookies

©2017 Healthy Homestead Living, a division of Strive 4 Savvy, LLC
All rights reserved. Do not duplicate, distribute, train from, or create derivative works from without permission.

Friday:

Breakfast: Breakfast Hash, Herbal Tea
Lunch: Leftover Tomato Basil Parmesan Soup, Side Salad
Dinner: Steak or Pork Chop, Baked Sweet Potato
Snacks: String Cheese, small bowl of lacto-fermented veggies
Treats: Lemon or Lime Sorbet

Saturday:

Breakfast: Leftover Breakfast Hash, Herbal Tea
Lunch: Antipasto Mediterranean
Dinner: Stuffed Acorn Squash, Green Beans
Snacks: Sliced Fresh Cucumber, Mediterranean Hummus
Treats: Leftover Meringues or Thin Mint Cookies

Sunday:

Breakfast: Scrambled Eggs with Sautéed Veggies, Herbal Tea
Lunch: Cabbage Soup, Fried Green Tomatoes
Dinner: Any remaining leftovers from the week
Snacks: Spiced Nuts, Sardines
Treats: Baked Cinnamon "Apples"

©2017 Healthy Homestead Living, a division of Strive 4 Savvy, LLC
All rights reserved. Do not duplicate, distribute, train from, or create derivative works from without permission.

Grocery List for Week 2

Now that it's the second week, you will have several pantry items already on hand from last week. You may also have deviated from the menu plan somewhat and have extra items that didn't get prepared. Those items can just transfer over to week 2 instead. I find that one menu plan can sometimes carry over for two weeks, depending on how many left-overs we have. If you're feeding a larger family, you'll need to adjust accordingly. Feel free to substitute per your personal preference.

Produce:

12-15 Medium Zucchini
2 yellow squash
1 lb fresh mushrooms
2-3 Avocados
5-6 Fresh Tomatoes
2 Lemons
2-3 Limes (optional or use Essential Oil)
Lettuce of Choice
Fresh Asparagus (if in season for Omelets)
Celery*
Carrots*
Onions*
Bell Pepper (3 per person)
Garlic*
Fresh or Frozen Brocolli
Fresh or Frozen Peas
3 Sweet Potatoes per person
1-2 Acorn Squash
2 medium Eggplant
1-2 Cucumbers
2 Green Cabbage
1 large head Cauliflower
1 bag radishes or 2 turnips
Green Tomatoes (if in season)
Cushaw Squash (if available)

Refrigerator Items:

2-3 dozen Eggs (depending on how many you have left from last week)
Cream
Milk/Almond Milk (or make your own)
3-4 packages Cream Cheese*
Fresh Parmesan Cheese
String Cheese*
Cottage Cheese*
Hard cheeses*
Yogurt*

Meats:

Smoked Trout
2-3 lbs grass-fed ground beef
Steak of Choice or Pork Chops
Ground Pork or breakfast sausage (optional)

Canned/Jar Items:

2-3 Quarts Organic Chicken Broth (Homemade is best but you can buy it if preferred)
3 cans Green Beans
5 cans Diced Tomatoes

2 cans organic Pumpkin
1 can evaporated milk
1 can black olives
1 jar green olives
Bubbies Sauerkraut (or other lacto-fermented brand)
Bubbies Pickles (or other lacto-fermented brand)

Spices/Herbs/Nuts:

Celtic Sea Salt*
Almond Flour*
Almonds*
Pecans*
Cashews
Cacao Powder*
Basil*
Oregano*
Parsley*

Vanilla (or make your own with Vanilla Beans and Vodka)*
Almond Butter (or make your own)
Hopefully you have most of these already in your pantry.

Other:

Nori Sheets (for Sushi)
Balsamic Vinegar*
Lily's Stevia Sweetened Chocolate Chips*
Tea of Choice (we love Chai)*
Liquid Stevia*
Cup-for-Cup Stevia Powder*
Baking Soda*
Baking Powder*
Peppermint (Food-Grade) Essential Oil
Lemon and/or Lime (Food-Grade) Essential Oil

©2017 Healthy Homestead Living, a division of Strive 4 Savvy, LLC
All rights reserved. Do not duplicate, train from, or create derivative works from without permission.

Prep Day Recommendations for Week 2

To save time as the week progresses, take a couple hours on a prep day to set things up for the week. Here are a few recommendations that go along with the menu plan for Week 2:

- Hard Boil 1 Dozen Eggs (10-15 minutes) if needed. You may have plenty left from last week. If so, skip this step.
- While eggs are boiling, brown ground beef with onions. Drain grease and let cool. Place half in the fridge to be ready for Tacos, and half in the freezer for future use. (10-15 minutes)
- Clean and wash all vegetables, then chop up items for snacks or salads. Prepare "Salad-in-a-Jar" if you want a couple on hand for the week or to prep for the "side salads" on the menu list.
- For added time saving, cut zucchini into ½ inch slices then freeze so they're ready to pull out for each recipe.
- Shred Cheeses if you ran out from last week. (5 minutes)
- Make Thin Mint Cookies (15-20 minutes)
- While cookies are baking, make Meringue Cookies. (15 minutes)
- Make Spiced Nuts. (10-15 minutes)
- Make Bone Broth if making your own. (5 minutes)
- If you have extra time, make pumpkin pie/s.

Total Prep Time: Less than 2 hours

A few final thoughts from Coach Green:

We hope you enjoyed the recipes and tips offered in this cookbook. I love cookbooks and cherish each and every one of mine. They're so wonderful to have in my kitchen and I write personal notes in the pages to remember events, personal tweaks I tried, what we liked best, and thoughts that come to mind as I try the various recipes.

We hope you can do the same in the pages of this cookbook. Where a cookbook is great to have in your hands, the only disadvantage is that physical copies cannot be easily added to or changed. It is our hope that we may have revisions in the future with additional recipes for you to enjoy. In the meantime, we currently also offer an online version of this book. That way, we can continually be updating the recipes, adding more as we try new ones and develop new favorites, or as new products become available that inspire us.

In the online cookbook, we have also created a community…with the ability for members to comment under each recipe to share their thoughts, suggestions, variations, and preferences. Connect with others who are winning the battle against Candida, hear their stories, and be encouraged.

Best of all, our online version has a full 8 weeks of Menu Plans to save you time, and our menu plans make deciding what to eat so much easier. We also included a few bonus sections including a few of our favorite recipes for the holidays.

Finally, the online version of this cookbook includes over 20 support videos with tips, suggestions, and encouragement.

Visit **www.DitchCandida.com** today to enroll.

It is our hope and prayer that you find abundant health and happiness. Enjoy the journey. Love life. Eat to live; don't live to eat.

God Bless.

Rebecca Austin (Coach Green)
Healthy Homestead Living

Made in the USA
Monee, IL
03 February 2020